Remaking Black Power

Remaking Black Power

How Black Women Transformed an Era

Ashley D. Farmer

The University of North Carolina Press CHAPEL HILL

This book was published with the assistance of the Authors Fund of the University of North Carolina Press.

Set in Espinosa Nova by Westchester Publishing Services
Manufactured in the United States of America

The University of North Carolina Press has been a member of the
Green Press Initiative since 2003.

Library of Congress Cataloging-in-Publication Data
Names: Farmer, Ashley D., author.
Title: Remaking black power : how black women transformed an era /
    Ashley D. Farmer.
Other titles: Justice, power, and politics.
Description: Chapel Hill : University of North Carolina Press, [2017] |
    Series: Justice, power, and politics | Includes bibliographical references
    and index.
Identifiers: LCCN 2017015698 | ISBN 9781469634371 (cloth : alk. paper) |
    ISBN 9781469634388 (ebook)
Subjects: LCSH: Women, Black—United States—History—20th century. |
    African American women—United States—History—20th century. |
    Black Power—United States—History—20th century.
Classification: LCC HQ1161 .F37 2017 | DDC 305.48/896073—dc23
    LC record available at https://lccn.loc.gov/2017015698

Cover illustration by Marcus Kiser.

Portions of chapter 3 were previously published as "Renegotiating the 'African
Woman': Women's Cultural Nationalist Theorizing in the Us Organization
and the Congress of African People, 1965–1975," *Black Diaspora Review* 4:1
(Winter 2014): 76–112.

For my mother, Madeline Farmer, who instilled
in me the love of black women's history;
For my niece, Madeline Wright, who embodies the
fearless spirit of the women in this book;
And for Madelines in my family yet to come, with
the hope that they can build on the freedom dreams
that the women in this book inspire

Contents

Illustrations

Acknowledgments

This book, like all things in life, would have not been possible without a village of professionals, professors, friends, and family who have helped me along the way. I'll never be able to fully express how thankful I am to each and every one of them. However, I hope that what follows conveys how grateful I am for each of the communities that helped me reach this point.

The most exciting, humbling, and challenging aspect of this project has been getting to know the lives and thoughts of the women in this book. I want to express my sincere gratitude to the numerous activists who were willing to reflect with me in interviews, invite me into their homes, and chat with me over coffee. These organizers generously shared their memories, personal papers, and possessions with me, broadening my understanding of the meaning of power and the possibilities of black empowerment. Those who could not speak to me personally did so through the archive. I will always be grateful for the many black women who wrote fearlessly and publicly in order to ensure that future generations would have a road map to guide us in developing differently constituted futures.

The wonderful intellectual community at and around Harvard University nurtured my nascent ideas about how to capture these activists' thoughts in ways that honored their contributions to our current understandings of race, gender, and empowerment. I owe a debt of gratitude to Nancy Cott, Evelyn Brooks Higginbotham, Peniel Joseph, and Tommie Shelby, who were vital intellectual mentors and thought shapers and without whom this project could not have developed. They set the scholarly bar high, provided a model for rigorous scholarship, and always pushed me to produce my best work. My community at Harvard also extended to people like Linda Chavers, who supported me personally, listened during the bad days, and provided insight and advice on the worst days. Most importantly, on the days I insisted that I was going to quit, she never let me (seriously) consider it. Peter Geller has listened, with patience, to my many ridiculous ideas—academic and otherwise—and offered great advice and a good laugh. I have no doubt that this process would have been far more difficult without him. I would also like to thank Laura Murphy and Amber Moulton. These two women have consistently been a sounding board and offered advice and insight that has helped me navigate the academic maze. I am extremely grateful for their wise words about both academia and life.

This project continued to take shape within a vibrant community in the African and African Diaspora Studies Department at the University of Texas at Austin. In addition to providing funding so that I could complete the first stages of this project, the department offered a welcoming community in which to work. I owe a great deal of gratitude to those scholars who were there during my tenure: Daina Ramey Berry, Tshepo Chery, Tiffany Gill, Kali Nicole Gross, Frank Guridy, Minkah Makalani, Stephen Marshall, Eric Tang, Lisa Thompson, and Shirley Thompson. This community welcomed me and nurtured me in more ways than I can express, and I appreciate their support more than they know.

Friends and colleges at the Clayman Institute for Gender Research were also great writing partners, readers, and friends as the project continued to develop. The institute provided funding and a work space in which I was able to complete book revisions. It also cultivated an intellectual community that fostered my scholarly and professional growth. I am especially grateful for the company and support of Alison Dahl Crossley, who was and remains a wonderful friend, and who has constantly encouraged me to push through the hardest parts of completing and publishing this book.

Duke University not only offered funding and a space within which to work but also provided me with a wonderful scholarly community. Whether it was in the History Department colloquia or through funding from the Dean's Office, Office of the Provost, and the Women's Studies Department to workshop the book in its earlier stages, this project benefited from a gracious community that offered critical insights into its subject matter and form. I also benefited from a supportive writing and scholarly community that included Annabel Kim, Eli Meyerhoff, Jecca Namakkal, David Romine, and Gabe Rosenberg. I owe special thanks to Adriane Lentz-Smith for her formal and informal mentorship throughout my years in Durham, Alisha Hines for her generous support, and Monica Huerta for her friendship and endless supply of laughs. Thanks, team!

My scholarly and professional community at Boston University helped me cross the finish line. The funding and time that the History Department and African American Studies Program offered, as well as the generous support from friends, colleagues, and students, all provided a welcoming community within which to work and helped further my thinking on the project in its final stages.

A community of scholars also helped shaped this project more than they will ever know. I want to thank Jelani Cobb, who set me on the course to graduate school and to becoming a historian, mentoring me along the way. I am also extremely grateful to Mia Bay, Sally Deutsch, Jolie Olcott, Kennetta Perry, and Robyn Spencer for taking time out of their busy schedules to read rough drafts of the book. My cohort of bloggers at the African American Intellectual History Society offer daily pieces of brilliant writing that challenge and reshape my thinking. I am grateful for the digital and in-person intellectual community that they consistently provide. Other scholars, including Ibram Kendi, Erik McDuffie, Russell Rickford, Stephen Ward, and many others not listed here, have offered invaluable advice and scholarly support on this project. My online writing group, and, in particular, Keisha Blain and Annette Joseph-Gabriel, has been a constant source of support throughout the years. I also owe a great deal of gratitude to the many scholars I have had the opportunity to encounter digitally, particularly on Twitter. Some I have met; some I haven't. However, they have all generously shared their thought processes and knowledge, and this book has no doubt benefited from their thoughts. Our scholarly practices for acknowledging intellectual influence lag behind our daily practices of knowledge formation. But I want to take this moment to say to those scholars: I see you, and I appreciate your allowing me to be an interlocutor in your brilliant minds.

I have also been blessed with a team of cheerleaders outside academia without whom I would have never finished the book. Bridget Billups has been a faithful friend since the first days of college. Although she has not always been close by, she has never, throughout this entire process, wavered in her encouragement and support. I know that without her insight, her encouragement, and her willingness to pick up the phone no matter what time of day or night, this book would not have been possible. Amissa Miller has consistently created both a physically and an emotionally encouraging space after long days at the archives or writing. I am very thankful for her ability to help me stay focused on this project while encouraging me to broaden my perspective and my goals. Brandy Canady cheered me on at every stage of this project, cajoling me out from under the covers and reminding me of what awaited me when I crossed the finish line. Thank you to each of you for your unwavering support throughout a process that has taken the better part of our friendships to complete.

Books never become fully formed without the help of a wonderful editing and press team. I want to extend my sincere thanks to Amadi Adamson,

Helena Holgersson-Shorter, and Kristin Thiel. I am also enormously grateful to my UNC Press editor Brandon Proia and the editorial staff. Brandon has been an incredible editor, always honest and encouraging and effortlessly pushing me to make this book the best that it could be. Thank you for seeing the potential in this project in its early stages and helping me reach the finish line. I am also extremely appreciative to the Justice, Power, and Politics editors, Rhonda Y. Williams and Heather Ann Thompson. Your generous support of this project, scholarly examples, and critical reading have made both the book and me as a scholar stronger. Equal thanks go to the UNC Press Board of Governors for supporting this project and the anonymous reviewers who invested time in it. Your suggestions helped mold this book into the best version it could be.

Without generous funding from multiple centers, this study would not have been possible. In addition to the many institutions that supported my research through fellowships and colloquia, the American Association of University Women, the Center for the History of Print and Digital Culture at the University of Wisconsin–Madison, the Carrie Chapman Catt Prize for Research on Women and Politics at Iowa State University, and the Center for American Political Studies at Harvard University also provided funding for various stages of this project.

I am also thankful to the librarians, archivists, and artists who helped me through this process. Without the staff support at Harvard University Libraries, the Stanford University Special Collections, the Auburn Avenue Research Library, the Wisconsin Historical Society, the Moorland-Spingarn Research Center, the Schomburg Center for Research on Black Culture, the Mary McLeod Bethune Council House, the National Parks Service, the Tamiment Library and Robert F. Wagner Labor Archives, and the Stuart A. Rose Manuscripts, Archives, and Rare Book Library, among others, this book would not be possible. Finally, a huge thank-you to Marcus Kiser for creating the incredible cover art for this book.

I have a wonderful family who have been very patient and understanding even as this book has stolen much of our time together. My in-laws always have encouraged me and offered a supportive atmosphere. My brother-in-law, Keith Wright, has always had an uncanny way of being able to show me how far I have come while reminding me not to drink the Kool-Aid. I am thankful for his humor, his support, and his honest perspective throughout this process. My amazing sister, Sylvia Wright, has played the roles of life coach, friend, mentor, and cheerleader throughout this process. I will never be able to thank her enough for her ability to pick me up and dust me off on my bad days, call me out when I am not giving my best effort, and remind me how fortunate I am. She is, in many ways, the kind of scholar and woman I have always aspired to be. I can only hope that in completing this book, I have made her as proud of me as I am of her.

My parents were my first history teachers, filling my mind with stories of the black imagination. My wonderful father, Absolom Farmer, is responsible for teaching me patience, endurance, perseverance, and the importance of hard work. I will always be thankful for his unwavering support and pride in my choice to follow, in his words, "the road less traveled in our family." My mother, Madeline Farmer, studied history, but life got in the way of her becoming a professional historian. This did not keep her from making history and living her life with strength and defiance, making her the kind of woman that historians like me love to write about. This book is dedicated to her, with my wish that she could be here to see what her hard work, support, and love of history have inspired.

Finally, my husband, Ade Adamson, has been my proverbial North Star, steady and ever present in the daylight but also lighting the path when it seemed darkest and I was sure that I had lost my way. This book has benefited in tangible and intangible ways from his gracious partnership throughout this process. Words cannot express how grateful I am to him for his love and support. But I am most thankful for the many moments when he believed in me, in us, and in this book, enough for the both of us.

Abbreviations in the Text

AAWC	All-Africa Women's Conference
AAWO	Alliance against Women's Oppression
ALD	African Liberation Day
ALSC	African Liberation Support Committee
ANT	American Negro Theatre
BART/S	Black Arts Repertory Theatre and School
BCD	Black Community Defense and Development
BWA	Black Women's Alliance
BWLC	Black Women's Liberation Committee
BWUF	Black Women's United Front
CAP	Congress of African People
CAWAH	Cultural Association for Women of African Heritage
CBE	Center for Black Education
CFUN	Committee for Unified Newark
Comintern	Third Communist International
CORE	Congress of Racial Equality
CP	U.S. Communist Party
DNC	Democratic National Convention
DWU	Domestic Workers Union
FRELIMO	Mozambique Liberation Front
ILD	International Labor Defense
LCFO	Lowndes County Freedom Organization

MDC	Monroe Defense Committee
MFDP	Mississippi Freedom Democratic Party
NAACP	National Association for the Advancement of Colored People
NBAWADU	National Black Antiwar and Antidraft Union
NNC	National Negro Congress
NOI	Nation of Islam
PAC	Pan-African Congress
SNCC	Student Nonviolent Coordinating Committee
SNYC	Southern Negro Youth Congress
TALO	Temporary Alliance of Local Organizations
TWWA	Third World Women's Alliance
UNIA	Universal Negro Improvement Association
WOCRC	Women of Color Resource Center

Remaking Black Power

Introduction

As readers finished the July 1, 1972, edition of the Black Panther Party's newspaper, they found a full-length, mixed-media image of a middle-aged black woman on the back page. The woman, dressed in hair rollers, a collared shirt, an apron, and no shoes, stares directly at the viewer, one hand on her hip; the other supports a bag of groceries from the Panthers' free food program. The woman also prominently displays her button in support of Panther leader Bobby Seale's mayoral campaign. The caption above contextualizes the woman's politics and party support: "Yes, I'm against the war in Vietnam, I'm for African Liberation, voter registration and the people's survival!"[1] This image was one of over a dozen pieces of artwork that Panther Party member Gayle Dickson created, many of which featured black women leading protests and championing party programs.[2] Not only did her artwork translate the party's expansive political agenda, it also reflected how the Panthers—often thought to be a male-dominated organization—expressed and promoted its agenda through images of black women.

Dickson's artwork was emblematic of the diversity of black women's political expression in the Black Power era. Beginning in the 1950s, black activists and intellectuals increased their efforts to develop oppositional institutions and practices designed to bring about black political, cultural, and social autonomy. By the time that Dickson became an artist for the Black Panther Party in the late 1960s, Black Power had coalesced into a worldwide movement dedicated to fundamentally redefining race, class, and gender hierarchies. The image described here was one of myriad expressions of Black Power that black women developed during the early 1970s, the height of the era in which black activists fundamentally reimagined black manhood, womanhood, and empowerment through political expressions that ranged from electoral politics to Pan-African solidarity efforts.

More than simply party propaganda, Dickson's art was a window into some of the common ways in which black women imagined their political roles and potential during the Black Power era. In this image alone, she illustrated how they envisioned themselves as militant domestics and revolutionary black women. She also showed how they often identified as

Mixed-media image by Gayle Dickson from the *Black Panther*, July 1, 1972.

Pan-Africanists through their solidarity with African liberation struggles. Many black women organizers imagined themselves as part of a Third World community, linking their fates and struggles with those of other women in Vietnam and Africa. Dickson's artwork reflected black women's global solidarities by featuring their rhetorical assertions of support. Through this image and other texts, black women collectively constructed ideas about how women should articulate and express their political and philosophical leanings. They also deployed these representations as a way to reshape Black Power–era symbols and politics to fit their needs and lived experiences.

Such images and intratextual conversations were ubiquitous during the Black Power era. Black women across regions, organizations, and political ideologies produced artwork and articles that challenged popular, masculinist perceptions of Black Power and asserted the centrality of black women to the era's political projects. Multiple members of the Panthers' rank and file submitted articles outlining their ideas of what constituted a "Black Revolutionary Woman." Meanwhile, women who belonged to cultural nationalist organizations, like the Committee for Unified Newark (CFUN), created the "Nationalist Woman" handbook, a guide for teaching members how to embody the "African Woman" ideal. Others developed weekly series in black radical newspapers to promote an idealized, militant, working-class womanhood. Some activists crossed organizational and ideological lines, developing position papers aimed at redefining their roles in Pan-African organizing at major international conferences. They also joined forces with other women of color to position black women as part of black and Third World collectives and as the vanguard of antiracist, anticapitalist, antisexist liberation struggles. Dickson's artwork was part of a multifaceted and long-standing conversation among black women activists during this era, one in which they used their intellectual and cultural production to challenge hegemonic and patriarchal perceptions of black womanhood and to develop unifying symbols that could incite other women to radical political action.

Black women's collective, and, at times, conflicting, debates over black womanhood show that the gendered imaginary—or activists' idealized, public projections of black manhood and womanhood—was a critical site of Black Power activism and theorizing. To be sure, activists' social and political organizing transformed race relations in the second half of the twentieth century. However, organizers were also expressly interested in redefining black identity outside white, Eurocentric norms and values. To achieve this goal, Black Power activists collectively reimagined black identity and gender constructs by developing oppositional, black-centered models of manhood and womanhood. These were collective symbols that united activists around a set of ideas and organizing goals. Many activists rooted their ideas about manhood and womanhood in a particular group's temporal, geographical, and ideological commitments. Taken together, they constituted idealized projections of organizers' gendered, raced, and classed political identities.

Activists' models of black womanhood were often utopian and symbolic; yet they were never apolitical.[3] If a central goal of Black Power mobilization was to overturn existing structures and cultures and replace them with black-centered ones, then redefining men's and women's roles, activists argued, was a seminal first step in the "revolution of the mind" required to effectively engage in this political project.[4] Individual and collective redefinition was the bedrock on which black Americans could reject white hegemonic cultural, political, and economic structures. New ideas about black manhood and womanhood were the scaffolding on which they could erect new ideas about Black Power and empowerment.

The common perception is that black men controlled these conversations and constructed the Black Power gendered imaginary. Yet images like Dickson's counter this claim. Black women activists developed distinct but overlapping bodies of literature and artwork dedicated to diversifying public perceptions of black womanhood. At times, they played on existing ideas about racialized gender roles and reshaped them to convey their gender-specific interpretations of ideologies and political agendas. In other moments, they pushed beyond racial lines to formulate capacious ideas about their roles in radical freedom struggles. Black women activists expressed their organizational and ideological commitments through their new formulations of black womanhood. They also used these ideals to reshape popular perceptions of black women's roles in political mobilization, masculinist ideas of black liberation, and the meaning of Black Power. Their attempts to theorize and embody these idealized political identities reveal how the gendered imaginary was an important space of political and ideological activism, and they demonstrate the centrality of black womanhood to the era's debates about race, class, and gender.

Black women activists' ubiquitous engagement with redefining black womanhood illustrates the importance of not just studying what black women did but also examining who and what they aspired to do and be. Black Power organizers participated in extensive and contested conversations over the definitions and contours of black womanhood *precisely* because they believed these new gendered ideals to be legitimate forms of political opposition and a vital component of personal and collective self-liberation. As a result, we must treat the complex and highly idealized aspects of Black Power with the same seriousness that we examine political and social organizing. This approach can not only reformulate our archival methods for examining this period in history, it also has the potential to offer new insights into how we might better understand the future that black women imagined for themselves and those around them. If activists used the gendered imaginary to imagine new worlds, I am suggesting that it's equally useful for reimagining how we study Black Power.

Bringing together their political speeches, essays, pamphlets, and artwork, *Remaking Black Power* explores how black women's efforts to produce new models of black womanhood shaped the Black Power era. The book documents how activists developed different and, at times, competing models of black womanhood—such as the "Black Revolutionary Woman" or the "African Woman"—to advance Black Power tenets and assert the primacy of women in political organizing. It shows how their gender-conscious writings often bent the ideological and organizational trajectory of the movement toward more radical, intersectional approaches to black liberation and how they pushed activists and organizations to articulate a critique of patriarchy along with their critique of racism. Despite their efforts, black women activists were not able to completely subvert the very real Black Power–era sexism and misogyny. However, their reformulation of political and popular ideas about black womanhood did have palpable effects. Using their new models of black womanhood, black women activists reformulated Black Power ideas and symbols and bent the era's major organizations toward more inclusive emancipatory models.

Black women activists' idealized forms of womanhood were not hermetically sealed categories. They were fluid and porous identifications that black women created, occupied, and moved between in their efforts to inch closer to freedom. The contours of these political categories changed over time, both shaping and being shaped by the political moment in which activists constructed them. This book identifies and explores *some* of the ways in which black women collectively constructed new ideals about gender roles in the Black Power era. However, it is not a complete account of black women's Black Power–era freedom dreams. It joins and contributes to a growing body of scholarship that explores black women's organizational, cultural, and theoretical contributions to presumed masculinist spaces. Adding to this scholarship, this study centers the theoretical, textual, and visual representations of black women's ideas about the nexus of political ideologies and gender roles. In doing so, it shows how their flexible formulations of black womanhood challenged, reshaped, and, at times, even reaffirmed patriarchal imaginings of black women and their roles. Ultimately, the book argues that black women's formulations of womanhood were important sites of Black Power expression and explores how they represented black women's purposeful efforts to reformulate racial and gender hierarchies within the movement and society at large.

Black Women and Black Power

Black Power activists' reformulations of womanhood foregrounded ideas that were more than a half century in the making. By the early 1900s, laborers, grassroots activists, and political leaders alike glibly surmised that, for black Americans, the new century would look much like the last. The racist rituals that characterized the postslavery era would remain intact in the first decades of the twentieth century, manifesting in turn-of-the-century Jim Crow laws and rampant black disenfranchisement. Black Americans migrated en masse to U.S. cities in the hopes of finding economic relief and a refuge from racial violence.[5] As migrants gathered in cities across the country, black activists, ideologues, religious officials, and political leaders attempted to make sense of black people's relationship to the modernizing American nation-state. On street corners and church pulpits, they debated which political philosophies and organizing strategies had the most potential to bring about black liberation.[6] Early twentieth-century luminaries such as Ida B. Wells and Anna Julia Cooper penned articles and theses weighing the merits of various liberation strategies, such as integration, separation, and expatriation. Whatever formulation these activists and intellectuals supported, they all grappled with concepts such as race pride, self-determination, black identity, black manhood, and black womanhood.[7]

In the face of rampant racial oppression and economic depression, black nationalist ideologies and groups gained widespread support. In the 1920s and 1930s, organizations including the Universal Negro Improvement Association (UNIA) and the U.S. Communist Party (CP) garnered significant black followings due to their backing of the idea that black Americans composed a separate nation within the United States, defined by their shared identity, culture, and heritage. Early twentieth-century women organizers made the advantages of radical organizing apparent. The activist Amy Jacques Garvey, wife of UNIA founder Marcus Garvey, published a weekly column, "Our Women and What They Think," in which she stressed the emancipatory potential of black nationalist organizing for black women. Meanwhile, Williana Burroughs and Maude White showed their fellow female activists how the CP's support of the black working-class generated spaces for them to organize to end their race, class, and gender oppression.[8] Other women, such as Grace Campbell, helped found the African Blood Brotherhood in 1919, a group that combined nationalism and socialism to address black Americans' race and class discrimination; cultural workers including Jessie Fauset used novels and essays to reevaluate black womanhood and motherhood amid early twentieth-century nationalist and Pan-Africanist discourses.[9] In women's columns, on Harlem street corners, and at political rallies, these and other women debated issues of race, womanhood, black identity, and nationalism, sometimes collaborating and at other moments clashing. They also planted the seeds of Black Power–era ideologies and protest strategies that would germinate in the interwar and postwar years.

After two world wars, back home, black Americans still found themselves on the losing end of America's global campaign for peace and democracy. During World War I (1914–18) and World War II (1939–45), black women watched as their brethren went off to battle racist and fascist regimes abroad while they still experienced the same discrimination at home. CP members such as Louise Thompson Patterson and Victoria (Vicki) Garvin capitalized on wartime discourses of freedom and equality to push the American government to live up to its democratic ideals. They were important leaders of the Popular Front, a group of ideologically and racially diverse organizations dedicated to advancing an antifascist, anticolonial, and antiracist agenda from 1935 through the 1940s.[10] These activists' support of mainstream, liberal reforms and programs did not mean they relinquished their radical politics or nationalist principles. Leftist organizers and theoreticians such as Claudia Jones and Audley Moore actively promoted Garveyite and Communist frameworks in their wartime publications and political work, sustaining these ideological and organizing traditions amid the leftist populism that characterized the era.[11]

The lack of economic and racial advancement, the rise of independent African nations, and the onset of the Cold War in the 1940s rekindled black Americans' widespread interest in nationalist frameworks. Former Garveyites joined with other radical women in an effort to achieve personal and collective freedom, making the late 1940s a period characterized by their transnational solidarities with other people of color.[12] By the early 1950s, their calls for black separation and independence gained momentum as, year after year, another African nation threw off the yoke of European colonialism and gained its freedom. These activists also recognized the urgency to mobilize as the previous generation of black women activists, including Jones, Garvin, and Patterson, weathered governmental attacks for their support of nationalist and communist causes during what is now known as the McCarthy era.[13] Indeed, the news of self-governing black nations abroad contrasted sharply with the antiblack attacks on activists at home, adding weight to the predictions of rising leaders such as Malcolm X who portended the potential of black nationalism.[14] Alongside, and in the absence of, these established organizers, a new generation of activists—including Alice Childress and Lorraine Hansberry—took up the mantle of nationalism and anti-imperialism in the 1950s.[15] By the early 1960s, women's groups such as the Cultural Association for Women of African Heritage and the Universal Association of Ethiopian Women inaugurated a new period of black nationalist organizing through their protests in support of black nationhood and self-determination on both sides of the Atlantic. Operating amid a shifting midcentury political landscape, these activists and organizations established the politics, style, and rhetoric now associated with post-1965 articulations of Black Power.[16]

Between 1961 and 1966, Black Power ideals and grassroots activism proliferated. In 1962, Moore revitalized UNIA members' earlier calls for reparations and African repatriation through the modern reparations movement.[17] The following year, Gloria Richardson, a member of the Cambridge Nonviolent Action Committee, an affiliate of the Student Nonviolent Coordinating Committee (SNCC), made her way to Detroit for the Northern Negro Grassroots Leadership Conference. The event combined the organizational spirit of the 1963 March on Washington with decolonization-inspired nationalist militancy. Along with her friend Malcolm X, who gave his iconic "Message to the Grassroots" speech, Richardson broke with SNCC's nonviolent mantra and voiced her support of armed self-defense and black community control at the event.[18] If Malcolm's call for black people to achieve freedom by "any means necessary" inspired Richardson, his appeals for them to reclaim their African culture captured the attention of activists such as Dorothy Jamal and Brenda Haiba Karenga. In 1965, they joined other local organizers in creating the Us Organization, a Los Angeles–based cultural nationalist group that advocated for cultural reclamation as a precursor to political revolution.[19] Black women's distinct but coinciding calls for economic independence, armed self-defense, cultural restoration, and political mobilization in the early 1960s were all manifestations of their increasingly unapologetic demands for control and autonomy.

By 1966, black women's various strands of activism became part of the fabric of the Black Power movement. The term *Black Power* evolved from a grassroots murmur into a national movement after Stokely Carmichael's June 1966 exclamation of the phrase in Greenwood, Mississippi. That same year saw the national debut of the original SNCC-supported Black Panther Party in Lowndes County, Alabama, and the Black Panther Party of Oakland, California, which Huey Newton and Bobby Seale created.[20] While the various iterations of the Black Panther Party challenged white supremacy through the ballot or the bullet, other black activists, including Amina Baraka, fused art, education, and community control through the African Free School, an independent educational institution supported by the CFUN in New Jersey. By the 1970s, members of these and other groups participated in national and international meetings such as the Black Power Conferences and the Sixth Pan-African Congress. Others joined the Congress of African People (CAP), a federation of Black Power organizations intent on realizing black self-determination and self-sufficiency on a global scale.[21] Black women consistently debated their roles and the meaning of black womanhood within these various Black Power projects and projections. Other times, women like Gwendolyn Patton and Frances Beal created independent, women-centered organizations, such as the Black Women's Liberation Committee (BWLC) and the Third World Women's Alliance (TWWA), designed to integrate Black Power, black feminist, and socialist principles.[22] Whatever form of Black Power they practiced, organizers, cultural workers, and theoreticians all engaged in the central slogans and principles of the era. Far from being marginal, violent, anti-intellectual, or male dominated, the Black Power movement of the late 1960s and 1970s was widespread and multifaceted in scope.

The new and proliferating histories of the Black Power era celebrate its diversity and challenge simplistic characterizations of its organizations, organizers, and political and cultural goals. They also reveal the rich, complex, and interlaced layers of the era by tracing postwar Black Power expressions, studying black women's Black Power politics, and considering the relationship of Black Power activism at the local, national, and international levels.[23] Although this new scholarship indicates that black women were an indispensable part of the movement, such activists still often remain ensconced in the popular imagination as a singular revolutionary persona or as marginal figures within organizations and collectives.[24] This is due, in part, to Black Power's lingering reputation as a sexist and male-dominated movement. It is also because black women's interventions into these conversations are not always legible within our current conceptualizations of Black Power, gender roles, intellectualism, and identity politics. However, black women left a record of direct and copious engagement with Black Power theoretics, symbolism, and politics expressed through their ideas about their rights and roles. Acknowledging and historicizing the scope and reach of their Black Power praxis requires exploring their activism in concert with their political imaginings. It also means reconstructing and analyzing their diverse visions of black womanhood within the context of their political and cultural organizing.

Regendering and Reimagining Black Power

Black female activists inaugurated the scholarship on their organizing and intellectual production. Well-known intellectuals and organizers such as Angela Davis, Assata Shakur, and Elaine Brown published personal and political autobiographies in the decades immediately following the movement. These texts documented their various routes to political activism and highlighted black women's critical contributions to Black Power organizing.[25] They also foregrounded the gender constructs, sexism, and misogyny within individual organizations and the movement at large. Historians quickly complemented these volumes with biographies of individual activists, such as Amy Jacques Garvey and Ruby Doris Smith Robinson, showing how black women consistently positioned themselves on the organizational and intellectual front lines of black nationalist projects and groups before and during the Black Power era.[26] Scholarly essays published alongside and shortly after these biographical accounts situated individual activists in the constellation of Black Power organizations and ideologies.[27] Many of these initial studies focused on national organizations such as the Black Panther Party. The pioneering work of Angela LeBlanc Ernest and Trayce Matthews, for example, explored women's participation in the party, illustrating how they shaped and were shaped by its gender dynamics.[28] Although contemporaneous and post hoc assessments glorified black men as the hypermasculine leaders of the movement, these initial personal accounts, biographies, and organizational studies indicated that black women held key leadership positions, challenged sexism, and advanced Black Power philosophies and organizing.

Historians have since continued this trend, diversifying our understandings of women's contributions to well-known Black Power organizations. Robyn Spencer and Mary Phillips have led the way in developing a body of scholarship that documents black women's stewardship of the Black Panther Party. Their research not only charts the evolution of the organization, paying particular attention to how black women shaped its stance on women and gender roles. It also shows how Panther women integrated their feminist priorities into their party work.[29] Ula Taylor has challenged popular and scholarly perceptions of black women's participation in the Nation of Islam. Focusing on female members, she reveals how they balanced the organization's conservative gender prescriptions with their personal and political goals by regendering their familial and social relationships.[30] Other scholars have begun to reexamine cultural nationalist groups such as the Us Organization and the CAP. Women in these organizations have often been overlooked because of the sexist reputation of these collectives. New analyses move beyond indicting male leaders for their patriarchal practices and document how women in these groups foregrounded their gendered priorities and challenged patriarchal interpretations of Kawaida, an ideology designed to counter white cultural hegemony through black-centered practices and values.[31] This scholarship provides more nuanced understandings of organizational dynamics and goals, highlights women's visible and previously undetected influence, and documents how black women navigated national Black Power organizations, at times challenging patriarchy and at other moments acquiescing to it.

Others have turned their focus toward black women's grassroots and extraorganizational activism. In the process, they have exposed the ways in which black women engendered and regendered the principles and rhetoric of the era. Whether it was Rhonda Williams's study of how black women in Baltimore mobilized "outside of, but in the context of, Black Power radicals" or Premilla Nadasen's assessment of how welfare rights activists including Johnnie Tillmon advocated a form of Black Power politics "attuned to the specific interests of poor women," historians have documented how black women have adopted and transformed Black Power principles to fit their lived experiences.[32]

If exploring black women's grassroots activism has proved productive, so too has examining their organizing in women-centered and feminist groups. Previously, studies of this period indicated that Black Power masculinism forced black women to create separate groups in order to organize around their gender-specific concerns.[33] To be sure, patriarchal interpretations of black nationalist ideologies fostered antagonistic relationships between male and female activists. However, the focus on these clashes has obscured instances of ideological and organizational convergence among nationalists and feminists. Recent scholarship by Stephen Ward and Sherie Randolph, among others, has delineated how black women fused Black Power and black feminist ideologies and protest strategies to create a women-centered radical identity and political agenda. Such scholarship argues for a new understanding of the relationship between Black Power and black feminism, one in which the former played a more generative role in cultivating the latter.[34]

The aforementioned studies have expanded our understanding of Black Power and challenged phallocentric readings of the era by focusing on black women's activism, particularly in a single organization or geographical locale. Such studies have now become an indispensable part of developing a holistic understanding of this era precisely because they show how black women challenged limiting ideas of their roles and responsibilities in daily organizing. They have also generated new questions. If we now know that black women disagreed with the real and imagined roles that black men assigned to them, what new models of womanhood did they developed in response? How did this differ within and among organizations? What role did ideology play in their reformulations of black womanhood? And what material effects did their gendered reimaginings have on the era's organizational and ideological trajectory?

I argue that some of these questions can be answered by mapping black women's engagement in the Black Power gendered imaginary. I begin with the premise that although activists' definitions of Black Power differed, they were united in their declaration of a new militant racial consciousness and driven by the collective goal of creating a new black identity. On the surface, this manifested in a cumulative shift from identifying with the term *Negro* to adopting the moniker *black*. It was also a deeper, more encompassing effort to transform the black condition by developing interpretations of black manhood and womanhood unbridled by Eurocentric definitions. Activists' new assertions of black identity were more than simply rhetorical expressions of militancy. They were the cornerstones of Black Power–era radicalism.[35] Reimagining themselves as Black Revolutionary Women or Pan-African Women empowered female activists; the Black Revolutionary's or Pan-Africanist's agenda became the rubric for their social, cultural, and political organizing.

Remaking Black Power documents *some* of the popular models of black womanhood that female Black Power–era activists produced. Historicizing black women's engagement in the Black Power–era gender debates means reconstructing their gendered political visions from multiple vantage points. As a result, my analysis spans from the political essays and satire of postwar women radicals of the 1950s, to the artwork of the Black Panther Party of the late 1960s, to the editorials of women's groups such as the TWWA, a Black Power–era feminist organization in which members reimagined black womanhood throughout the 1970s.[36] I show how black women remade black identity from multiple ideological and organizational positionalities; they did not always agree on how black womanhood should be redefined, and they both reinforced and defied the patriarchal parameters in which they worked. Comparing activists' visions of black womanhood foregrounds black women's pervasive engagement in Black Power principles and highlights the complexities and contradictions of the era. It also reveals the need for a conceptual remapping of the Black Power era, one in which their definitions of black womanhood were indispensable to organizational activism and critical to the era's ideological advancement.

A study of the gendered imaginary invites us to reconfigure previous conclusions about the Black Power era and women's roles within it. Centering black women's debates about black womanhood, for example, suggests the need for a temporal reframing of the era. Histories of Black Power often begin in 1966—the year Carmichael introduced the "Black Power" slogan into the mainstream, national consciousness. However, a closer examination shows that, in reimagining black womanhood, postwar women radicals developed and sustained "Black Power–style radicalism" before and alongside the civil rights movement of the 1950s and well before the rise of the New Left movements of the 1960s and 1970s.[37] It also indicates that black women continued to theorize and enact Black Power principles after 1975 and the demise of well-known Black Power organizations.

Remaking Black Power locates the origins of Black Power and its gendered debates amid the political organizing of postwar black women radicals who moved in and through leftist organizations including the CP and the Sojourners for Truth and Justice in the 1940s and 1950s. Chapter 1 shows how activists such as Claudia Jones, Alice Childress, and Mae Mallory revived black nationalist frameworks espoused in the 1920s and 1930s and infused them into a new political identity for black women in the postwar era. Organizing in a period in which 80 percent of black women were employed as domestic workers, Jones, Childress, and Mallory, among others, collectively created the trope of the "Militant Negro Domestic" as a way to reimagine working-class black women as nationalist political actors. Using political tracts, satire, fiction, and autobiographical accounts, they reimagined the black domestic worker as a militant activist who espoused a politics that fused Garveyite nationalism, communist class critiques, and gender-inclusive (later called feminist) visions of black liberation. In theorizing new ideas about black womanhood, postwar black women radicals challenged the common gendering of the black working-class as male. They also sustained and further developed early twentieth-century black nationalist formulations, laying the groundwork for future expressions of Black Power. This expansive temporal frame shows that black women's gendered redefinition was more than simply a response to popular male activists' sexism in the 1960s. It was a driving force behind the development and evolution of this era.

Examining black women's ideas about black womanhood also reframes our understanding of Black Power ideology, intellectuals, and intellectualism. Activists' formulations of black womanhood reflect a preoccupation with advancing a particular doctrine—such as revolutionary nationalism or cultural nationalism—as part of their gendered political redefinition. The new Black Power scholarship emphasizes the importance of the ideological development and trajectories of men like Malcolm X, Huey Newton, and Maulana Karenga.[38] Important additions to the historiography, these studies reveal that Black Power was a generative ideological era replete with liberal, radical, and revolutionary political philosophies. However, they also position men as the primary progenitors of Black Power thought and imply that the flow of ideas moved in only one direction: from the top-ranking male leaders down to the female rank and file.

This book moves beyond a framework in which men theorized and women organized. Heeding the advice of scholars like Ula Taylor, who has argued that we must pay attention to the ways in which black women "ground their ideas in the personal, antidotal, and subjective modes," this book illustrates how they devised more expansive understandings of political theory by reimagining and enacting new gendered political identities.[39] In chapter 2, I show how women in the Black Panther Party theorized new ideas about the Black Revolutionary Woman in concert with the party's changing political ideology. Charting the evolution of this ideal from 1967 to 1975 reveals how Panther women engaged with the organization's evolving ideological outlook, applied it to their lived experiences, and then promulgated their gender-specific interpretations of the organization's philosophy in their writings and artwork. I show how their debates over the contours of the ideal female revolutionary actor shaped how party leadership perceived and enacted the ideological tenets to which they were beholden. This and other chapters indicate that black women's writings about black womanhood were critical sites through which they constructed more inclusive applications of political theory. Their influence on the ideological direction of organizations foregrounds the importance of considering black women as Black Power theorists in their own right and interrogating the reciprocal relationship between their intellectual and activist work.

Centering these activists' writings about black womanhood also transforms the body of evidence on which much of the history of the Black Power era has been written. Previously, studies of this period have primarily relied on white and black men's characterizations of black womanhood and black women's rights and roles. This archival method stems from a position that assumes that black women did not articulate their own perspectives on the intersection of political ideology and gender. It also derives from bias in what we decide "counts" as intellectual production during this period.[40] The same periodicals, publications, and collections that scholars often use to frame Black Power as a male-dominated era are brimming with information about black women's thoughts, actions, and philosophical leanings. These sources are often overlooked because they do not take the "traditional" form of ideological expression or because they undermine popular perceptions about black women and gender politics during this era. In reading black women's intellectual production as authoritative sources on gender politics and political thought during this period, this book destabilizes dominant perspectives and archival practices and highlights how, by redefining black womanhood, black women developed a vibrant genealogy of black thought.

These same documents also transform conventional understandings of what constituted Black Power activism. For many of the women in this study, a key part of redefining black identity and liberation was reimagining their roles and responsibilities within movement organizing. They based their claims on their lived experiences as activists. Black women also drew on the larger Black Power–era goal of overturning the social order to push for more expansive understandings of women's roles within the era's organizations or groups. Many argued that heading voter registration drives, creating black community schools, developing black cultural practices, leading community programs, heading organizations, and myriad other forms of activism were the purview of women. Irrespective of how they reimagined black womanhood, these activists consistently argued that they should not be confined to traditional interpretations of "women's work."

A focus on black women's ideas about black womanhood foregrounds their ideas about their roles and responsibilities in political organizing. Chapter 3 explores women who were part of two cultural nationalist groups: the Us Organization and the CFUN. Both of these groups originally practiced the philosophy of Kawaida, a culturally driven doctrine that originally relegated black women to marginal activist roles in the private sphere. I show how, by redefining their roles and responsibilities as African Women, women in these groups expanded the range of organizing activities for which cultural nationalist women were responsible. Not only did they consider developing new cultural ceremonies, such as birth rites, wedding ceremonies, and naming rituals, as the purview of the African Woman, in their columns and handbooks on "African Womanhood," they also pushed for women to be active participants in protests, voting drives, community education, and ideological debates. This chapter illustrates how, by constructing more expansive definitions of the African Woman, Kawaidist women encouraged this faction of the Black Power movement to adopt more equitable conceptualizations of gender roles. They also played on activists' goals of redefining black manhood and womanhood to theorize more inclusive ideological and organizational expressions of cultural nationalism.

Black women did not confine these expressions to specific organizations or groups; they also reimagined black womanhood in ways that traversed organizational, ideological, and geographical boundaries. Recognizing that Black Power was not a strictly U.S. phenomenon, many activists expressed global solidarity and formulated imagined communities through the lens of Pan-Africanism, a political ideology based on the belief that peoples of African descent around the world share a common past and destiny, as well as similar political aims. Black American activists developed gendered political identities that reflected their appreciation, solidarity, and identification with other women across the diaspora. One of the many ways that they accomplished this goal was by envisioning themselves as Pan-African Women, or by identifying as members of the African diasporic rather than the American populace. Women from across the political spectrum, including some from the aforementioned groups, theorized forms of black womanhood that embraced a unified, African-centered politics and subjectivity across sectarian lines. They rhetorically repositioned black American women as part of the vanguard of diasporic liberation struggles, challenging black men's real and imagined positions as leaders of the global black liberation struggle.

In chapter 4, I explore how black women extended these gendered debates beyond American borders. I contextualize their interest in and identification with African and Pan-African liberation struggles within Black Power activists' deepening investment in internationalizing the movement. I then read their speeches, working papers, and conference resolutions from the 1972 All-Africa Women's Conference and the 1974 Sixth Pan-African Congress as examples of how some female activists articulated the ideal of the Pan-African Woman. Black American women's formulations of Pan-African womanhood reflect the global scope of Black Power, as well as their interest in redefining their roles on an international scale. Their ideas about the intersection of Pan-Africanism and black womanhood highlight the need to look beyond organizational, ideological, and geographical borders for evidence of black women's intellectual activism. It also shows the gendered imaginary to be a critical but understudied site of Black Power internationalism.

Similarly, black women's ideas about black womanhood invite us to rethink the relationship between black feminism and Black Power. It is traditionally assumed that male activists promoted a monolithic form of black identity that did not account for women's gendered or class-based identifications. As a response to and as a criticism of this approach, some argue, black women created separate women's or feminist organizations and developed a political identity based on their intersecting race, gender, and class oppression.[41] Many female activists did critique this aspect of Black Power organizing and formed independent women's or feminist organizations during the early 1970s.[42] Others challenged sexism and pushed for multifaceted ideas of blackness from *within* Black Power groups. Whichever avenue these activists chose, they were typically addressing sexist *interpretations* of black nationalist philosophies and principles rather than a given ideology itself. Nevertheless, post hoc assessments of these debates have positioned black feminism and black nationalism as oppositional theoretical and activist pursuits.

Exploring Black Power–era debates about gender roles reveals a more complicated story. Black women's formulations of black womanhood indicate that they consistently simultaneously identified as nationalists and feminists. A survey of their intellectual production also illustrates how, as members of multiple Black Power–era organizations, ranging from the Sojourners for Truth and Justice to the Black Panther Party, they developed definitions of black womanhood with these concurrent ideological allegiances in mind. Chapter 5 reflects this point in greater detail by exploring the TWWA. I chart how this group created the identity of the Third World Black Woman, a radical, intersectional model of womanhood based on their real and imagined commonalities with women in and from Third World countries. In this particular formulation, alliance members imagined black women as activists who retained their commitments to Black Power principles while also integrating feminist and socialist principles into their political and cultural work. Tracing the evolution of the alliance's redefinition of black womanhood challenges long-held assumptions about the incompatibility of black feminism and black nationalism. It also shows that intersectional approaches to identity formation and activism that we uphold today emanated from Black Power activists' efforts to envision black women's liberation in holistic and generative ways.

Black Power activists continued to engage in debates over women's roles throughout the late 1970s. However, their freedom dreams were not enough to overcome the very real obstacles that their groups faced due to government repression, internal divisiveness, and financial crises. After Black Power organizations and collectives fell apart, a new generation of activists continued to debate the meaning of manhood and womanhood, albeit amid very different historical circumstances and political conditions.[43] Subsequent activists often looked to the Black Power–era generation to develop liberatory models and identities to meet the political and economic challenges of their day. Here again debates about black manhood and womanhood played an important role, as later generations have both rehearsed the gendered antagonisms of the era and drawn from the symbols and political models that female activists produced. Even if the organizations and activists of the Black Power era were blunted by the late 1970s, their ideas about gender roles and women's liberation live on in popular and political organizing and theorizing traditions.

In the pages that follow, I historicize and analyze the alternative roles and identities that black women imagined for themselves. This book is not a definitive history of women in the Black Power era. Rather, it is a history of Black Power told through black women's ideas about black womanhood. It is a study of how black women rhetorically and imagistically engaged in the Black Power–era goal of identity making, as well as of the effect of their gendered identity models on this period and how we understand it. My purpose is to foreground some of the nuances, complexities, and possibilities imbedded in black women's attempts to imagine a different world and their roles within it. I also aim to illustrate that histories of the Black Power era that do not account for black women's gender-specific freedom dreams are incomplete.

I undertake this task by detailing some of the many definitions of womanhood that female Black Power activists produced. Balancing the inherent messiness of identity politics with the usefulness of gender as an analytical category, I have isolated and named these different models of womanhood in each chapter of the book. My titles for these categories stem from the historical record in which these activists implicitly or explicitly referenced them and the political moment or organization in which they were created. This is an inexact approach. However, I maintain that in embracing rather than shying away from the ambiguities of these debates, we might be better able to see the possibilities and limitations of Black Power ideals and reframe well-worn debates about this period. This approach also extends to the source material of the book. Its emphasis on intellectual and artistic production biases the book toward well-known organizations that produced substantial amounts of print media. This means that I offer an analysis of only a handful of the many important actors and organizations that defined the era. However, this method also provides the opportunity to focus on black women's engagement and racial redefinition in some of the most well-known and male-dominated groups. Ultimately, the book invites a conversation about how black women's real and imagined ideas about black womanhood shaped the Black Power era and how they can help us move toward different understandings of Black Power, as well as its present and future lessons.

The Black Power era was transformative not only for its critique of American race relations but also for the generative models of black identity that activists created. *Remaking Black Power* shows that black women's theorizing, particularly their new tropes of black womanhood, was an important engine of this ideological and political experimentation. Just as their male counterparts challenged racial hierarchies by redefining gender roles, black women worked to promote revolutionary change among their peers by redefining their roles and communal gender constructs. Their models of womanhood were, at times, contradictory, problematic, and essentialist. Nevertheless, by demonstrating the different radical identities that black women could adopt, and how these models were related to the liberation of black men and women everywhere, they shaped the evolution of the era and molded a movement that redefined the meaning of race and identity in American life.

CHAPTER ONE

The Militant Negro Domestic, 1945–1965

"The revolution is on, and it isn't just tonight," seventy-year-old radical activist Audley Moore told a group of protesters and schoolteachers in 1968.
"I want you to know that it isn't just this week. This revolution has been
going on for the last fifty years, because when I came into the movement,
I came in only because it was revolutionary. This is something for you
to think about, so don't just think that because Carmichael said 'Black
Power' that all of sudden people today are thinking in terms of their freedom."[1] These New York City–based activists and educators had invited
Moore to the "Priorities in Urban Education Conference" to help garner
support for their campaign for community control of Brooklyn public
schools.[2] As one of the movement's midwives, Moore had been fighting
for black self-determination longer than most of her audience members
had been alive. She used the speaking invitation to proffer an alternative
genealogy of the Black Power era, one in which 1960s protests were the
continuation rather than the origin of the movement.

Moore counted herself among a cadre of activists who were instrumental in developing the ideological frameworks of the Black Power era and
in formulating gendered expressions of its central principles. Although
the story of the movement typically begins in 1966, with Stokely Carmichael's speech in Greenwood, Mississippi, Black Power was much larger
than the slogan he introduced into the popular and political discourse.[3] A
lifelong black nationalist, Moore consistently argued that black women
radicals developed and sustained radical emancipation projects well before
the 1960s. She also credited these women with creating the new definitions
of black "self-identity" that Carmichael and others would later argue were at
the core of Black Power projects.[4]

Moore located the origins of the Black Power movement in the intellectualism and activism of postwar women radicals. Coming of age in the
1920s and 1930s, many of these women were politicized by Marcus Garvey's Universal Negro Improvement Association (UNIA), a global black
nationalist organization that advocated for black self-determination, African repatriation, and separate black cultural and political institutions. As

the Depression hit and the UNIA dissipated in the 1930s, many of these women joined the Communist Party (CP). Employed almost exclusively as maids and cooks in white households, they found the CP attractive because it combined Garveyite nationalist frameworks with sophisticated critiques of domestic workers' class oppression. As CP members, they espoused a black nationalist, working-class, women-centered political agenda and organized around their unique experiences with racism, sexism, and capitalism.

In the first half of the twentieth century, black nationalists and Communists often theorized black liberation through the lens of the working class. Moreover, these activists and organizations framed the struggle for black self-determination and liberation as the fight to regain black manhood.[5] Popular and political perceptions of black womanhood, on the other hand, often focused on the domestic worker as a symbol of black working-class womanhood. Although leftist organizations identified black women's "special" race, class, and gender oppression, they did not always articulate a gender-inclusive emancipatory vision. Instead, leading activists and groups often marginalized the domestic worker and the plight of black women more broadly, reinforcing popular perceptions of black women that were steeped in the ideal of the "docile" mammy figure and entrenched in the legacy of slavery.[6]

From the 1940s to the 1960s, black women radicals both centered and reimagined the political identity of the black domestic worker. Drawing on Garveyite frameworks, they maintained that black Americans constituted a distinct cultural and political group entitled to separation and self-determination. These activists' communist-inspired analyses of their intersecting race, class, and gender oppression also led them to view black working-class women as the vanguard of black Americans' self-deterministic pursuits. Combining these positions, they collectively constructed the idea of a Militant Negro Domestic, a political identity that framed the domestic worker as a political activist who advocated for community control, black self-determination, self-defense, and separate black cultural and political institutions. By reimagining this dominant symbol of black womanhood, black women activists reshaped contemporary masculinist conceptions of the black working-class political subject. They also linked the ideologies and symbols of early twentieth-century black nationalism to the burgeoning Black Power movement of the early 1960s, making both black women and womanhood foundational to Black Power–era thought.

Radical Networks and Domestic Worker Politics

Many Black Power foremothers started the backbreaking work of cleaning white women's homes at the same time that the UNIA began its ascent as the preeminent, global black nationalist organization.[7] Marcus Garvey's organization reached its zenith in the United States in the early 1920s and was a powerful antidote to black Americans' daily experiences of disenfranchisement, discrimination, and dehumanization. Garvey's sermons about racial pride, black-controlled business enterprises, and plans to redeem Africa through repatriation prompted many black Americans to join their local chapter of the UNIA.[8] Garveyites created independent schools, cultural programming, medical services, and economic relief funds to enact their leader's calls for black autonomy and self-determination.[9] The UNIA's uplift-oriented nationalism, formulated through extensive symbolism and catechism, galvanized black people worldwide and created a substantial black nationalist base within the United States.

Despite its middle-class leadership, Garveyism was a working-class movement, and black working-class women were critical to its success.[10] They supported the organization's many parades and programs; became part of the UNIA women's auxiliary, the Black Cross Nurses; and subscribed to the organizational newspaper, the *Negro World*.[11] Garvey's second wife and fellow UNIA leader, Amy Jacques Garvey, emphasized black women's special role in the UNIA and black nationalist activism more broadly. Through her column, "Our Women and What They Think," she roused many domestic workers to spend what little money they had on UNIA dues and stock in Garvey's black-owned shipping company, the Black Star Line.[12] Countless black women radicals identified Garveyism and the UNIA as progenitors of their activism. Audley Moore, who was a domestic worker in New Orleans and Harlem, found Marcus Garvey's emphasis on black pride and global solidarity promising. Throughout her life, she maintained that it was the UNIA leader's ideology that showed her the "nature of [her] oppression," revealed that she was part of a diasporic community, and taught her how to formulate nationalist claims.[13] Moore was among the many black working-class women who remained committed to the ideological and programmatic tenets of Garveyism well after 1927, when the U.S. government convicted and deported the UNIA leader for mail fraud.[14]

While Garvey battled federal authorities, the CP gained a foothold in black communities. During the 1920s, the CP's governing body, the Third Communist International (Comintern), identified black workers as important partners in ending global capitalism and imperialism. By 1928, the Comintern had developed a formal position on what it called the "Negro Question," or the larger issue of how black people fit into its ideological frame. At the Sixth World Congress held that same year, officials announced their support of the Black Belt Thesis, or the claim that black Americans in the southeastern United States and northern urban centers constituted a nation set apart from other Americans by their shared cultural heritage, economic subjugation, and political exclusion.[15] According to the CP, black Americans in the Deep South constituted an oppressed nation within a nation and were entitled to self-determination, political and economic power, and the right to secede from the United States.[16] By adopting the Black Belt Thesis, the Comintern made black nationalism and black self-determination central components of the CP's U.S. agenda. It also positioned the CP—both ideologically and programmatically—to capture Garvey's membership base in the United States.

The party's stance on black political and economic self-determination gained traction among black Americans during a period in which both the UNIA and the U.S. economy were weakening. In the aftermath of Garvey's deportation and the failure of the Black Star Line, UNIA membership declined. Far more detrimental, however, was the economic collapse of 1929 and the subsequent depression that engulfed the country.[17] The Great Depression affected black women workers more than any other segment of the population. Before the nationwide crisis, Jim Crow laws and hegemonic gendered divisions of labor relegated black women to domestic work in white households.[18] As jobs and money became scarce, more white women sought domestic work. An overcrowded labor market led many black women to seek employment through exchanges such as the Bronx Slave Market, a term activists Ella Baker and Marvel Cooke used to describe the process in which black women lined the New York City streets "waiting expectantly" for white "housewives to buy their strength and energy for an hour, two hours, or even for a day."[19] The popularity of these street-corner markets made it clear that, despite President Franklin D. Roosevelt's efforts to ameliorate suffering through New Deal programs in the 1930s, black women would continue to be shut out of other occupations and shoulder the brunt of the discrimination brought on by universal economic hardship. In an effort to gain better pay and treatment, some turned to progressive organizations like the National Association for the Advancement of Colored People (NAACP) and the New York–based Domestic Workers Union (DWU).[20] Others joined the CP.

Bronx Slave Market (detail). Smithsonian American Art Museum, Museum Purchase; copyright 1938 by Robert McNeill.

The CP attracted thousands of black women through its working-class, nationalist, and gender-conscious ideology exemplified by its vigorous attacks on racism and imperialism. Domestically, the CP's backing of the Scottsboro Boys, nine black teenagers accused of raping two white women in 1931, confirmed its support of black working-class women.[21] Within days of the boys' arrests, the CP's legal advocacy wing, the International Labor Defense (ILD), had successfully turned the trial into a powerful symbol of race and class injustice. The organization also supported the mothers of the Scottsboro Boys, some of whom were domestic workers. With its help, mothers such as Ada Wright framed their arrest and trial as another example of black working-class women's oppression, emphasizing the unique hardships they faced in trying to provide for and protect their sons.[22] Party members' involvement in the Scottsboro case showcased the organization's ability to recognize and mobilize around black women's concerns. Many former Garveyites found their way to the CP through ILD-sponsored Scottsboro protests, where they joined in with hundreds of black and white protesters carrying "red banners, the hammer and sickle," and placards reading, "Death to the Lynchers" and "End Jim Crow."[23]

Black women also appreciated Communist support of global black self-determination. When Italian dictator Benito Mussolini invaded Ethiopia in an effort to annex it to Italy in 1935, CP members framed the incursion as both an imperialist atrocity and an affront to black sovereignty. They also joined with local black nationalist groups to protest the violation of the African nation's autonomy and self-determination. In Harlem, CP members participated in large, multiorganizational demonstrations and formed the Provisional Committee for the Defense of Ethiopia in order to publicly denounce Italy's imperialist and racist aims.[24] This and other protests attracted black women who found ideological and organizational congruence between the UNIA and CP platforms. Claudia Jones, who had migrated to Harlem from Trinidad, recalled that she joined the party because she, "like millions of negro people[,] ... was impressed by the communist speakers who explained the reasons for this brutal crime against young Negro boys; and who related the Scottsboro case to the struggle of the Ethiopian people against fascism, and Mussolini's invasion."[25]

Although the CP advanced an antiracist and anti-imperialist agenda, it, like other nationalist organizations at this time, framed black nationalism and liberation in masculinist terms and imagery.[26] Party literature emphasized the revolutionary potential of a black male proletariat and heralded figures like the Haitian Revolution's Toussaint Louverture and U.S. slave revolt leader Nat Turner as exemplars of black self-determination.[27] The cultural realm reflected the political. The CP valorized black working-class or folk culture but "gendered the folk" as male.[28] Its masculinist characterization of the black proletariat contrasted sharply with the lived experiences of working-class black women, who represented a rapidly growing segment of CP membership.

As they joined the party ranks, black women challenged this patriarchal perception of the black working class, developing an organizational structure and political culture that centered their lives and work.[29] In the 1920s, women such as Grace Campbell and Hermina Dumont Huiswoud became leaders of the CP-supported Harlem Tenants League, a group that coordinated demonstrations, blocked evictions, led rent strikes, and demanded fair housing-regulation enforcement for black Americans during the Great Depression. Along with other organizers, they shaped the ideological and organizational agenda of the league, which combined strategies such as neighborhood marches for lower rent with rhetoric that framed housing struggles as part of a global fight against white supremacy and capitalism.[30] These first recruits also published articles foregrounding black women's oppression and political potential. Fanny Austin and Bell Lamb argued that black women were the most exploited segment of the working class and that their domestic and factory work helped them develop a "considerable degree of class consciousness" that made them "material for the foundation of a labor movement" in the industrial world.[31] These and other women capitalized on Black Belt Thesis directives for black self-determination and working-class-led activism and fit them to meet their gendered experiences and goals. They also laid the foundation for future black women members to focus on and retheorize the position and potential of the black domestic worker.

Black women's influence in the CP increased significantly during the Popular Front era of the 1930s. The rise of fascism in Germany and Italy, and the threat of an eminent global war to stem it, caused the CP to shift its focus to meet the needs of the changing global political order. From the mid-1930s to the 1940s, the organization de-emphasized its critique of the American nation-state, supported Roosevelt's New Deal programs, championed American democracy, and appealed to trade unionists, intellectuals, artists, and women's organizations. Members also formed coalitions with progressive and liberal groups in an effort to create an anticolonial, antiracist, and antifascist political front.[32] This strategy not only swelled party ranks, it also created a host of new programs, committees, and political campaigns through which black members could develop as activists and intellectuals.[33] Black women led the expansion of many Popular Front organizations, which included a host of diverse, civil-rights-focused leftist groups such as the Southern Negro Youth Congress (SNYC), the National Negro Congress (NNC), and the Civil Rights Congress.[34]

These same women capitalized on Popular Front rhetoric and organizing in order to foreground the plight of domestic workers and reformulate prevailing perceptions of black womanhood. Esther Cooper Jackson joined the CP-supported SNYC after completing her master's thesis, "The Negro Woman Domestic Worker in Relation to Trade Unionism," at Fisk University.[35] As a SNYC leader, Jackson was a key part of the party's Southern front. She worked with the youth wing of the NNC for twelve years, serving as its executive secretary and mobilizing young Southern activists to fight for racial and economic justice through voter and union rights protests.[36] Women such as Louise Thompson Patterson, who joined the organization in 1933, created new analytical frameworks to address domestic workers' unique oppression.[37] In "Toward a Brighter Dawn" (1936), she recounted the exploitation of the Bronx Slave Market and emphasized how it was a microcosm of the race, class, and gender discrimination, or the "triple exploitation," that black women faced.[38] Thompson was the first to use this term to describe the intersectional oppression of black women workers. Other activists would continue to develop this framework, emphasizing black women's position at the epicenter of oppressive systems. Jackson's and Thompson's analyses were emblematic of the second generation of black Communist women, who framed the domestic worker as a symbol of black women's oppression and political potential.[39]

Although the Popular Front opened doors for black women organizers, it also foreclosed their opportunities to champion black nationalism and self-determination. Wartime realities forced black leftist activists to advocate for their rights through a prodemocratic, antifascist discourse and downplay calls for black self-determination and decolonization. During this period, the party de-emphasized nationalist and separatist rhetoric, opting to promote desegregation and integrationist approaches instead.[40] After World War II, the CP continued this strategy of building leftist alliances and a populist base. In 1944, party leader Earl Browder reconstituted the organization as the Communist Political Association.[41] In that same year, he ended the organization's formal support of the Black Belt Thesis, arguing that black Americans had opted for "their complete integration into the American nation as a whole, and not for separation."[42]

Many black women activists remained convinced of the emancipatory potential of both the Black Belt Thesis and black domestic workers despite the CP's shifting stance. Some members had never relinquished their support of Garvey-inspired nationalism; they simply viewed the party as a vehicle through which to assert their politics.[43] Others recognized the value and enduring relevance of the nationalism promulgated by their compatriots in the pared-down, but still active, UNIA.[44] Many recognized that, after two world wars, black Americans still lacked basic freedoms and civil rights, despite their willingness to "close ranks" and work and fight alongside their white counterparts at home and abroad.[45] Most compelling, perhaps, for these black women activists was the fact that by the 1950s, they were still exploited and largely relegated to domestic work. Accordingly, black women radicals reconfigured the idea of the domestic worker in the gendered imaginary, often framing her as prototypical Marxist and nationalist activist. Their writings not only fostered radical, gender-conscious frameworks amid an increasingly liberal political climate; they also laid the foundation for future cultural and political expressions of Black Power and empowerment.

Reimagining Domestic Militancy

Theorist and activist Claudia Jones was one of many black women who refused to let the concept of black nationhood and self-determination disappear from party debate and discussion. She arrived in the United States in 1924 when she was eight years old. Like many West Indians, her family relocated from Port of Spain, Trinidad, to New York City with the hopes of thriving in America. "This dream was soon disabused," Jones recollected, as the Depression hit, and she and her family "learned the special scourge of indignity stemming from Jim Crow national oppression." As an adolescent, she navigated the streets of Harlem, buoyed by her father's teachings about the "pride and consciousness of [her] people" and "[their] relation to Africa from which [their] antecedents sprang."[46] Her introduction to political writing came shortly after high school, in 1935, when she began publishing "Claudia's Comments" for a nationalist newspaper, a column in which she addressed the invasion of Ethiopia, civil rights protests, trade union struggles, and antilynching fights.[47] She joined the CP in 1936 and was active in the Young Communist League soon thereafter. In 1937, she became the associate editor for the league's newspaper, the *Weekly Review*, and, by 1943, she was the editor of the publication.[48] She also authored "Half the World," a women's column in the CP news organ the *Daily Worker*, and nine essays in *Political Affairs*.[49]

Jones used her prominent position in the Communist Party to reinvigorate debates over black nationhood and reenvision the role of black domestic workers within this political frame. Responding directly to Browder's disavowal of black Americans' claims to nationhood, the theorist argued that not only was the Black Belt Thesis ideologically sound, but it was also vital to black liberation.[50] In "On the Right to Self-Determination for the Negro People in the Black Belt" (1946), she maintained that black Americans were "an historically developed community of people, with a common language, a common territory, and a common economic life, all of which are manifest in a common culture." Therefore, "Negro people in the Black Belt constitute[d] a nation."[51] For Jones, nationhood was a prerequisite for the right to self-determination; yet enacting self-determination did not require an act of physical separation. Browder claimed that black Americans had chosen to integrate rather than form a separate nation. Jones argued that this dichotomy between separation and integration was a false one. "Integration cannot be considered a substitute for the right of self-determination. National liberation is not synonymous with integration, neither are the concepts mutually exclusive," she wrote.[52] Integration entailed "breaking down the fetters which prohibit the full economic, political, and social participation of Negroes in all phases of American life." It did not mean that "a merger, or an assimilative process necessarily [took] place."[53] Jones combined Soviet ideas of nationality, Western nation-state frameworks, and Garveyite goals of racial redemption in her defense of black nationhood. Writing in the late 1940s, she used this argument to encourage activists to renew their commitment to the Black Belt Thesis as a viable liberation schema.[54]

Jones asserted the emancipatory potential of black nationalism for black working-class women in "An End to the Neglect of the Problems of the Negro Woman!" (1949). She used the black domestic worker as evidence for this claim. Her reasons for adopting this approach were twofold. According to Jones, the discrimination that black domestic workers faced represented the "crassest manifestations" of race, class, and gender oppression in the United States. In addition, black women's "almost complete exclusion from virtually all fields of work except the most menial and underpaid, namely, domestic service," meant that the experiences and representations of domestic workers were a powerful symbol of black womanhood.[55] As she explained, the "lot of the domestic worker [was] one of unbearable misery." When not suffering the "additional indignity, in some areas, of having to seek work in virtual 'slave markets' on the streets where bids are made, as from a slave block," these women labored in poorly defined and ever-expanding jobs in white homes. Confined to the gender-specific work of cleaning and cooking, and facing perpetual racial discrimination, Jones declared that the black domestic worker was "superexploited" and the lowest member of the social stratum.[56]

The theorist asserted that black domestic workers had the potential to be emancipated and an emancipatory force, but only if they rejected demeaning definitions of black womanhood and ascribed to newer, radical ideas about their rights and roles. Jones explained that in "film, radio, and press, the Negro woman is not pictured in her real role as breadwinner, mother, and protector of the family, but as a traditional 'mammy' who puts the care of children and families of others above her own." She argued that this demeaning image of black womanhood "must be combatted and rejected as a device of the imperialists to perpetuate the white chauvinist ideology that Negro women are 'backward,' 'inferior,' and the 'natural slaves' of others." Jones encouraged the CP and her female readership to reject this characterization and replace it with one that appreciated black women's militancy and black-centered political ethos. Emphasizing the tangible effects of reimagining black women's personal and political attributes, Jones asserted that the "bourgeoisie [was] fearful of the militancy of the Negro woman," as "the militancy of the whole Negro people and thus of the anti-imperialist coalition" would be enhanced if black women eschewed traditional gendered stereotypes and adopted a militant political persona.[57]

Jones then encouraged black women to envision and enact this persona using the theoretical and programmatic demands of the Black Belt Thesis. If party members based their support of black self-determination on the black proletariat's shared experiences with slavery and its "remnants," then Jones urged black women to ground their political self-conception in their gender-specific experiences within these oppressive systems. She explained that "the history of the Negro woman shows that the Negro mother under slavery held a key position and played a dominant role in her own family grouping. This was due primarily to two factors: the conditions of slavery, under which marriage, as such, was nonexistent, and the Negro's social status was derived from the mother and not the father; and the fact that most of the Negro people brought to these shores by the slave traders came from West Africa where the position of women, based on their actual participation in property control, was relatively higher in the family than that of European women." Jones found it "impossible within the confines of th[e] article" to chronicle the "degradation" of black women in slavery and its remnants that led to black women's "superexploited" status. However, she connected her historical analysis to the present day by noting that "during and after slavery, Negro women had to support themselves and the children," had taken on "an important role in the economic and social life of [their] people," and "became schooled in self-reliance, in courageous and selfless action."[58] Jones's discussion of the "historical aspects" of black women workers became the foundation of her new projection of militant black womanhood predicated on the principles of self-determination and self-reliance. She also laid the foundation for an alternative, positive conception of the black domestic worker, defined by gender-specific racial and cultural signifiers to a greater extent than Marxist and Eurocentric characterizations had allowed.

Jones then demonstrated how black women domestic workers could build on the historical legacy of black women's militancy, offering concrete examples of black women's enactments of self-defense and self-determination. She heralded women such as Rosa Lee Ingram, a mother and sharecropper who "faced life imprisonment in a Georgia Jail" when police arrested her and two of her sons after an altercation with their neighboring white tenant farmer, John Stratford. Stratford attempted to sexually assault Ingram, and she and her sons retaliated, killing him in self-defense.[59] Jones argued that Ingram epitomized working-class black militancy and exemplified principles such as self-determination over one's body and land by defending herself against the "indecent advances of a 'white supremacist.'"[60] The CP leader also cited other examples of black women's "militancy and organizational talents," including their successful fights for partial demands such as employment equality, their support for Ingram, and their lobbying of the United Nations for civil rights. For Jones, these examples served as evidence of the need for black domestic workers to reimagine themselves as radical women committed to achieving black liberation through self-determination, self-defense, and "concrete" demands for black liberation.[61]

What emerged from "An End to the Neglect" was a new vision of the black woman worker as the Militant Negro Domestic. Jones took the most prominent symbol of black womanhood—the black domestic worker—and reformulated it using the principles of the Black Belt Thesis. She chronicled black women's shared cultural and political heritage, as well as their gender-specific experiences with oppression. She then argued that this could be the basis of black women's militancy if they rejected predominant characterizations of black women workers and invested in nationalist-inspired principles. Ultimately, Jones transformed the downtrodden black domestic from a "superexploited" worker into a powerful nationalist activist. She projected an image of the domestic worker as a radical political actor mobilized by her intersectional oppression, guided by her African heritage, committed to race-based politics, and insistent on black women's right to self-defense and self-determination.

The theorist's projection of the Militant Negro Domestic both aligned with and subverted other ideas about black womanhood circulating at this time. In her effort to redefine black womanhood, she, like her nationalist contemporaries, relied on undifferentiated understandings of African societies and heritage. In the essay, Jones claimed that "the love of the African mother for her child was unsurpassed" and that "East African mothers offered themselves to the slave traders" in order to save their children.[62] Her statements confirmed black women's strength and militancy and challenged popular perceptions of black women as weak and marginal. However, such claims also proffered an undifferentiated perception of African societies that did not account for cultural, regional, or community differences. Jones departed from Garveyite-like constructs, however, by rejecting the UNIA leader's calls for capitalist-based economic advancement in favor of black working-class-led socialist revolution. Similarly, she eschewed popular models of black womanhood predicated on middle-class ideals of female domesticity, or ones that envisioned black women primarily as mothers and caregivers in the home and the private sphere. She consistently proffered a conception of the black domestic worker who engaged in public expressions of militancy and nationalism rather than withdrawing from civic life or aspiring to assimilate into white society.[63]

Jones recognized that her formulation of black womanhood contrasted with existing ideas about gender roles within radical black organizing. Anticipating her contemporaries' critiques, she situated her vision of the Militant Negro Domestic within the larger context of nationalist, communist, and women-centered organizing. In "An End to the Neglect," she noted that in reimagining themselves as militants, black women did not "fail to recognize that the Negro question in the United States [was] *prior* to, and not equal to the woman question; that only to the extent that [they fought] all chauvinist expressions and actions as regards the Negro people and fight for the full equality of the Negro people, [could] women as a whole advance their struggle for equal rights."[64] At first glance, Jones's statements appeared to rehearse a "race first" approach, or a perspective that prioritized black liberation over women's equality in political struggles. However, her vision of the Militant Negro Domestic situated black working-class women at the epicenter of both black and women's liberation struggles and framed their militancy as indispensable to both movements. Her vision rested on the idea that black women could simultaneously advance both black nationalist and women-centered emancipatory projects by challenging cultural, historical, and economic forces that had come to define black oppression at large. In doing so, Jones underscored black women's commitments to nationalist projects while also suggesting that the ideology was broad enough to encompass and advance black women's subjectivities and political priorities.[65] If, as Robin D. G. Kelley has argued, the CP's patriarchal vision of black nationalist liberation "precluded a serious theoretical framework that might combine the 'Negro' and 'Woman' questions," then, through the Militant Negro Domestic, Jones offered a plausible and practical resolution to both issues.[66]

Although "An End to the Neglect" reinvigorated the party's attention to black domestic workers and black nationalism, by 1950, few black women found it to be a viable conduit through which to assert this militant identity. When World War II ended, President Harry S. Truman's administration pursued an aggressive policy of containment against the Soviet Union that adversely affected the CP and its affiliates. From the late 1940s to the early 1960s, state and federal government officials targeted leftists across the political spectrum, instigating a period of arrests, trials, and deportations of activists based on their known or perceived association with communism.[67] During the McCarthy era, progressive organizations and activists began to distance themselves from the CP and its members, fearing persecution or incarceration for supposedly violating the Smith Act, a law that penalized anyone whom members of the House Un-American Activities Committee determined was advocating for the overthrow of the government.[68]

As their larger networks and organizations shrank, black women activists turned to smaller groups to enact the militancy that Jones prescribed. Some joined the Sojourners for Truth and Justice, an intergenerational group of activists, domestic workers, and factory employees that rallied around black women's political priorities.[69] CP members such as Patterson, Jones, and Moore brought their experience to the group. Younger Sojourner leadership included budding writers and cultural critics Alice Childress and Lorraine Hansberry. From 1951 to 1952, members rallied around high-profile cases of women such as Ingram as profound examples of the government's unwillingness to protect black women's "lives and liberties."[70] They also pursued a platform that included charging the American government with the genocide of black Americans and waging a campaign to bring the murderer of Harriette Moore, a Florida NAACP leader, to justice.[71] Under heavy government surveillance, the group was short-lived.[72] Yet the Sojourners was a key organization through which CP and Popular Front activists transmitted their politics and organizing strategies to a younger generation of radicals.

Although the Sojourners did not let McCarthy-era inquests quell their radicalism, government repression forced members to express their politics in divergent ways. Jones continued to champion working-class women and support antiracist struggles in London after she was deported under the auspices of the Smith Act.[73] Others, including Esther Cooper Jackson, became "Smith Act wives," a group of women who valorized traditional family structures and roles in order to cast McCarthyism and the state as the "destroyer of family freedom, security, and happiness."[74] Audley Moore renounced her party membership and returned to her former Garveyite networks, creating the Universal Association of Ethiopian Women in her home state of Louisiana.[75] Younger Sojourners, such as Childress, followed Jones's directives for "cultural workers to write and sing of the Negro woman in her full courage and dignity."[76] In the 1950s, Childress created a body of cultural production dedicated to reimagining the black domestic worker.

Mildred, the Model Militant Domestic

As a Sojourner, Childress learned about the plight of domestic workers from veteran members such as Jones. She also experienced the dehumanizing nature of domestic work firsthand. Without a high school diploma and with little other financial support, Childress found herself among the black women who depended on work in white households to survive.[77] Born in Charleston, South Carolina, in 1916, she moved to Harlem to live with her maternal grandmother, Eliza Campbell, around the age of five.[78] Childress's adolescence was filled with encounters of a thriving political milieu that included Garvey's UNIA, the Scottsboro protests, CP strikes, and Popular Front organizing. Her grandmother introduced her to the sights and sounds of Harlem culture and politics, encouraging her to pay as much attention to the people lining the streets as to the preacher in church on Sunday. Childress later recalled that these experiences showed her the importance of writing about "those who come in second, or not at all."[79]

Like Jones, Childress found Popular Front and postwar spaces to be productive arenas in which to proffer new conceptions of the black working class. She began her artistic career in leftist community theater in the 1930s. In 1941, she joined the American Negro Theatre (ANT), a cooperative of black actors that counted Ruby Dee, Ossie Davis, Harry Belafonte, and Sidney Poitier among its membership.[80] Childress worked as an actress, director, and playwright during her eleven-year tenure at the ANT, garnering a Tony nomination for her portrayal of Blanche in the theater's production of *Anna Lucasta*.[81] When the ANT folded in the early 1950s, she joined the Committee for the Negroes in the Arts, the cultural division of the Civil Rights Congress. She also became a columnist for *Freedom*, activist Paul Robeson's radically minded newspaper. Childress's association with these groups and publications garnered the attention of both the FBI and the

House Un-American Activities Committee. By 1955, she was blacklisted for her association with these and other organizations that McCarthy-era officials deemed subversive.[82]

Childress was purposely ambiguous about her affiliation with the CP. Some of her contemporaries suggested that she did not establish a formal membership with the group in order to maintain creative freedom. Others claimed that she fostered strong associations with the party even if she was not an actual member. As a result, her membership status within the CP was nebulous; yet her engagement in party protests and politics was clear.[83] Childress was active in CP-supported cultural production and political protests. She participated in May Day parades and rallies in support of blacklisted Hollywood stars and writers.[84] She also published widely in Communist-backed publications like the *Daily Worker* and *Masses and Mainstream*.

The cultural and political imperatives of the CP's Black Belt Thesis bent Childress's pen toward nationalist-influenced art. In her 1951 article, "For a Negro Theatre," she championed the value of black working-class, self-deterministic cultural production. Like Jones and other black women CP members, Childress argued that the black working class occupied a negative space in the gendered imagination. The playwright noted that film, plays, and media took "little interest in the cultural or historical background of the Negro people," reinforcing racist tropes of manhood, womanhood, and the working class.[85] She also argued that redefining black working-class manhood and womanhood in popular culture could be a valuable political tool. Childress suggested that black Americans' shared heritage and culture could be the basis of a radical political movement, but only if they adopted a new, black-centered artistic method that reflected their lived experiences. Accordingly, she added her name to calls for the creation of a "Negro people's theatre," or a black cultural archive and practice that drew its inspiration from the lived experiences and cultural production of "domestic workers, porters, and laborers, white-collar workers, churches, lodges, and institutions." Childress called on black writers, actors, and artists to study their communities in order to produce authentic portrayals of black life.[86] She also instructed them to use the theater as a way to engage in and amplify themes like race pride, black self-determination, and black political struggle. By infusing a nationalist-driven, oppositional culture into their artistic work, Childress argued, they could "eventually create a complete desire for the liberation of all oppressed peoples" and incite black audiences to radical action.[87]

The writer took these directives to heart in her midcentury cultural production, developing a body of literature that promoted black autonomy, self-determination, and working-class black women's militancy. Her first play, *Florence* (1950), set in a Southern, segregated train station, featured Mrs. Whitney, striving to support her daughter Florence's dream of escaping domestic work by becoming an actress. In *Gold through the Trees* (1952), Childress offered a sweeping portrayal of black resistance across the African diaspora. The first act featured Harriet Tubman as a domestic laundress, working to raise money for the abolitionist movement.[88] "Conversations from Life," a serial featuring Mildred Johnson, a domestic worker in Harlem, was her most popular and widely read work from this period. Subscribers to *Freedom* encountered the series from 1951 to 1955. She also published the columns in book form in 1956.[89]

"Conversations" chronicled the fictional exploits of Mildred, a domestic worker who refused to acquiesce to traditional perceptions of black womanhood. Each entry in the series featured Mildred recounting her conversations, expectations, estimations, and denunciations of contemporaneous politics, culture, race relations, and society. Throughout the series, Childress turned the contingency of domestic work into an asset. Popular and political literature about domestic workers often focused on the precarious nature of the job, magnified by black women being "rented" by different women each day "at unbelievably low rates for house work."[90] Childress created a world in which this benefited Mildred, affording her the opportunity to move freely about Harlem, in and out of white homes and community meetings and on and off street corners. Mildred's mobility allowed her to violate racialized and gendered physical, cultural, and social mores as she frequented places and discussed issues often considered outside the domestic worker's purview.[91] Through these conversations and confrontations, Mildred modeled black domestic militancy in the theaters of everyday life.

"Like One of the Family" was the signature vignette of the series. In it, Mildred takes offense when her employer, Mrs. C., tells her houseguest, "We *just* love [Mildred]! She's *like* one of the family and she *just adores* our little Carol! We don't know *what* we would do without her! We don't think of her as a servant!" When the guest leaves, Mildred has a talk with Mrs. C. Speaking pointedly, she remarks, "Mrs. C. . . . you are a pretty nice person to work for, but I wish you would please stop talkin' about me like I was a *cocker spaniel* or a *poll parrot* or a *kitten*. . . . In the first place you do not *love* me, you may be fond of me, but that is all. . . . In the second place, I am *not* just like one of the family at all! The family eats in the dining room and I eat in the kitchen. Your mama borrows your lace tablecloth for company and your son entertains his friends in your parlor. . . . So you can see I am not *just* like one of the family." Mildred tells Mrs. C. that she would prefer that her employer not pretend as if she viewed her, and, by association, domestic workers, as equals. Instead, if Mrs. C. would accept the power dynamics of their relationship, they would "get along like a good employer and employee should."[92]

Readers often learned of Mildred's militancy when she relayed the events of the day to her fellow domestic worker and friend Marge. In "All about My Job," Mildred tells Marge that she is glad they are friends because they both migrated from the South and did the "same kinda work: *housework*." Mildred explains that she was reminded of the value of domestic work while volunteering at her church bazaar. A woman came by and asked Mildred and her fellow volunteer what they did for a living. Although her booth mate stuttered through her answer, Mildred responded, "I do housework, and I do it every day because that is the way I make my livin' and if you look around at these pictures on the wall you will see that people do all kinds of work, I do housework." After the patron left, Miss Timid told Mildred that she was ashamed of stating that she was a domestic worker. Reflecting on this conversation, Mildred tells Marge, "Domestic workers have done a awful lot of good things in this country besides clean up peoples' houses. . . . And it's a rare thing for anyone to find a colored family in this land that can't trace a domestic worker somewhere in their history. . . . Yes there's many a doctor, many a lawyer, many a teacher, many a minister that got where they are 'cause somebody worked in the kitchen to put 'em there." Mildred ends by framing domestic workers as the vanguard of black advancement: "Of course a lot of people think it's *smart* not to talk about *slavery* anymore, but after freedom came, it was the domestics that kept us from perishin' by the wayside. . . . So I told this little Miss Meek, 'Dear, throw back your shoulders and pop your fingers at the *world* because the way I see it there's nobody with common sense that can look down on the domestic worker!' "[93]

Childress paired stories of Mildred's workplace militancy and pride with columns that framed her as an enlightened, politically conscious member of the black community. The February 1952 issue of *Freedom* featured "The 'Many Others' in History," in which Mildred wakes Marge to tell her about a "Negro History" meeting she attended. She tells her fellow domestic worker about the list of speakers on the program: "There was one pretty

The 'Many Others' In History

A Conversation from Life
By ALICE CHILDRESS

Good evenin', Marge. I am sorry I woke you up.... Yes, I know it's 12 o'clock.... Well, I got to work tomorrow too but I just have to tell you about your friend Mildred....

Honey, I went to a Negro History meetin' tonight. It was held on account of this is either Negro History week or month.... Why, of course it should be a year-round thing, but a week or a month is better than a "no time," ain't it?

Marge, I realy 'fell in' at that meeting! Let's admit it—I look good, don't I? Well, they had several speakers. There was one pretty young colored girl who was a little nervous but she came through fine and gave a nice talk about Harriet Tubman, Sojourner Truth, and many others . . . and a distinguish lookin' man who was kinda grey at the temples

spoke about Frederick Douglass, Nat Turner and many others.... Then a middle age white woman delivered a rousin' speech about John Brown, Frances Harper and many others.

I noticed that everybody would name a couple of folk and then add "and many others." Well, when the talkin' was over they asked the people to speak up and express themselves.... Why of course I did! I got up and said, "This has been a delightful evenin' and I'm glad to be here but you folks kept talkin' about 'many others.' . . . But you didn't tell much about them.

"Now I can't think about the many others without thinkin' of my grandmother because that's who you are talkin' about.... My grandpapa worked in a phosphate mill in South Carolina. He was

a foreman and made eight dollars a week. He and grandma had seven children and paid eight dollars a month rent. It cost ten cent a week for each child to go to school, ten cent apiece for the nine in the family to belong to the burial society . . . and the pickings were lean. Each child had to have a penny a week for Sunday School and grandma put in two dimes a week for the church.

"Once in a while she squeezed out seven nickels so's the children could go see lantern slides. Them kids wanted at least one picnic during the summer. They ate up one can of condensed milk a day . . . a tablespoon in a glass of water . . . that's how they got their milk.

"Christmas and Easter was a terrible time of trouble and worry to my grand-

(Continued on Page 3)

Alice Childress, "Conversations from Life: The 'Many Others' in History," *Freedom*, February 1952 (article detail). David M. Rubenstein Rare Book and Manuscript Library, Duke University.

young colored girl who ... gave a nice talk about Harriet Tubman, Sojourner Truth, and *many others* ... and a distinguish lookin' man ... [who] spoke about Frederick Douglass, Nat Turner, and *many others*.... Then a middle aged white woman delivered a rousin' speech about John Brown, Frances Harper, and *many others*." Fed up with repetitive stories of larger-than-life black heroism, Mildred stood up and exclaimed, "This has been a delightful evenin' and I'm glad to be here but you folks keep talking about 'many others.' ... But you didn't tell much about them.... Now I can't think about the *many others* without thinkin' of my grandmother because that's who you are talkin' about." Mildred regaled the audience with stories of her grandmother, who found ways to financially and emotionally support her family in the face of seemingly insurmountable odds and discrimination. Editorializing the meeting, Mildred tells Marge, "Well, the way they took it you could tell that I was talkin' about their grandmas too.... So I told 'em, 'I bet Miss Tubman and Miss Truth would like us to remember and give some time to the *many others*.'"[94] Mildred modeled a form of women-centered race consciousness that challenged top-down, masculinist narratives and inserted black working-class women into the history of black revolt. The goal of the Negro Theatre was to give black Americans a more accurate way of "seeing and viewing" themselves. Through vignettes like "Many Others," Childress debunked stereotypes of black domestic docility by reflecting black women's quotidian militancy.[95]

Mildred also takes issue with degrading representations of black working-class womanhood in popular culture. In "About Those Colored Movies," Mildred tells Marge that she gets "real salty sometimes" because every movie she sees featuring black people shows "colored maids and handymen and such" who were "always passin' for white" or "talkin' the same old line." According to Mildred, white America's popular cultural projections of black womanhood had appreciable effects on domestic workers' lives. Their white employers expected the maids they hired to behave like the caricatures they saw in films and on television. Mildred rejects this idea of the docile domestic figure in the popular imagination and asserts her refusal to adopt that model of black womanhood. She claims that if a white employer came "walkin' up to [her] expectin' [her] to laugh and grin, sing 'em a song," she would "probably cuss 'em out." Simultaneously echoing Jones's cultural critique and presaging Black Power activists' call for a black cultural movement, Mildred concludes by telling Marge that she wishes that old and new actors would "make some pictures and plays sometimes that [they] could be real proud about."[96]

Childress also framed black domestic workers as leaders in the fight for global black liberation and self-determination in vignettes such as "What Does Africa Want? . . . Freedom!" In the June 1953 edition of *Freedom*, Mildred tells Marge that she attended a meeting about Africa where she heard from "speakers tellin' things about Africa and how Africans are different groups of people and not all one single thing." At first, Mildred was content to hear about the "real stuff" happening in Africa rather than the essentialist and racist narratives that many inside and outside her community promoted. However, she soon objected to the direction and tone of the meeting when attendees started "arguin' back and forth about "WHAT THE AFRICAN WANTS" and "WHAT THE AFRICANS DON'T WANT." Mildred took exception with the group for being "uppity 'bout 'Are Africans fit to govern themselves.' " She interrupted them and proclaimed, "There ain't no mystery about that! Africans want to be free! . . . Stop all this pussyfootin' pretense. . . . Right is right and wrong is wrong, FREE AFRICA!"[97] Mildred hardly concealed her critique of the black middle class's perspectives on global politics or her support of internationalist, anticolonial, self-deterministic positions. Instead, she disrupted and contributed to communal debates about global black emancipation, proving that domestic workers were at the forefront of the theorization of diasporic liberation.

Through Mildred, Childress proffered a nationalist-oriented, working-class, militant form of womanhood for black women to adopt. Childress's "Conversations" appeared during a period in which ideas about black women teetered from the expectation that black women adopt white, middle-class models of womanhood to permanently ensconcing them in idyllic, domestic roles through cultural depictions of the mammy or maid figure.[98] Mildred forcefully countered both of these ideals. Whether in the workplace or at community meetings, the domestic worker advocated for herself and her community, promoted black culture and institutions, and supported global black liberation. She also affirmed that militancy and self-determination were organic to domestic workers' lives. Childress's character challenged male-dominated conceptualizations of the black working class and showed that a black-centered, gender-conscious, pro-labor political stance could advance black liberation. Ultimately, "Conversations" presented readers with a Marxist-influenced, nationalist, political identity manifested through the character of an uncompromisingly black domestic worker.

Mildred's daily acts of self-assertion and self-definition also provided concrete examples of protest that female readers could adopt. Childress received "floods of beautiful mail" from black women workers in which they "gave their approval to Mildred's exploits," validated Mildred's politics, and "told their own stories of protest."[99] Although Mildred's militancy may have been idealized, her calls for accurate black representation, race pride, and black self-determination had tangible effects for black women readers. "Conversations" became a space that bridged the gap between theoretical tracts, like Jones's, and the lived experiences of black domestic workers. The series also anticipated and extended the relevance of early twentieth-century nationalist formulations throughout the 1950s.

Mildred moved to the pages of the *Baltimore Afro American* newspaper as Popular Front networks unraveled. Like many other black leftist organizations and periodicals during this period, *Freedom* collapsed under the weight of targeted McCarthyite attacks against its staff.[100] Childress continued to publish stories of Mildred's exploits in the *Afro American*, under the title "Here's Mildred," until the late 1950s. In 1960, Childress joined the editorial staff of *Freedomways*, the successor to *Freedom*, founded in that same year. The brainchild of black female leftists such as Esther Cooper Jackson and Shirley Graham Du Bois, the periodical chronicled black activists' transition from Cold War warriors to Black Power militants.[101]

From Militant Domestic to Black Power Militant

Freedomways documented the shifting racial and political terrain of the early 1960s. Contributors chronicled the sit-ins and school desegregation struggles of the coalescing civil rights movement, the multiple African nations resisting their colonial oppressors, and charismatic leaders including Malcolm X and Dr. Martin Luther King Jr.[102] The periodical also documented what one observer called the "New Afro American Nationalism," or a rise in activists' public support of black separatism, African decolonization struggles, and their idolization of a triumvirate of emerging African leaders: Patrice Lumumba, Kwame Nkrumah, and Sékou Touré. Described as a "new manifestation of old grievances," this early 1960s nationalism drew on earlier ideas proposed by Garveyites and CP members and reformulated them to meet a moment during which the goals of African independence and self-determination were moving from the hypothetical to the actual.[103] These activists helped construct black American radicals' real and imagined relationships with Africa and the political and cultural frameworks that would later come to characterize Black Power.

Black women midwifed this early 1960s nationalist moment. On February 15, 1961, the Cultural Association for Women of African Heritage (CAWAH), an artistic and activist group that included writers Maya Angelou and Rosa Guy and jazz singer Abbey Lincoln, led hundreds of progressives and nationalists in taking over the United Nations building in midtown Manhattan.[104] The demonstrators' goal was to interrupt a UN Security Council meeting in order to express their outrage at First World nations' complicity in the assassination of Patrice Lumumba, the first democratically elected prime minster of the Congo. Many black Americans believed that both the American and Belgian governments were complicit in his murder. Hundreds of activists picketed outside on Forty-Second Street while another group simulated a funeral procession inside the halls of the UN to mourn the leader's death.[105] The CAWAH-led protest united Popular Front organizers and budding Black Power radicals under the banner of black nationalism and anticolonialism and showcased black women's organizing power.

A young Harlem activist named Mae Mallory made headlines during this protest when she put up a "terrific battle" while being arrested on the steps of the UN.[106] Born in Macon, Georgia, in 1927, Mallory's family, like Jones's and Childress's, migrated to Harlem with the hopes of economic and educational advancement. However, the black mecca looked different to Mallory, who was younger than the women leftists who spearheaded black organizing during the Popular Front years.[107] As a child, she would have walked to school past protests organized by CP women such as Jones, Childress, or Thompson and newsstands filled with periodicals like *Daily Worker*, replete with their tracts and essays about militant black womanhood. As a teenager and young adult, Mallory would experience the "triple exploitation" they often wrote about. By the age of seventeen, she had married, divorced, and entered the workforce. She joined the millions of black women who worked in factories and as maids in white women's homes, experiencing what her predecessors called the "special scourge" of domestic work.[108]

Mallory was, in many ways, an embodiment of the Mildred character. When not working in white homes, she navigated the Harlem landscape, attending meetings, debating CP leaders and black nationalist speakers, and voicing her support for African liberation. Mallory recalled that she was "introduced to the Communist Party during the McCarthy Era." She claimed that she joined the CP briefly in the 1950s but quickly grew disillusioned with the organization when she discovered the leaders' unwillingness to take a stand on racial discrimination and black self-determination.[109] Mallory then turned to local black nationalist groups. She found her way to the CAWAH protest through a collection of organizations such as the On Guard Committee for Freedom and the Afro-American Alliance for Action. These groups were among the many that represented the rising black nationalist sentiment of the early 1960s. Both expressed their support of black self-defense and self-determination by backing Robert F. Williams, the militant president of the Union County, North Carolina, chapter of the NAACP.[110]

Williams and his wife, Mabel, were paragons of black nationalism in the early 1960s. An army-veteran-turned-activist, Williams returned home from World War II armed with a new global political consciousness and an interest in unequivocally asserting his humanity and equality. Black residents elected Williams as the president of the NAACP, a position that he and Mabel Williams used to launch an aggressive assault on local expressions of white supremacy.[111] Together, they pursued an activist agenda that combined protests to desegregate local schools and swimming pools with armed self-defense of their home and community.[112] Williams's armed protests and unabashed calls to "meet violence with violence" clashed with the progressive, nonviolent message of the NAACP. By 1959, the organization's national leadership expelled Williams and censured his radical politics and rhetoric.[113] As liberals denounced the Monroe leader, black nationalist activists flocked to him, forming support groups and publicizing the Southern nationalist's efforts.

Mallory was one of the many activists who came to Williams's aid. In August 1961, she went to Monroe to help Williams host the Freedom Riders, a trip that would transform her into an internationally recognized black nationalist organizer. A group of nonviolent, interracial activists, the Freedom Riders rode buses to challenge local noncompliance with Supreme Court decisions that outlawed segregation on interstate public transportation. They arrived in Monroe, North Carolina, in August 1961 in the hopes of revealing the depths of white Southern racism and converting the local, militant, Williams-led movement into a nonviolent one.[114] Their week of local, nonviolent protests ended when a white mob attacked the Freedom Riders on Sunday, August 27, jump-starting waves of violence across the city. While black residents gathered at Williams's house seeking safety and a retaliation strategy, Bruce and Mabel Stegall, an elderly white couple, drove down his street.[115] In an effort to defuse the racial tension, Mallory, Williams, and his wife allowed the Stegalls to come inside the Williamses' home and remain there until the black crowd dispersed. The couple left the house unharmed and by their own volition. Yet they later claimed that they had been kidnapped. Fearing a lynch mob, Williams and Mallory fled. Williams escaped to Cuba.[116] Mallory went underground briefly before police arrested her in Cleveland, Ohio, on October 19, 1961.[117]

While incarcerated and awaiting trial in Cleveland, Mallory wrote extensively about the black condition and black liberation. Her prison writings represented a blend of Popular Front politics and her burgeoning interest in black nationalist frameworks and principles.[118] Published in black newspapers across the country, leftist magazines such as *Freedomways*, and through the Monroe Defense Committee (MDC)—her nationalist-inspired support group—her letters and essays often used the ideal of the domestic worker to personify her militant politics. Mallory's prison writings were part of a growing body of black women's intellectual production that not only ushered in the Black Power movement but also situated black women as pivotal figures in nationalist projects.

In her 1962 prison letter, "Of Dogs and Men," Mallory played on Childress's tales of domestic defiance to forge a new model of black militant womanhood. Drawing on the signature vignette of "Conversations from Life," Mallory opened, "A White woman I used to baby-sit for when I was but a teenager once said that having me around was like having a pet. I wondered about that statement; for it was different. The usual statement of this nature concerning a Black servant goes something like 'She's just like one of the family.' This time it was like having a pet around the house. The usual American pet is a dog. Could this woman have intended to imply that having me around was like having a dog around? No doubt she did!"[119] This exchange between domestic workers and employers became the basis of

Mallory's open letter, a meditation on black dehumanization, black self-determination, and the potential militancy of black domestic workers.

Mallory then used her experience with domestic work to advance her analysis of racism and promote black women's militancy. "When I used to ride the 5th Avenue bus in New York City in my threadbare coat, I would look out the window and see rich White ladies of fashion with their dogs—all pedicured, clipped, and perfectly groomed. . . . For both the lady and her dog to be dressed in mink and 'go strolling down Fifth Avenue' was considered smart. But if I were paid a decent salary by her, it would have been considered stupid; if I would have demanded more money, it would have been considered impudent." Echoing Jones's claim that the domestic worker was the lowest member of the social stratum, Mallory concluded that black women were so dehumanized, that "the dog really led the best life."[120]

Despite her exploited status, Mallory, like Mildred, refused to acquiesce to white society's attempts to define and dehumanize her. She explained that her employer "lived in a very comfortable upper middleclass apartment house" with a sign that said "NO DOGS OR NEGROES ALLOWED." Even when she "was without [her] little charge, [she] was instructed to use the 'Service Entrance.'" Refusing to know her "place," Mallory violated the spatial and racial mores designed to confine black domestic workers: "Since I did not come to service the building, I paid no heed to such instructions and went brazenly through the front door."[121] Mallory showed how she engaged in everyday acts of defiance while on the job, refusing to accept her role as a "pet," or, as Mildred might put it, a "poll parrot."[122]

Whereas the black domestic worker resisted dehumanization, Mallory argued that black middle-class leadership welcomed it. "Just as there are dogs for show, there are some Negroes 'for show.' The master dresses these Negroes up just as he does his dog. These Blacks are put on display as Exhibit-A for the people of Africa, Asia, and Latin America to see." Mallory argued that there were benefits to being a show dog, as "this Black is allowed a living wage and sometimes he is allowed to live in the same neighborhood or building with his master." In exchange, however, he or she had to produce "foolish propaganda on how well the Blackman is treated in America and the 'progress we are making.'" She noted that "dogs are never made to stoop this low. For [she had] never heard of a dog having to propagandize other dogs as to the benevolence of his master." Mallory encapsulated this point in her final assessment of the political distance between civil rights leadership and the domestic worker: "Most Negroes do not choose to lead a dog's life—whether it is a lap dog, hunting dog, or one from the kennel. They do not want scraps from the master's table, neither do we choose to be masters—only masters of our fate."[123]

Mallory combined Jones's political analyses and Childress's tales of defiance in order to formulate a new model of the Militant Negro Domestic and promote radical, internationalist, and anti-integrationist politics. In "Of Dogs and Men," she framed black domestic workers as figures who had a vested interest in self-determination or in becoming "masters of [their] fate." They were also among the "thinking" masses that supported global black and Third World sovereignty by resisting the "blockade of Cuba" and "Atomic War to protect imperialistic interests." Domestic workers were also a part of the group of black Americans who realized that they needed "liberation—the same as other oppressed peoples in Asia, Africa and Latin America."[124] Her letter connected the domestic worker's local agenda to global politics. It also showed the disconnect between the black masses and the mainstream (male) leadership, implying that the latter did not represent the majority of black Americans' interests or self-definition; rather, they undermined the oppressed on a global scale.

"Of Dogs and Men" was also a direct attack on dehumanizing definitions of black womanhood and an attempt to reimagine black women's role in radical liberation projects. By the 1960s, black women still made up over half of the domestic workforce, reinforcing Jones's contention that white Americans still thought black domestics to be the "natural slave of others."[125] Mallory showed that black women had an incisive, militant, and radical perception of the world and cast them as freethinking intellectuals rather than docile mammy figures. Her published prison letters encouraged black women readers to view themselves as defiant and politically engaged rather than as the pets or property of others.

Mallory continued to integrate the idea of the Militant Negro Domestic into her prison writings after she was extradited back to Monroe in 1964 to stand trial for the kidnapping charges. Now imprisoned in North Carolina, Mallory composed "Memo from a Monroe Jail" (1964), an account of the Monroe events in which she foregrounded the radicalization of domestic workers and modeled black domestic militancy. She opened the essay by contextualizing her kidnapping charges within racial politics and black women's militancy in Monroe. She recounted stories of black domestic workers' abuse, including a story of "a black woman who worked as a maid" who was "kicked down the stairs of the local hotel in Monroe because a white patron decided that 'she was making too much noise.'"

According to Mallory, this and other instances moved local black domestic workers to action. She recalled, "The black women of Monroe, fed up with this kind of treatment, vowed that 'never again would a black woman sit and be belittled before a crowd.'" Positioning black women workers at the forefront of racial politics in the city, Mallory argued that it was their militancy that "moved Robert Williams to declare that there was no justice in the courts for black people and that there was no other alternative but to 'counter mob-violence violently.'"[126]

Mallory then turned to her own case, recounting her role in Monroe, and subsequent flight and capture, through the lens of domesticity and domestic work. Although she had been an avid supporter of Williams through Harlem-based nationalist groups, Mallory maintained that she agreed to go to North Carolina only after fellow New York activist Julian Mayfield "explained that Mabel (Mrs. Robert Williams), could use [her] moral support." The activist claimed that she embraced a domestic role during the Freedom Riders' weeklong demonstrations, remaining at the Williams residence and helping "Mabel Williams with her household chores." However, Mallory warned against reading her domesticity as a recusal of her radical politics. She explained that she did not stay at the Williams home because she was uninterested in the protest. Rather, she could "not let someone hit [her] or kick [her] and remain passive." Given that her promotion of self-defense could be a liability for others, she explained that "it was agreed by all that [she] should stay at home."[127]

In her recounting of the events, Mallory advanced a narrative of black female domestics' radicalization and politicized traditional, women-centered spaces. The activist located the origins of the Monroe "frame up" not in Williams's insolence but in local black domestic workers' quotidian acts of defiance. In doing so, she proffered an alternative genealogy of grassroots radicalism and challenged popular characterizations of domestic workers as docile figures. Mallory's assessment of her and Mabel Williams's roles in the incident also complicated ideas about women's "place" in political protest. By 1961, both she and Mabel Williams were established radical activists who advocated direct action, armed self-defense, and black self-determination.[128] However, Mallory rooted their role in the Monroe protest in the Williamses' home. She indicated that both occupied domestic roles within the protest without renouncing their radical tendencies or affiliations. She also framed her and Mabel's assistance as vital to the overall success of the protest. The activist indicated that black women's domesticity, domestic work, and radical politics were not mutually exclusive. Rather, they could work, organize, and support radical or nationalist principles in multiple political spaces and acts.

The activist then explained how she played on dominant perceptions of the racialized gendered imaginary in her attempts to avoid capture and incarceration. She recalled that she thought it would be best if she "left New York and went to a strange town with a black population. Cleveland, Ohio came to [her] mind. The bus station was so crowded that the authorities couldn't tell [her] from any other black workingclass [sic] woman."[129] Newspaper reports confirmed Mallory's assessment. The *Cleveland Call and Post* indicated that she eluded capture for six weeks because "she looks like a million other domestics or nurse's aides. There's nothing special about her, except her ideas."[130] Like Jones and Childress, Mallory recognized that in the dominant view of black women, they were downtrodden, indistinguishable domestic workers. She used the explanation of her escape to foreground hegemonic characterizations of black women and undergird her claims about the devaluation and potential of black working-class women.

Mallory juxtaposed this docile, domestic characterization with examples of her militancy. She explained that initially she was arrested and released on bail, after which she began organizing against her extradition in black communities in Cleveland. She claimed that the majority of the local black community did not welcome her or the MDC because they were "a group with a way-out philosophy of self-defense." Mallory also maintained that the "so-called respectable organizations slammed the doors in [their] faces." However, with the help of the MDC, she was eventually able to garner support for her case and her nationalist politics. Mallory indicated that she had such widespread support for her pro-black, self-defense agenda that when "election time rolled around every candidate that had publically denounced [her and the MDC] lost except one." Despite her ability to politicize the black community, it was not enough to stymie her extradition back to North Carolina for her to stand trial on the kidnapping charges. Sitting in a Union County, North Carolina, jail cell awaiting bail funds and a trial date, she ended the "Memo" by remarking that she and the other activists charged were "all victims of an outlandish frame-up" and "on the sacrificial alter to pay obeisance to the decadent god of white supremacy."[131]

In "Memo from a Monroe Jail," Mallory offered a multilayered narrative of black working-class women's redefinition and radicalization told through the lens of the black domestic worker. In her recounting of events, black working-class women were not simply the "help" but also militant activists who espoused "way-out" philosophies of self-defense and self-determination during a period in which civil rights events, such as the 1963 March on Washington, eclipsed nationalist activism. Moreover, Mallory positioned domestic militancy at the epicenter of the burgeoning black nationalist movement, arguing that black domestic workers were the impetus behind the calls of well-known black nationalists like Robert F. Williams for self-defense and self-determination and that they were responsible for fostering Cleveland's radical grassroots organizing. In her account of the Monroe incident and its aftermath, she, like the "black women of Monroe," moved from a domestic or domesticated role to a militant one, drawn to radical politics due to the ubiquitous nature of white supremacy.

Through the "Memo," Mallory made an important connection between black domestics' lived experiences with oppression and the necessity of embracing nationalist politics. She argued that, for black working-class women, adopting a nationalist political agenda and militant persona was a viable path to liberation, but only if they were willing to reimagine themselves as vital nationalist political actors. By centering them in her analyses and accounts and offering autobiographical examples of domestic workers' defiance, Mallory politicized black women workers' everyday acts of resistance and offered a militant, internationalist, and class-conscious political program for readers to consider. She positioned black domestics at the vanguard of the black liberation struggle and characterized them as the leaders of a "Black non-intellectual working class," fighting not "for accessibility" but "for freedom."[132] Part of black women's corpus of writings about black domestic workers, Mallory's early 1960s publications transformed the Militant Negro Domestic into a Black Power militant, poised to lead the nationalist movement in the ensuing decade.

"Save Mae from the KKK" became the rallying cry across the political left in the early 1960s.[133] The movement to free Mallory, who stood trial for the kidnapping charges in February 1964, also fostered relationships between older and younger black radicals and introduced them to the nationalist aspects of the black freedom struggle. Student-activist Muhammad Ahmad met his future political mentor, Audley Moore, at a Free Mae Mallory Meeting held at her Philadelphia home.[134] He would become one of the leading theoreticians and activists of the Black Power era, blending old and new left nationalist frameworks to develop the Revolutionary Action Movement, a cadre-based group that fused nationalism and Marxist-Leninism. Moore, Ahmad, and other supporters rejoiced when the North Carolina Supreme Court voided Mallory's conviction in January 1965, overturning the all-white jury's conviction due to jury selection bias.[135] Once freed, Mallory returned to New York and entrenched herself in black nationalist communities, leading women's Black Power groups such as the Organization of Militant Black Women. Yet, well before this and other groups encouraged black Americans to seek their freedom by "any means necessary," Mallory advanced the black nationalist tradition by foregrounding black working-class women's political potential and modeling the militancy that her predecessors prescribed.[136]

Mallory's prison letters sustained postwar black women radicals' tradition of redefining black womanhood using the Militant Negro Domestic as a model. Throughout the 1940s, 1950s, and early 1960s, black women radicals used this ideal to reimagine domestic workers, and, by extension, all black women, as nationalist, Marxist, gender-conscious political actors who were at the vanguard of race, class, and gender liberation struggles. They remained invested in this perception of black womanhood even as liberalism and McCarthyism overshadowed radical and nationalist political frameworks during the 1950s. In the early 1960s, when Garveyite frameworks again gained traction due to advances in civil rights and African independence struggles, black women activists continued to reimagine black domestics' radical activism, producing literature that modeled the transformation of the black domestic into a black nationalist activist. Ultimately, they carved out a place for working-class black women within the black left and reshaped static perceptions of women, the working class, and black radicalism.

Although postwar black women activists' theorizing of the Militant Negro Domestic reached it apex in the early 1960s, the political identity models that they developed reflected their ongoing interest in reimagining black womanhood as a way to advance radical and nationalist political and cultural frames. A new generation of black women activists would continue this trend. As the decade proceeded, female Black Power activists developed different, and at times conflicting, definitions of black womanhood that combined their gendered priorities with the ideological frameworks of the Black Power movement's most popular organizations. Their ideas advanced postwar women radicals' intersectional approaches to defining black womanhood and compelled members of multiple organizations to rethink their perceptions of black women, gender roles, and black liberation.

CHAPTER TWO

The Black Revolutionary Woman, 1966–1975

Mae Mallory went to jail as the "new" nationalism was taking root in black communities across the country. By the time the Union County court exonerated her in 1965, black activists had begun to weave their nationalist-inspired grassroots struggles into a united, militant organizational front. Along with other experienced radicals such as Audley Moore and Vicki Garvin, Mallory continued to mobilize around a class-conscious, nationalist agenda.[1] These women also mentored younger activists, instilling in them the lessons they learned from organizing at the intersections of Garveyism and communism. The convict-turned-Muslim-minster Malcolm X was perhaps their most prized pupil. Malcolm garnered their attention in the late 1950s when he rose to fame within the Nation of Islam (NOI), the premier black nationalist organization of that decade. After he left the NOI in 1964, Malcolm rapidly became the crown prince of the growing black nationalist movement, often collaborating with postwar women radicals to help legitimize his throne.[2] As an early adopter of self-defense and self-determination, Mallory was an ideal ally for the nationalist leader. She began appearing alongside him at events at Harlem's Audubon Ballroom in 1964.[3] She was also in the audience when he was gunned down in that same auditorium on February 21, 1965.[4]

Hailed as a black prophet killed in his prime, Malcolm X's assassination helped stoke the embers of black nationalism into the flames of the Black Power movement. In the wake of his death, a new generation of activists, including Huey Newton and Bobby Seale, fashioned themselves as his political and ideological heirs. In 1966, they created the Black Panther Party for Self-Defense in Oakland, California. They also injected the ideal of the black revolutionary—a Malcolm X–styled black nationalist and anti-imperialist radical—into the black radical imaginary.[5] The Panthers used their revolutionary ideal to galvanize black communities, convince them of the efficacy of the party's ideology, and assert the inevitability of their radical political vision. In the years following Malcolm X's death, the party, and the model of black revolutionary manhood that it projected, became one of the most visible and popular expressions of Black Power worldwide.

As the Panthers' popularity soared, so too did its female membership. Only a few years after the party's inception, women were close to half of the rank and file.[6] Like their activist foremothers, Panther women engaged in extensive conversations over how to best conceptualize black womanhood in the party and society at large. In an effort to align their activism, political theory, and emancipatory goals, Panther women theorized a gender-specific version of the Panthers' political identity: the Black Revolutionary Woman. An ideal that personified gendered formulations and applications of the Panthers' political ideology, the Black Revolutionary Woman became a conduit through which female members reimagined their political and social roles.

From 1967 to 1975, Panther women expanded the party's gendered imaginary and organizing ethos through their debate over black womanhood in the *Black Panther* newspaper. Early female Panther recruits used the publication to theorize new ideas about the Black Revolutionary Woman as a way to challenge the Panthers' patriarchal political imaginary. As the organization evolved, Panther women began to define the female revolutionary in ways that purposely transgressed organizational and societal gender constructs. By the early 1970s, they solidified the Black Revolutionary Woman as a viable form of self-representation and a symbol of their radical politics. Their rhetorical and pictorial constructions of the Black Revolutionary Woman expanded and diversified the party's collective subjectivity, political identity, and everyday culture. It also shifted Panther leaders' stance on sexism and gender equality, making the party more inclusive.

The Rise of Black Power and the Black Panther Party

The origins of the Black Panther Party's revolutionary symbolism lay in the Student Nonviolent Coordinating Committee (SNCC), formed in April 1960. During a year in which Robert F. Williams led armed self-defense protests in Monroe, North Carolina; Cuban Revolution leader Fidel Castro visited Harlem, New York; and more than ten African nations declared their independence from their colonial oppressors, four black college students staged a sit-in at a Woolworth's lunch counter in Greensboro, North Carolina.[7] Their protest spawned a wave of sit-ins in more than thirty locations across the county.[8] Seasoned activist Ella Baker, known for her NAACP organizing as well as her exposés about black domestic workers in the Bronx Slave Market, called these students together to develop an organizational infrastructure for their protests.[9] They created SNCC, a student-led civil rights organization dedicated to direct action and grassroots mobilization. At Baker's urging, the students structured SNCC to promote autonomy and self-determination. They formed an independent organization without formal ties to established civil rights groups. The student group also had a decentralized organizational structure in order to cultivate indigenous black leadership and protest.[10]

Across the country, SNCC members spearheaded voter registration drives and desegregation protests, however the primary thrust of their early programming was the 1964 Mississippi Freedom Summer Project.[11] Thousands of black and white college students poured into the Magnolia State to participate in SNCC's efforts to draw the nation's attention to the rampant disenfranchisement of Southern blacks, register black Mississippians to vote, and create the infrastructure for a homegrown civil rights movement.[12] Organizers including Ruby Doris Smith Robinson and Joyce Ladner raised money for and led literacy schools, voter education rallies, and courthouse protests that gradually increased the state's black electorate.[13] SNCC members such as Gwendolyn Patton and Gwendolyn Simmons developed similar projects in the neighboring states of Alabama and Georgia, empowering black communities and foregrounding the rampant racial violence and disenfranchisement throughout the southeastern United States.[14]

SNCC activists made significant inroads in challenging segregation and increasing black enfranchisement. However, translating this freedom and voting bloc into political power proved more difficult. Although black names slowly populated Southern voter rolls, state parties still barred them from participating in political life. In response, SNCC members worked with local activists to develop separate, black-led political parties to represent their interests. In Sunflower County, Mississippi, local leaders Fannie Lou Hamer, Victoria Gray, and Annie Devine created the Mississippi Freedom Democratic Party (MFDP). Throughout the spring and summer of 1964, MFDP leaders and SNCC organizers educated local residents about the electoral system, registered black voters, and held a statewide convention to elect delegates to represent the MFDP at the national level. That August, MFDP delegates—including Hamer, Gray, and Devine—attended the Democratic National Convention (DNC) in Atlantic City, New Jersey, with the goal of unseating their white counterparts from the Mississippi State Democratic Party.[15] Their challenge of the legitimacy of the all-white Mississippi Democratic Party delegation made national headlines when Hamer testified in a nationally televised speech before the DNC Credentials Committee about the rampant violence black women faced when attempting to vote. Looking to quell racial tensions and avoid intraparty feuding, DNC officials offered two "at large" seats to two male MFDP delegates, a gesture meant to placate the MFDP and avoid alienating Southern white democrats. Hamer and the other members of the MFDP rejected the proposal. Their Atlantic City challenge was unsuccessful.[16]

The MFDP's challenge exposed the depth and breadth of white power. In response, SNCC vowed to expand black power. The original Black Panther Party in Lowndes County, Alabama, epitomized this new political direction. SNCC workers including Gwendolyn Patton and Stokely Carmichael recognized that the residents of the 80 percent black Lowndes County would need to create their own party to secure local political power. Working with residents, they created the Lowndes County Freedom Organization (LCFO), an independent, third political party designed to grow the black electorate and "control the county" by electing local black residents to county positions.[17] SNCC volunteers helped brand and promote the organization, with local field secretary Ruth Howard developing the black panther image that became the symbol and name of the group, and that would capture the imaginations of Newton and Seale.[18] Throughout the spring of 1966, SNCC and LCFO members registered black voters and campaigned for black candidates to be elected to positions on the Lowndes County school board, as county sheriff, as coroner, and as tax assessor under the banner of the snarling black panther.[19]

Although the LCFO Panther Party candidates lost the November 1966 election, they helped win the battle over Black Power brewing within SNCC. Discussions about the importance of self-defense, all-black organizing, and black separatism had been fermenting in the organization after Freedom Summer.[20] The potential of the LCFO Black Panther Party, combined with Carmichael's June 1966 "Black Power" speech and members' growing disillusionment with the promise of integration, spurred SNCC toward adopting Black Power as its new political ideology and organizing mantra.[21] Although the media often framed the organization's adoption of Black Power, and its eventual expulsion of white members, as destructive and nihilistic, SNCC members asserted more complex analyses of the organization's shift. SNCC/LCFO volunteer Gwendolyn Patton, for example, did not see "the separation [from whites] as divisive, but rather complementary." "Black Power," she contended, "demanded a strategy in which black people would transform the powerless black community into one that could exert its human potential to be an equal partner in the larger society."[22]

Black women in the Alabama-based Black Panther Party were not the only ones thinking about embracing Black Power or the idea of a Black Panther Party. For Elendar Barnes and Judy Hart, Oakland residents and future members of Newton and Seale's Panther Party, the political climate demanded radical, black-led activism.[23] In the early 1960s, independent black female activists, and those involved in organizations like SNCC, waged protracted protests that accelerated the passage of the 1964 Civil Rights Act and the 1965 Voting Rights Act. However, they saw few tangible results from President Lyndon B. Johnson's efforts to equalize race relations through federal legislation. By and large, black women remained disenfranchised and barred from safe and fair housing, access to health care, and most educational and professional opportunities. In fact, the majority of black women were still relegated to employment as domestic workers.[24] Moreover, black women endured gender-specific forms of discrimination, including stigmatization for poverty and alleged promiscuity, as well as sexual assault.[25] When calls for black autonomy and separatism erupted in the late 1960s, such ideas appealed to many black women in search of capital and corporal control.

If black women's oppression exposed the reach of white supremacy, then their participation in urban uprisings represented their unequivocal rejection of white control. In July 1964, Harlem erupted in violence. Philadelphia followed suit that same year.[26] Incidents of police brutality were often the match that lit the raging fires of black rebellion in urban metropolises across the country. However, these mass revolts were also manifestations of black Americans' protracted frustrations with white flight, police surveillance, high unemployment rates, and rampant poverty.[27] Uprisings in cities across the country foregrounded their frustration with the gradualism of mainstream desegregation struggles, government policies, and state-sanctioned violence. They also fostered new ideological and organizational responses and propelled the popularity of black nationalism.

Many Black Power activists framed these rebellions in nationalist and imperialist terms, casting the uprisings as examples of America's internal black colony in revolt. Conjuring up nationalist frameworks akin to those championed by postwar activists such as Claudia Jones, younger organizers claimed that the black community was a nation within a nation, penned into urban ghettos and fighting for self-determination. These activists argued that black Americans' subjugated position was analogous to that of colonized people of color across the globe. They joined in with Third World communities in vocalizing their opposition to American imperialist intervention and neocolonialist practices. By 1966, many black organizers worked alongside, and, at times, with, a growing number of student and antiwar movements that cast the Vietnam War as the foremost example of American racism and imperialism run amok.[28] Students and future Oakland Panther members, including Janice Garrett-Forte, aligned themselves with international liberation groups like the Vietnamese National Liberation Front, or the Viet Cong. These collegiate activists often paired their anti-imperialist activism with demands for the end of their imperialist-inspired education at home. In the late 1960s, students across the country participated in sit-ins, strikes, and even violent clashes with university administrations in an effort to "decolonize" their education and their campuses.[29] These campus movements forced universities across the country to create black studies programs replete with classes on African civilization, African American history, and economic inequality.[30]

Coming of age in Oakland in the 1960s, Newton and Seale witnessed Black Power's ascent firsthand. The party founders were among the many black migrants from the South who found that the promise of a better life out west never materialized. Both leaders spent their boyhoods navigating the poverty, segregation, and criminalization that characterized black life in the Bay Area. Surviving a youth hounded by California's juvenile penal system, Newton and Seale eventually enrolled in Merritt College, a local university known for its radical student activism. They became politically engaged on and off campus amid a proliferation of black nationalist organizations on campus and in the local community. Lawyer-turned-activist Donald Warden and his Afro-American Association galvanized students across multiple local universities, while the Audley Moore–inspired African Descendants People's Partition Party revived Garveyite nationalist formulations among black San Franciscans.[31]

As Newton and Seale navigated the Bay Area's nationalist groups, news of the Lowndes County Black Panther Party made its way west. Mark Comfort, a well-known local activist, had traveled to Lowndes County to work alongside SNCC activists and register black voters. He brought information about the LCFO Panther Party, and its imagery, back to Oakland. LCFO leaders also visited the Berkeley-based chapter of the SNCC support group, Friends of SNCC, to speak about their grassroots organizing.[32] The Oakland-Lowndes connection was further solidified through two Black Power conferences held at the University of California, Berkeley, in October 1966. The first, sponsored by the Committee for Lowndes County, raised money for the LCFO Black Panther Party. The second, spearheaded by the white leftist group Students for a Democratic Society, brought local, regional, and national activists together to address the meaning and substance of Black Power. Comfort was among the local activists who attended, as was Los Angeles–based black nationalist Maulana Karenga. Lowndes County SNCC activist Stokely Carmichael also spoke at the latter conference, offering news of the Alabama Black Panthers along with his analysis of American race relations.[33]

Newton and Seale founded the Black Panther Party for Self-Defense in an Oakland antipoverty center that same month. Recalling the start of the Oakland party, Newton noted that he had heard about "how the people in Lowndes County had armed themselves against Establishment violence. Their political group, called the Lowndes County Freedom Organization, had a black panther for its symbol." "A few days later," when he and Bobby were talking, he suggested that they "use the panther as [their] symbol and call [their] political vehicle the Black Panther Party."[34] The Oakland founders attached the LCFO's black panther symbol to their founding document, "What We Want Now! What We Believe," a manifesto that announced the party's theoretical goals and practical demands.[35]

Originally, Newton and Seale framed their organization, programming, and goals in nationalist terms. Animated by Malcolm X's teachings, their original Ten Point Platform borrowed its structure and rhetoric from the NOI's weekly statement of demands published in their newspaper, *Muhammad Speaks*.[36] Although the party's ideological and programmatic demands differed from the NOI's, the document still located the burgeoning organization firmly within the black nationalist tradition. Using statements such as "We want a full and complete freedom" and "We want power to determine the destiny of our black community," the Panther founders framed black Americans as a racially subjugated group in need of ideological, political, and cultural separation and self-determination. Newton and Seale also addressed the local black community's racially specific concerns, including their need for decent housing and protection from police brutality. In early party literature, they called on black Americans to adopt "righteous BLACK POWER" in order to achieve liberation and extolled the teachings of nationalist icons such as Malcolm X.[37]

In its first year, the party garnered a following through an intricate balance of high-profile protests and local-level organizing. They earned the Bay Area black community's respect through their armed police patrols, designed to thwart the Oakland Police Department's constant harassment of black residents. Dressed in their now-iconic uniform—black leather jacket, black beret, and black boots—early Panther members would roam around observing police, challenging their treatment of black detainees, and loudly reciting the penal code so that both the police and observers could hear. When incidents of harassment resulted in the deaths of black people, the party led community efforts to ensure police accountability. The Panthers led the public outcry about and investigation into the death of Denzil Dowell, a twenty-two-year-old black construction worker who was harassed and eventually killed by police on April 1, 1967. Newton, Seale, and other early Panther recruits gained the Dowell family's and other residents' trust by protecting the family and publicizing the case. Their community support convinced black Oaklanders of the party's potential and the importance of armed self-defense and self-determination.[38]

If their protest of Dowell's death alerted the Bay Area to the Panthers' presence, their Sacramento demonstration made them a household name. In May 1967, a group of thirty armed Panthers—twenty-four men and six women—went to the state capitol building to protest the Mulford Act, legislation designed to criminalize the Panthers' armed police patrols. The party contingent appeared at the capitol, heavily armed and in search of the assembly chambers. Hounded by reporters, the Seale-led group spilled onto the assembly floor. The party exploited the media attention. After being escorted out of the courthouse, Seale read the Panthers' Executive Mandate #1 on the front steps, supported by members of the delegation, such as Mary Williams and Ruby Dowell.[39]

Williams's and Dowell's activism reflected women's early party activity. Women joined the party in 1967 and immediately became integral to organizational life. Tarika Lewis, a sixteen-year-old Oakland Technical High School student, joined the party that year. She quickly completed the Panthers' political education and weapons training and went on to become a local lieutenant in the party while also working as an artist for the *Black Panther*.[40] Roommates Judy Hart and Janice Garrett-Forte contributed to the *Black Panther*, attended rallies, and worked with the Panthers Free Breakfast Program, which began in 1968.[41] Audrey Hudson served as a secretary and a member of the editorial staff of the newspaper, while community elders such as Ruth Beckford helped the Panthers establish an office and served on an advisory board that Newton and Seale developed.[42] Belva Butcher and Majeeda Roman participated in firearms training and political education classes.[43] A number of other women marched alongside men in the Panthers' local police patrols. They also participated in the short-lived women's auxiliary of the organization, the Pantherettes.[44]

Despite women's formative role in early party protests, the Panthers' early organizational culture was decidedly masculinist. The rise of the party coincided with black male activists' unabashed calls for black women to relinquish their public roles so that black men could reclaim their manhood. To be sure, the black radical tradition was replete with narratives that equated black liberation with the restoration of black manhood. However, the 1965 Moynihan Report amplified these claims. Tasked with analyzing race relations and poverty during the Johnson administration, sociologist and Assistant Secretary of Labor Daniel Patrick Moynihan compiled *The Negro Family: A Case for National Action*. Ostensibly intended to explore and ameliorate the crux of the race problem in America, the report blamed black poverty and inequality on black women's dominance in the home and community.[45] Taking their cue from Moynihan, male activists often labeled women who assumed leadership roles or asserted their independence as "castrators" who undermined the movement. They called on these women to abandon their public positions in order to perform their "revolutionary" roles as mothers and caregivers for the black men and children of the black nation.

Newton and Seale initially framed the party as a conduit through which black men could redefine and assert their manhood. The first issues of the *Black Panther* newspaper cast the organization as a space explicitly designed for the "cream of black manhood," knowledgeable about "all the ins and outs of the problems facing Black People."[46] The Panthers also promulgated a series of powerful visual images to promote an idealized form of revolutionary manhood, publishing photos and artwork of black men in black leather jackets, black berets, and dark sunglasses and holding weaponry. Through this combination of rhetoric and images, the Panthers created a collective subjectivity, revolutionary identity, and radical culture. Their synthesis of nationalist rhetoric and symbols also codified a masculinist construction of the revolutionary figure in the popular and political imagination.[47]

The Origins of the Panthers' Black Revolutionary Woman Ideal

Although Panther leaders promoted a form of militant manhood, as Robyn Spencer notes, they did not endorse a form of submissive black womanhood.[48] As a result, soon after joining the party, black women created spaces in which to construct powerful images and ideas about black women's roles in party and political organizing. The short-lived "Sisters' Section" in the *Black Panther* newspaper was one of the earliest arenas in which Panther women articulated their gender-specific vision of the revolutionary figure. The articles in the section focused on two themes that would come to characterize Panther women's initial writings: party promotion and women's political self-conception.

Barbara Auther's "Sisters Unite" set the tone for this section of the Panthers' newspaper. Published alongside an image of an armed female activist with the caption "a revolutionary sister," the article emphasized the party's early goals of community protection and militancy. Auther denounced the "police brutality and black genocide" ravaging the local community. She also praised the black men with "guts" who stood up to the "white power structure" through armed self-defense. Speaking directly to her female readership, Auther called on black women to support the party, because it was where the "BLACK MEN [were]." She ended the article with a rousing call to arms for female readership: "Become members of the Black Panther Party for Self-Defense, Sisters, 'we got a good thing going.'"[49] Although it rehearsed Moynihan-inspired calls for male support, Auther's article was also an example of women's efforts to frame the party as an inclusive organizing space. If the Panthers created the "Sisters' Section" to convince black women of the party's efficacy and goals, then "Sisters Unite" invited them to envision themselves as part of the Panthers' revolutionary legion and protests from the outset.

Other early recruits used the "Sisters' Section" to expound on the importance of redefining black womanhood within black liberation struggles. In her July 1967 article, "Black Womanhood No. 1," Judy Hart began the public, intraorganizational debate about how to best redefine black womanhood within the party and the contemporaneous political terrain. Hart opened this discussion by offering a meditation on how the rising popularity of Black Power had necessitated shifts in the black gendered imaginary. She explained that, in the late 1960s, the black freedom movement reflected the "fusing of [black Americans'] separate frustrations, desires, convictions, and strengths toward a common liberation." As a result, "the relationships between black men and black women [were] taking on new and crucial meanings." Black women were beginning to "constantly analyze and evaluate [their] position and direction in relation to each other, [them]selves, to the black community, and to [their] enemy." Their analyses of their social, cultural, and political positions, Hart argued, led many black women to determine that they needed to develop new definitions of black womanhood unbridled by Eurocentric values and principles.[50]

Hart then explained how black women reshaped the gendered imaginary in light of this new political perspective, offering an extended comparison of the different definitions of black womanhood circulating in the public sphere. Previously, she argued, black women aspired to a white, capitalist-driven ideal of womanhood, or to be the "bourgeois-oriented female." This "ultra-boogie chick," Hart asserted, was immature, aspired to white beauty standards akin to images promulgated in "Glamour-Mademoiselle-Vogue" magazines, and emasculated black men.[51] In 1967, however, black women's cultural and political self-conception was shifting. Hart contended that the rise of Black Power caused black women to embrace black-centered ideals of beauty and politics and to redefine black womanhood within the context of movement organizing.

The Panther identified two factors that she believed influenced black women's shifting political self-conception: black men and white supremacy. The "Sisters' Section" author argued that black women could "not help but gravitate" toward black men who were fighting for black freedom and "join with [them] in the pursuit of a life together, removing the shackles of White Racist America and establishing a solid foundation of blackness from which to build." Hart also maintained that through their study of and participation in political organizing, black women had come to understand contemporaneous black oppression as a "repetition of history," or the latest iteration of a long history of black subjugation engendered by the ability of white supremacy to continually manifest itself in myriad ways. Black women's simultaneous recognition of the importance of black men, racism's resiliency, and their own "increasing possibility" as antiracist actors had led them to rethink traditional gendered models. Hart explained that black women now realized that they should bring their strength, will, and black heritage rather than their "leadership" and "domination" to bear on the black struggle, and they recognized that they should ardently reject Eurocentric, capitalist markers of womanhood, progress, and power.[52]

The Panther ended the article by announcing what she believed to be a new idea of black womanhood circulating with the party and the black community at large. "Politically, economically, and sexually, a new ethic is molded," Hart wrote, "constantly adapting itself to the needs of blackness." She described this new conception of black womanhood as one in which the revolutionary black woman rejected white cultural standards, or "stop[ped] pressing her hair," prioritized being "involved in her community with the end in mind of laying the foundation for the [white] man's destruction," and made "her man and thus his commitment . . . [the] essence of her life."[53]

Hart's characterization of black womanhood was propagandistic, patriarchal, and, in some ways, progressive. The new gendered political persona that she envisioned reflected the party's early Black Power agenda. In its first year, the party promoted a form of male-centered, separatist, class-conscious politics and called for black Americans to reject Eurocentric political, class, and cultural values and seize community control through armed confrontation. In line with this perspective, Hart envisioned the burgeoning Black Revolutionary Woman as an activist who was ardently opposed to white beauty standards and materialism and devoted to black community control and self-determination. The idealized trope of black womanhood that she promoted also reflected the Panthers' initial commitment to patriarchal ideas of black empowerment in that it defined black women's political promise largely through their support of black men.

Despite these patriarchal underpinnings, Hart established the real and imagined political potential of black women within the Panther Party in "Black Womanhood No. 1." Her explication of black women's evolving political self-conception confirmed that black women were capable of and interested in developing a new definition of black womanhood that responded to the political moment and organizational politics. By articulating a new idea of black womanhood in a Panther-sanctioned publication, Hart asserted that the party was a space in which black women could advance new, gender-specific definitions of their rights, roles, and revolutionary identities. Ultimately, Hart's article, and the "Sisters' Section" more broadly, illustrated how black women's commitment to Black Power politics and organizing shaped the gendered imaginary. These early articles also laid the groundwork for women to envision themselves as consummate revolutionaries alongside Panther men.

If articles in the "Sisters' Section" foregrounded Panther women's changing self-conception, then their early political artwork personified their redefinition. The party began incorporating Revolutionary Art—a collection of drawings, political cartoons, and mixed-media images designed to "enlighten" party members and "educate the masses"—into the *Black Panther* newspaper in May 1967.[54] Panther leaders used artwork as way to represent the black condition and to visually theorize black liberation.[55] The Panthers' minister of culture Emory Douglas explained that Revolutionary Art gave "people the correct picture of [their] struggle, whereas Revolutionary Ideology

[gave] people the correct political understanding of [their] struggle."[56] In every issue, the Panthers provided a set of imagistic lessons designed to instruct readership on the "correct" way to embody and enact their ideological and programmatic directives. It also highlighted the Panthers' revolutionary identity and ideology.

Tarika Lewis was the party's first Revolutionary Artist. Between 1967 and 1969, she created over forty images under the pen name Matilaba.[57] Although her drawings appeared alongside those of famed Panther artist Emory Douglas, they had a style and tone of their own. Readers could identify her artwork by its thin, angular lines and pen strokes and her use of light shading to provide contrast in her black-and-white drawings. Her demonization of police officers as "pigs" galvanized readership against law enforcement; her depictions of black Americans in armed confrontation reinforced the Panthers' real-life challenges to police brutality.[58] Lewis also foregrounded black women often, and she unfailingly depicted them engaging in the same activities and tasks as men. Not only did her artwork challenge monolithic perceptions of black militancy, it also reshaped Panther and public imaginings of the black revolutionary figure.

The December 21, 1968, edition of the *Black Panther* featured five of Lewis's drawings. On page 4 of the issue, readers saw her full-page illustration of point number three of the Panther Party's Ten Point Platform: "We Want an End to the Robbery by the White Man of Our Black Community." Lewis illustrated this Panther principle by centering the image of the upper body of a black woman against a white background. Outfitted in paramilitary clothing, an Afro, and earrings, the woman does not look down or at the viewer but stares off into the distance. With a gun on her back and a shell casing strung around her neck, and her angled body conveying a sense of motion and purpose, the woman is prepared to "off the pig," or to protect the black community, as the accompanying dialogue proclaims.[59]

After perusing articles about local-level politics, the Panthers' Free Breakfast Program, and cultural nationalism, readers found another one of Lewis's drawings on page 15 of the same issue. In this half-page illustration, Lewis depicted four armed Panthers in a room, peering through an open doorway. One man, wearing the Panthers' signature black beret, sits at the top of the staircase; another cautiously peers around the slightly open door. The third figure, another man, stands directly behind him in a defensive posture. The only unobstructed figure is that of a woman dressed in knee-high boots, a black skirt, and a white shirt, poised to be the first one to attack or to be attacked. Because of her vulnerable position, the woman is in a

Drawing by Tarika Lewis of armed black woman from the *Black Panther*, December 21, 1968.

Drawing by Tarika Lewis of group of Black Panthers from the *Black Panther*, December 21, 1968.

defensive stance, both hands on her rifle, eyes fixed just beyond the open door.[60]

Originally, the Panthers used pictorial representations of black men engaged in armed self-defense to assure the male readership that, through the organization, they could redefine and assert their manhood. Leadership of the black community was foremost among these rights, as long as they also engaged in what Farah Jasmine Griffin has called the "promise of protection," or a social contract that implied that black women would accept black men as the leaders and defenders of the community in exchange for protection and security.[61] The Panthers visually conveyed this idea by populating the *Black Panther* newspaper with drawings and images of armed black men.

Lewis questioned the gendered exclusivity of this contract. Through her artwork, she amplified party members' daily activities, such as their armed police patrols and confrontation with local law enforcement. The artist also transformed the masculinist underpinnings of these acts by integrating women into representations of black militancy and Panther tenets. Lewis's illustration of the third point of the Panthers' Ten Point Platform both reinforced and reconceptualized the party's approach to the promise of protection. Throughout the paper, party members often framed the organization as the one best poised to protect the black community from the avaricious white community. In her visual representation of point three, Lewis bolstered this claim by drawing a black figure armed and poised to attack. However, by illustrating this point through a stand-alone image of a black woman, Lewis confirmed party women's ability to embody and enact the Panthers' calls for armed self-defense and community control without the leadership or protection of men. When depicting the Panthers' collective armed confrontation, akin to their armed police patrols, Lewis visually positioned women as protectors of the community alongside men. The location of the female figure in the second image confirms this point. She is not behind the pack of men or unarmed. Rather, she stands shoulder to shoulder with her male comrades in clear command of her weapon and the situation. Through this and other images, Lewis showed that black women were capable of identifying with, adopting, and embodying the Panthers' revolutionary values, appearance, strategies, and politics. She also implied that the common bond among Panther members—and the core of their new revolutionary identity—was not maleness but militancy.

Panther women's early Revolutionary Art was also progressive and provocative because it subverted traditional visual constructions of black womanhood. As bell hooks notes, artists and photographers often portray black women as simplistic and transparent, particularly through frontal views of their faces and bodies.[62] Lewis disputed this characterization by insisting that the viewer take note of the force and purpose of the black women. She centered the face and upper body of the female figure in the first image, yet her body is angled, eyes transfixed elsewhere, and the remaining portion of her body is absent. In the second image, Lewis drew attention to women's militancy by outfitting the female figure in different clothing and positioning her on the outside of the Panthers' formation. Like her counterpart in the preceding drawing, this woman does not face front or meet eyes with the viewer. Both images gave readers the sense that black women were militant, aggressive, and volatile rather than stable, dependable, domesticated, or simplistic. Lewis's artwork reinforced the Panthers' early message of armed militancy while simultaneously broadening the scope of their revolutionary imagery and identity.

Panther women's initial projections of the Black Revolutionary Woman had important implications for black women's goal of collective redefinition. Although postwar activists like Mallory continually defined black women by their militancy rather than their maternalism, throughout the

1960s, the latter often remained the litmus test of their revolutionary acuity. Even the Panthers' Revolutionary Posters—reproductions of Emory Douglas's art sold for profit—often featured women carrying children or caring for them.[63] Lewis's artwork disputed characterizations of black women as docile servant figures and visually solidified their place among the burgeoning militant Black Power ranks. Similarly, Auther and Hart defined the new female revolutionary by her support of radical race-based politics, anticapitalist analysis of white supremacy, and resistance to dominant ideas of black womanhood. Early Panther women consistently depicted women as public, militant, and powerful protectors of their communities rather than as maids or mammies.[64] In the process, they divested black women of their domestic markers and cast them as self-defined and self-determining activists.

Black women who joined the party in its nascent years embodied the revolutionary attributes that Hart, Lewis, and other Panther women prescribed. SNCC activist Kathleen Neal Cleaver joined the party in 1967 after meeting her future husband, Eldridge Cleaver, a former-prisoner-turned-radical-activist who joined the party in February 1967.[65] Confrontations between the Panthers and police catapulted her to party prominence. On October 28, 1967, an early morning altercation between Huey Newton and Oakland police officer John Frey turned violent, resulting in Frey's death and Newton's incarceration.[66] The Panther leader's absence, coupled with the arrests of many early recruits after the Sacramento incident, left the party in disarray. The following month, Kathleen Cleaver relocated to the Bay Area and began working for the organization. She created leaflets, reported on court hearings, and organized demonstrations, laying the foundation for the Free Huey campaign, a national grassroots movement to free the Panther leader.[67] Her leadership of the movement led to her appointment as the organization's communications secretary, a position that made her the first woman to sit on its Central Committee and a Black Power icon. Party publications presented her as the real-life personification of the Black Revolutionary Woman that early Panther women described. Reflecting the reciprocal relationship between party literature and members, photos of Cleaver dressed in a black leather jacket and boots, with her hair styled in an Afro and a gun in her hands, began to populate the pages of the *Black Panther*.[68]

Kathleen Cleaver's popularity was indicative of women's growing participation in the Panther Party. Their presence in the collective increased amid a series of organizational and national events. On April 6, 1968, the police surrounded Bobby Hutton, Eldridge Cleaver, and six other party members in West Oakland. The Panthers and police exchanged words, then gunfire. Lil' Bobby, as the Panthers called him, was the party's first casualty.[69] Hutton's death hit a black community still reeling from the assassination of Dr. Martin Luther King Jr. just two days earlier. Newton's arrest, Hutton's murder, and King's assassination became the triumvirate of events that tipped the scales of popular opinion toward the Panthers' brand of insurgency. In the months following Hutton's funeral, seventeen new Panther chapters developed in cities including Boston, Seattle, and Chicago.[70]

Women founded or headed many of these new branches. Mary Rem established the Des Moines chapter; Ericka Huggins helped create and lead the New Haven branch of the group.[71] Audrea Jones cofounded and led the Boston branch of the party. Under Jones's direction, the chapter developed their local Free Breakfast Program, created liberation schools, and built medical centers for black Bostonians.[72] Shirley George-Meadors cofounded the San Diego branch.[73] Women also held key positions within individual chapters. Yvonne King was the minister of labor and a field secretary in the Chicago chapter.[74] Safiya Bukhari served as the communications and information officer of the East Coast Black Panther Party, while Elaine Brown, who came into the party through the Los Angeles chapter, became the local deputy minister of education.[75] Women's vital contributions led many to conclude that women "ran" the daily operations of the party and that the organization would have to promulgate new ideas of the revolutionary to reflect members' lived experiences.[76]

Panther women such as New Orleans member Linda Greene began to reconfigure the idea of the female revolutionary in the late 1960s. In her 1968 article "The Black Revolutionary Woman," she remarked, "There is a phenomenon that is beginning to evolve out of many other phenomenon [sic]. That is the revolutionary Black woman. She is a new, different creature, different from all women who have walked the face of the earth.... She is a change; she is inherently revolutionary." Greene explained what set this new, idealized woman apart: "She is a worker. She is a mother. She is a companion intellectual, spiritual, mental, and physical. She is what her man, and what her people need her to be, when they need her. She is the strength of the struggle.... She is militant, revolutionary, committed, strong, and warm, feminine, loving, and kind. These qualities are not the antithesis of each other; they must all be her simultaneously."[77] While Hart and Lewis were intent on proving that women could match men's militancy, Greene suggested that this was no longer the only axis on which black women's revolutionary potential should be measured. The Panthers' ideal of revolutionary womanhood could not rest solely on women's ability to perform "masculine" acts; rather, Panther women needed a model of womanhood that reflected the complete range of their activities and political organizing.

Political expediency may have prompted Greene to rethink existing definitions of black womanhood; however, her new formulation marked a turning point in the Panthers' gendered imaginary. Not only did her article establish the centrality of women to all aspects of party life, it also challenged popular conceptions of "masculine" and "feminine" revolutionary traits or acts. Greene continued early Panther women's strategy of linking the Black Revolutionary Woman to the traditional markers of revolutionary manhood, stating that she was *militant, revolutionary*, an *intellectual*, and *committed* to struggle. However, she did not disavow the importance of femininity or traditionally feminine traits. Greene instead proffered a holistic idea of the revolutionary figure, one that responded to the political moment rather than a gender-specific understanding of men's or women's roles. Her rhetorical reordering countered anti-intellectual and apolitical characterizations of black women. It also offered female readership a broader, more applicable model of womanhood to adopt. Ultimately, Greene advanced an argument for reimagining black women as revolutionaries and autonomous actors while also countering the limiting gender dichotomies and binaries that had previously governed the Panthers' gendered imaginary.

Greene's article also reflected Panther women's attempts to balance men's rhetoric of emasculation with their lived experiences organizing on the front lines. Like her fellow activists, she argued that the revolutionary woman should "put herself to the task and honor of inspiring" black men. She departed from this masculinist construction, however, in her rationale for calling for black women's support of black men. In the late 1960s, the predominant claim among Black Power organizers was that true, revolutionary black men were in short supply. Greene suggested the opposite. She claimed that it was "true, revolutionary Black women," rather than men, who were "more scarce than freedom."[78] The political climate demanded that versatile, rigorous, and committed activists lead both the party and the movement. The Black Revolutionary Woman, as Greene envisioned her, was the one who fit that bill. Greene's rhetorical reversal, in which she framed black women as the most sought-after liberation fighters, challenged male-centered frames of revolutionary activism. Her article, and those of other women who joined the party in 1968, highlighted Panther women's investment in theorizing a continually evolving definition of black revolutionary womanhood within the organization.

Revolutionary Nationalism and the Black Revolutionary Woman

Greene and her contemporaries formulated new definitions of revolutionary womanhood as the party entered a new organizational and ideological phase. Between 1968 and 1970, female membership in the organization peaked.[79] At the same time, Panther leadership also began to question the feasibility of their black nationalist and masculinist agenda. Women who joined the party during this period invested in the Panthers' expanding ideological frame, developing more capacious conceptualizations of women's real and imagined roles. Their reformulation of the Black Revolutionary Woman in the remaining years of the decade directly challenged patriarchal interpretations of party ideology and pushed Panther leadership to label sexist practices as counterrevolutionary.

Women poured into the Panther Party amid an increasingly repressive government order. In 1968, Richard Nixon won the presidency, garnering over 60 percent of the popular vote through an aggressive campaign that emphasized "law and order" and free enterprise. Nixon's approach to the black community reflected this two-pronged platform. Under his watch, the FBI extended the counterintelligence program—known as COINTELPRO—in an effort to stamp out black groups. He simultaneously embraced the idea of black capitalism as a form of Black Power, establishing the Office of Minority Business Enterprise, funneling money toward black colleges and black-owned businesses, and enriching the black middle class.[80]

As an anti-state and anticapitalist organization, the party drew the ire of Nixon administration. In 1967, state and federal officials escalated their attacks on the Panthers through COINTELPRO. The goal of the program was to "disrupt, misdirect, and discredit" what the bureau deemed to be subversive, black nationalist organizations and leaders.[81] In 1969 alone, the Panthers endured raids on offices and members in Des Moines, New York City, Chicago, Seattle, and Los Angeles, among other cities.[82] Most notably, government agents fostered antipathy between the Panthers and the Us Organization, a Los Angeles–based cultural nationalist group. The FBI-fueled animosity between Us and the party led to a January 17, 1969, shootout on the campus of the University of California, Los Angeles, and the deaths of Panther members John Huggins and Alprentice "Bunchy"

Carter.[83] Local police arrested two Us members, Larry and George Stiner, for their murders. The incident also initiated a wave of interorganizational attacks that adversely affected both groups.

Although patriarchal conceptions of leadership led law enforcement to target Panther men, women in the organization responded to state-sponsored violence in kind. Renee "Peaches" Moore, a nineteen-year-old member of the Los Angeles chapter, exchanged gunfire with the LAPD after officers raided the chapter's headquarters in December 1969. Catherine "Top Cat" Bourns, Leah Hodges, and Elaine "E-baby" Young of the New Orleans chapter garnered national attention for their involvement in a September 1970 shootout with local police.[84] Panther women's resiliency in the face of repression impressed their contemporaries and brought more women into the organization. Kiilu Nyasha (Pat Gallyot), for example, became a Panther after seeing photos from Huggins's funeral. She recalled that she joined the New Haven chapter in 1969 because she was "very impressed by the Black Panther Party and their seriousness and their militancy."[85]

Nyasha joined the party as its leaders were shifting their ideological perspectives on black liberation, capitalism, and imperialism. Initial members came of age during a period in which grassroots, independent, black-led political parties and the proliferation of independent black nations in Africa made calls for black political autonomy, self-determination, and physical separation appear feasible. However, party leaders soon found black nationhood to be a difficult goal to achieve on American soil. Lacking separate land on which to establish a new nation, many Panthers realized that black Americans would have to become a "dominant faction" within the United States to achieve their original nationalist goals. Achieving political and cultural dominance was virtually impossible without physical separation. This circular approach to nation building led many of them to conclude that this model of black nationalism was an untenable ideological approach to maintain.[86]

Drawing on the lessons that he learned as a student of revolutionary theorists such as Frantz Fanon, Kwame Nkrumah, and Mao Zedong, in 1969, Newton announced that the party had adopted the ideology of revolutionary nationalism. The Panthers' new goal was to join forces with "other people of the world struggling for decolonization and nationhood."[87] Not only would allying with other dispersed and dispossessed communities help black Americans achieve their nationalistic goals, it could also bring about a "people's revolution with the end goal of the people being in power."[88] The Panthers became "nationalists who want[ed] revolutionary changes in everything, including the economic system the[ir] oppressor inflict[ed] on [them]."[89] This elastic political frame led party members to amplify their anticapitalist and anti-imperialist critique of American society. It also laid the foundation for them to challenge other forms of oppression, including patriarchy, under the auspices of the organization's expanding revolutionary ethos.

Women in the party cited the organization's ideological evolution as the impetus behind their changing definition of black revolutionary womanhood. In a 1969 interview with the *Movement*, a white radical newspaper, a group of Panther women explained that the organization's emphasis on comprehensive revolutionary change had caused party members to scrutinize gender roles and their relationship with capitalist structures. According to these women, members' adoption of an explicit anticapitalist frame led party participants to "realize that male chauvinism and all of its manifestations [were] bourgeois," or that sexism and patriarchal gender roles were tools developed by white, capitalist society that mediated black community building. Further study led party members to develop an intersectional analysis of black women's oppression and to conclude that their emancipatory visions would have to account for the converging forms of racism and sexism that black women experienced. Echoing earlier radicals, such as Claudia Jones, the Panther women asserted, "In a proletarian revolution, the emancipation of women is primary."[90]

Party women's emphasis on women's liberation reflected conversations taking place inside and outside the black liberation movement. The surge of leftist activism in the late 1960s and, in particular, women's participation in the civil rights movement generated new debates about gender roles and hierarchies across multiple progressive and radical groups.[91] Black and white women began to develop collective and separate organizations dedicated to ending sexism in the home, the workplace, political organizing, and society at large.[92] By the end of the decade, the women's liberation movement was in full swing, with activists and protests attracting mainstream media coverage and the publication of a bevy of books, manifestos, and anthologies dedicated to defining feminism, eradicating patriarchy, and advocating for reproductive rights.[93]

Women in the party were often interested in women's liberation principles but not the movement itself. They, like many other black women, maintained that it was a white-centered movement, designed to end patriarchy while leaving racism intact. As Kathleen Neal Cleaver explained, many members found that the "problems of black women and the problems of white women are so completely diverse they [could not] possibly be solved in the same type of organization nor met by the same type of activity."[94] Other Panther women maintained that feminist organizations that did not incorporate a race or class critique into their political ideology were misguided, as women could only truly be liberated through the simultaneous destruction of racism, sexism, and capitalism. This led many party women, according to historian Mary Phillips, to "operat[e] as feminists" while distancing themselves from the term.[95] However, Panther women did, at times, collaborate with feminist organizations.[96] They also integrated feminist principles into their visions of revolutionary womanhood.

In the August 1969 issue of the *Black Panther*, member Candi Robinson characterized the Black Revolutionary Woman as a feminist and revolutionary nationalist activist. In her article, "Message to Revolutionary Women," she told readers, "Black Women, Black Women, hold your head up, and look ahead. We too are needed in the revolution. We too are strong. We too are a threat to the oppressive enemy. We are revolutionaries. We are the other half of our revolutionary men. We are their equal halves, may it be with gun in hand, or battling in streets to make this country take a socialist lead."[97] This parity, according to Robinson, meant that one of the key roles of female revolutionaries was to "educate [their] people [to] combat liberalism, and combat male chauvinism. Awaken [their] men to the fact that [black women were] no more nor no less than they." "For too long," she contended, women had "been doubly oppressed, not only by capitalist society but also by [their men]." Employing the rhetoric of the moment, Robinson encouraged her female readership to teach men to "bring their minds from a male chauvinistic level to a higher level" and to continually remind them that women were "as revolutionary as they."[98] The Panther promoted a vision of revolutionary womanhood in which party women were the intellectual and organizational equals of men, invested in the revolutionary nationalist goal of bringing about a socialist state, and dedicated to ending sexism within the organization and the movement at large.

Panther women like Robinson simultaneously codified Panther ideology and stretched the boundaries of the party's gendered ideals. Her formulation of this political identity retained earlier Panther women's efforts to envision the Black Revolutionary Woman as militant, political, and versatile. Reflecting shifting ideas about women's rights and gender roles, Robinson also envisioned the female revolutionary as a political actor who incorporated antisexist work into her litany of roles and responsibilities. In her estimation, the Black Revolutionary Woman brought the Panthers closer to their proletariat revolution by explicitly combatting the central disciplining structures of capitalism: liberalism and male chauvinism. She was also a woman who expanded the definition of revolution, and the Panthers' revolutionary ideal, by envisioning a world free from sexism and leading the fight to achieve gender equality.

If Panther women's articles were prescriptive, then their autobiographical accounts were demonstrative. Like postwar women radicals, they used their personal stories of politicization to both model and project new, more radical conceptions of black womanhood. New York chapter member Joan Bird's autobiographical essays highlighted this practice. Born and raised in the city, Bird joined the party in 1968. Her party activism led to her incarceration as one of the Panther 21, a group of New York members falsely accused of plotting to bomb department stores, police stations, and other local landmarks in 1969.[99] Like Mallory, Bird penned autobiographical accounts from her jail cell to call attention to her case and contextualize it within the larger framework of government repression and white supremacy. She also used her account of radicalization to model how Panther women adopted and enacted the identity of the Revolutionary Black Woman that members like Greene and Robinson described.

In "Joan Bird, N.Y. Panther 21 Political Prisoner," Bird provided readers with her personal narrative of persecution and politicization. She began her account with her upbringing and introduction to the Panther Party. "I was born and raised in Harlem in New York City. I went to a parochial elementary school from kindergarten through eighth grade, from there I attended Cathedral High School. . . . It was an integrated school and in there I found different sorts of racism present both among teachers and among the students. I can think of one incident where a group of Black sisters were sitting in the auditorium and we were rapping during a recess period. A White racist nun came over and said, 'get the hell outta here, this is all you niggers are good for.'"[100] Bird offered other examples of the gender-specific incidents of racism that framed her young adult life: "After graduation from Cathedral, I decided to go into nursing at Bronx Community College, I was instructed by a Zionist, who had a thing against Black women. She didn't dig us wearing our hair natural, and did anything to deprive us of being ourselves." Frustrated at every turn, Bird explained that she sought both refuge and community. She was attracted to the party because it offered "some sort of concrete ideology" to explain her oppression and community programs through which she could organize against it.[101]

The New York activist then gave *Black Panther* readers a detailed account of her arrest, incarceration, and trial. "In January of 1969, I was in a car and two pigs stopped and they asked us what was the trouble. A few minutes later the pigs, started shooting. A ten minute interval later, one pig, named McKenzie, (a Black pig by the way) says, cover me, I think there's a broad in the car and he came up to the car where I'm at. . . . I was dragged out and finally, I was placed on the ground, beaten with a blackjack by McKenzie, kicked, stomped, beaten in the head, given a busted lip and busted eye." Bird confirmed that once she was arrested and released on bail, she continued working for the Panthers until the police arrested her again. In closing, she remarked, "I have been in jail for over fourteen months now, along with my brothers, ten of them, and we have just finished our preliminary hearings which clearly shows that the racist system of America does not intend to give the Black Panther Party members justice or anyone else in this country any sort of justice."[102]

Bird's account not only established the party as an inclusive organization, it also foregrounded Panther women's revolutionary potential and reshaped the contours of the Panthers' revolutionary persona. The New York organizer cast the party as an ideologically and organizationally malleable organization, flexible enough to address her gender-specific experiences with oppression and equipped with an ideological framework that could offer "concrete" solutions for black women's subjugation. Her narrative indicates that she was not only welcomed into the party ranks but also able to apply the Panthers' revolutionary nationalist tenets to her lived experiences as a working-class black woman. Bird's recounting of her arrest and incarceration undergirded this message. In her retelling, she casts the state as the natural enemy of black women, emphasizing that it was the police, not her fellow Panthers, who targeted and abused her. Instead, Panther men were her comrades in arms, fighting alongside her and enduring the trumped-up legal charges. This narrative left the reader with the impression that the party was a conduit through which black women could assert their community based, anti-imperialist politics and challenge state-sanctioned political repression.

Bird also gendered black activists' prototypical stories of revolutionary transformation. Often published as essays in the newspaper—and later in book form—the autobiographical accounts that (male) Panthers produced offered a road map of how they became radical activists worthy of public recognition.[103] Bird's article was similar to those that black activists created, beginning with her upbringing and experiences with discrimination. She departed from masculinist radicalization narratives, however, by fore-grounding her personal moments of politicization in gendered and racial terms. Bird consistently citied incidents of racism particular to her girlhood in order to foreground how oppression manifested differently for black women. Her narrative challenged claims that black women did not experi-ence the same level of police harassment or racial violence as black men.[104] It also indicated that black women could be radicalized through their gender-specific experiences with repression. Bird's use of this genre had important implications for Panther women's theorizing of the female rev-olutionary identity and subjectivity. Her recounting offered an alternative genealogy of politicization and transformation outside the traditional tropes that male activists produced and presented readers with a model of black revolutionary womanhood steeped in black women's personal or subjective modes.

Ultimately, Bird's autobiographical account challenged the imagined uni-versality of the Panthers' masculine revolutionary subject and shaped pub-lic perceptions about black women's political personas and organizing.[105] Her narrative and the others like it can be thought of as what Sidonie Smith calls "autobiographical manifestos," which can contest dominant narratives "by working to dislodge the consolidations of the Eurocentric, phallogo-cenric 'I'" and replacing them with black, women-centered understandings of the political subject.[106] Bird literally and rhetorically reconfigured her-self as a true revolutionary, physically and ideologically in step with Pan-ther men. She also provided readers with a gender-specific story of personal transformation, framed the party as a gender-inclusive and ideologically generative space, and modeled a gender-specific form of the black revolu-tionary that other black women could adopt. Her account exemplifies Pan-ther women's attempts to dislodge universal, male-dominated conceptions of the black revolutionary subject and assert a women-centered political identity in service of advancing the Panthers' revolutionary nationalist politics. Bird, along with many other Panther women, used autobiographi-cal manifestos to insist on the potential and equality of the female revolu-tionary actor and to chart a path to redefinition and radical action for the party's female readership.

Panther women's rhetorical reformulations and real-life representations of the revolutionary figure altered the male leadership's perspectives on men's and women's roles. One of the starkest examples of this shift was in the public declarations of party leader Eldridge Cleaver. Cleaver rose to prominence after the publication of his controversial book *Soul on Ice*, an autobiographical account that included graphic tales of misogyny and heterosexual, oppressive sexual politics.[107] When he became the minister of information for the party in 1967, the Panthers implicitly endorsed his sexist positions along with his political vision. Several years later, Cleaver revised his public statements on women's rights and roles, citing Panther women's real and imagined acts of revolutionary activism as evidence for his claims.

Writing from the Panthers' International Section in Algeria, a chapter he and Kathleen Cleaver formed in 1968, Eldridge Cleaver championed gender equality within the organization and women's revolutionary potential.[108] The Panther leader used Ericka Huggins's imprisonment and trial as evidence for the need for gender parity within the organization. Huggins was jailed on charges that she, along with Seale and several other Panthers, tortured and killed member Alex Rackley in May 1969 because they suspected him of being an FBI informant.[109] Local police incarcerated her for years while the State of Connecticut engaged in a long and costly trial in an effort to convict the group of Panthers, known as the New Haven 9, and undermine the party's reputation and leadership.[110]

In "Message to Sister Ericka Huggins," Eldridge Cleaver argued that Huggins's political commitments and activism made her the ideal revolutionary actor and that her experiences with government repression discredited claims of women's inferiority. In a full-page spread on the back page of the July 5, 1969, edition of the *Black Panther*, Cleaver claimed that Huggins was "a shining example of a revolutionary woman," and that her "incarceration and suffering" should serve as a "stinging rebuke to all manifestations of male chauvinism in [party] ranks." "We must purge our ranks and our hearts, and our minds, and our understanding of any chauvinism, chauvinistic behavior or disrespectful behavior toward women," Cleaver told the Panther readership. "We must too recognize that a woman can be just as revolutionary as a man and that she has equal stature [with men] . . . that we cannot prejudice her in any manner, [and] that we cannot relegate her to an inferior position."[111]

Cleaver's "Message" marked an important moment in the evolution of the Panthers' ethos and gendered imaginary. As a party leader, Cleaver's *rhetorical* disavowal of patriarchy served as prong of the organization's de facto repudiation of sexism. Moreover, his message reflected the changes in the Panthers' culture brought about by women's political and personal sacrifice, as well as their assertions of women's revolutionary identity and potential. Huggins, according to Cleaver, was a revolutionary black woman because she eschewed traditional, gender-specific roles and embodied and enacted the traits of revolutionary womanhood that women like Greene, Bird, and Robinson described. If Panther women sought to reformulate the black revolutionary as an empowered female actor, then Cleaver's public endorsement of their assertions reflected the inroads they had made in infusing this ideal into party culture.

Individual chapter leaders took Cleaver's message to heart. At the local level, members advanced a progressive, if uneven, line on gender equality that codified Panther women's framing of the Black Revolutionary Woman as men's powerful, political, and militant equal. Women in the Chicago chapter maintained that their leader, Fred Hampton, demanded that women be treated as equals and purged members who did not comply.[112] Ruby Morgan, a member of the Houston chapter, indicated that local leaders such as Charles Freeman illustrated their commitment to equality by assigning men and women to the same jobs and posts and by following women's leadership when they became ranking officers.[113] Debating, organizing, and studying with women caused rank-and-file men to rethink the masculinist image of the revolutionary figure. Austin Allen, who worked alongside many women in Oakland, later noted that his female fellow members clearly embodied and articulated the Panthers' ideological platform and revolutionary culture.[114] Panther women's rhetorical and pictorial constructions of the Black Revolutionary Woman gave members, and the broader public, the tools with which to reimagine and enact alternative understandings of manhood and womanhood. By 1970, they had solidified a party discourse and ideological ethos that framed black women as leaders and revolutionary equals.

Internationalism, Intercommunalism, and the Black Revolutionary Woman

In the 1970s, women emerged as formal leaders within the party. They filled multiple organizational positions, becoming directors, newspaper editors, and heads of the group's community programs. Panther women led efforts to transform the party into a locally driven, globally minded grassroots organization during its final years. They also capitalized on the organization's shifting focus to expand the boundaries of the party's gendered imaginary. From 1970 to 1975, female members developed an expansive political identity that integrated black mothers, feminists, and caregivers into the party's revolutionary fold. Their broadening of the definition of the Black Revolutionary Woman diversified the Panthers' political identity during a period in which the party was in need of wide-ranging community support. It also transformed the organization into a space that openly championed women's and feminist causes.

On August 5, 1970, the Free Huey campaign declared victory when the California Court of Appeals overturned Newton's manslaughter conviction.[115] The Panther leader walked out of Alameda County Jail and back into an organization that had changed significantly in his three-year absence. Between 1967 and 1970, the party proliferated, growing from a local, Bay Area group to an organization with chapters across the globe. The group's meteoric rise was matched only by the FBI's efforts to curtail its power. Local and federal law enforcement cells launched violent attacks on the organization, decimating party ranks and casting the organization as destructive and nihilistic. By the time the Panther founder resumed leadership of the organization, it was disjointed, reeling from the assassinations of major figures such as Chicago chapter leader Fred Hampton and in need of infrastructure and a political vision for the new decade.[116] In an attempt to consolidate and streamline the party, Newton demilitarized its image and turned its focus toward community organizing.

To create ideological and administrative coherence, the Panther founder shifted the party's ideological stance to intercommunalism. At the Panther-hosted Revolutionary People's Convention in Philadelphia, held in September 1970, Newton postulated that the United States was no longer simply a nation—it was an empire that controlled "*all* the world's land and people" and transformed other nations into oppressed communities. The global power struggle was divided along the axis of a "small circle that administered and profited from the empire of the United States" and those peoples and nations caught under the weight of American imperialism. As intercommunalists, the Panthers' goal was to work with other oppressed communities to create a global network of revolutionaries dedicated to ending all facets of American imperialism.[117] A position that drew on the Panthers' previous Marxist-Leninist and internationalist stances, intercommunalism amplified rather than completely redefined the organization's existing revolutionary nationalist position.

Intercommunalism also brought about a new organizing mantra: survival pending revolution. As member Gwen Hodges explained, the Panthers maintained that the "overthrow of one class by another [had to] be carried out by revolutionary violence." However, until they could achieve this goal, the party was going to "concentrate on the immediate needs of the people" in order to "build a unified political force" to fight racism and imperialism.[118] To this end, members created survival programs, or a network of services designed to mitigate the daily effects of oppression in black communities. The Panthers had already instituted this type of programming through initiatives such as the Free Breakfast Program that Seale started in 1968. In the early 1970s they expanded these programs—which included free health clinics and clothing and food programs—and framed them as "a first-aid kit," triaging and treating the black community so that it could "see the next day or see the revolution."[119] The party's survival programs, and the intercommunal ideology that framed them, allowed the Panthers to lay claim to their earlier revolutionary rhetoric while also engaging in progressive and practical community-based activities that improved their image and deepened their community relationships.[120]

A key part of this new image was party leaders' public endorsement of women's equality. In an August 1970 statement, Newton announced his formal support of women's and gay rights and framed sexism and homophobia as counterrevolutionary positions. "I do not remember our ever constituting any value that said that a revolutionary must say offensive things toward homosexuals, or that a revolutionary should make sure that women do not speak out about their own particular kind of oppression," Newton warned. "As a matter of fact, it is just the opposite: we say that we recognize the woman's right to be free."[121] Newton's public pronouncement simultaneously validated Panther women's contributions to political struggle and highlighted the distinction between party rhetoric and the quotidian experiences of Panther women. During the time that the party leader was incarcerated, female members not only directly challenged organizational sexism, they also linked women's liberation and proletariat revolution through their political writings, public speeches, and everyday activism. Reflecting these influences, Newton's statement was a rhetorical disavowal of the Moynihan-induced discourses of hypermasculinity, violence, and homophobia that had characterized the organization's political positions and perspectives in previous years. As was often the case, the party put the ideals Newton professed into practice unevenly. It would be up to women in the party to close the gap between rhetoric and reality by imagining and enacting new definitions of black womanhood.[122]

Although Newton's affirmation of women's equality may have been popular, his new approach to party organizing was not. In the early 1970s, Panther leadership deepened their support of community programming and deemphasized armed revolution. Members of the New York chapter were especially vocal about their disagreement with this new stance.[123] On

January 19, 1971, the New York Panther 21 published an open letter denouncing Newton's gradualist approach. The East Coast group maintained that revolution required armed struggle, violence, and bloodshed and that a revolutionary organization developed through political education, "extreme violence, and radicalization."[124] In response, Newton expelled this group and other Panthers who disagreed with the party's new direction.[125] Some members of this expulsed faction created the Black Liberation Army, an underground group designed to defend the black community and prepare them for armed revolutionary warfare.[126]

On the heels of this schism, Eldridge Cleaver, who sided with the Panther 21, publicly challenged Newton about this ideological turn. On February 26, 1971, Newton appeared live on San Francisco's locally syndicated *A.M. Show* with Jim Dunbar. Cleaver called in to the show from Algiers, challenged Newton's new survival program strategy, and demanded that he reinstate the expelled members. After the program, Newton expelled Cleaver and members of the International Section of the party.[127] FBI agents fueled the animosity between the two Panther leaders, using Connie Matthews, a Jamaican woman who served as the Panthers' international coordinator in Europe, as a mark in their efforts.[128] The sectarian split escalated in the following months, with calls from each side for the removal of members, damaging claims published by each faction in the mainstream and underground press, and the murders of Robert Webb and Sam Napier, which members blamed on this dispute. During this period, numerous chapters broke away from the national body, reducing the number of chapters by nearly half.[129]

In the face of dwindling support, an ideological schism, and internal mutinies, Newton and the Central Committee decided to consolidate the party. In July 1972, they closed all remaining chapters and asked members to relocate to the Panthers' central headquarters in Oakland.[130] In the years leading up to this organizational consolidation, women made up a large portion of the rank and file. They were also the majority of members who relocated to the Bay Area. By the fall of that year, there was a critical mass of women at the helm of the party in Oakland working to reconstitute it as an intercommunalist organization.[131]

The Central Committee envisioned Oakland as the epicenter of the Panthers' new political movement. To that end, the Panthers focused on turning the Bay Area city from a "reactionary base into a revolutionary one" using a three-pronged approach.[132] Members formed alliances with progressive groups such as the East Bay Democratic Club and black politicians such as

Congressman Ron Dellums and congresswoman and 1972 presidential candidate Shirley Chisholm.[133] They also expanded their existing community programs to create a complex network of services to meet the local community's needs.[134] Finally, the organization concentrated on winning political power in Oakland through electoral politics. The organization's Black Community Survival Conference in March 1972 epitomized their multilayered approach to transforming the city. At this massive rally, held at Oakland's DeFremery Park, the Panthers combined political speeches from candidates like Chisholm with coalition building, voter registration drives, food and clothing giveaways, and health care screenings. Such conferences raised the consciousness of local residents and advanced the Panthers' political agenda. The events also created a black voter base for party political office candidates Elaine Brown and Bobby Seale.[135]

Panther women headed this phase of party organizing. By 1973, they had developed the organization's Oakland-based survival programs, which included the Free Plumbing and Maintenance Program, the Legal Aid Educational Program, the People's Free Clothing Program, and the People's Free Shoe Program, among others. Female members also created Liberation Schools and the Intercommunal Youth Institute, an "alternative to established learning institutions" that provided "black and other oppressed children with a scientific method of thinking and analyzing things."[136] Many Panther women had been in charge of survival programs in their local chapters and continued to lead them after relocating to the Bay Area. Audrea Jones, who established the Panthers' free medical clinics in Boston, also headed their clinics and health services in Oakland.[137] As members of the Detroit chapter, Jonina Abron and Gwendolyn Robinson helped run the Free Busing to Prison Program. They also picked up where they left off when they relocated to the West Coast, helping to run similar programs in Oakland.[138]

Women were also the face of the group's electoral efforts. After supporting party-backed candidates in the early 1970s, Elaine Brown became the Panthers' candidate for Oakland City Council in 1973 and 1975. Challenging the city's Republican stronghold, she garnered an impressive 44 percent of the vote in the 1975 election.[139] Panther women also occupied other local and municipal seats. In addition to serving as the campaign manager for Seale's mayoral run, Audrea Jones was one of four Panthers who won a seat on the Berkeley Community Development Council board of directors, a local board that controlled the distribution of millions of federal dollars for antipoverty programs. Ericka Huggins, who was also elected, joined

Jones on the board because she "found it hard to ignore the unending harassment, poverty, and racism Black and poor people" faced.[140]

Female Panthers also took over editorial leadership of the *Black Panther* newspaper, now called the *Intercommunal News Service*. Under the direction of Brown and Huggins, the paper often featured women on the cover and published articles that foregrounded the gender-specific concerns of black women in inner-city communities.[141] Readers encountered articles about forced sterilization from women such as Lula Hudson, who wrote about her "fascist ordeal" in "They Told Me I Had to Be Sterilized or Die."[142] They also heard from female prisoners about their fight for self-determination and human dignity in the face of inhumane carceral conditions.[143] The *Intercommunal News Service* featured interviews with Margaret Sloan, founding member of the National Black Feminist Organization. It also chronicled Angela Davis's 1972 trial, informing readers on how the former UCLA professor and activist was falsely accused of supplying the guns used in the August 7, 1970, Marin County Courthouse takeover that ended with the deaths of the judge and three other men.[144] The party's newspaper had always been an ideologically and organizationally generative space. With female editors and artists at the helm, it continued to foreground the intersections of black womanhood, community organizing, and political theory.

In command of the party's programming and propaganda, Panther women expanded their real and imagined representations of black revolutionary women. The front-page story of the February 12, 1972, issue of the paper, for example, featured a photo of Inez Williams, mother of Fleeta Drumgo, as part of the article "Another Mother for Struggle."[145] Drumgo was one of the Soledad Brothers—three black Soledad prison inmates, including George Jackson and John Clutchette, charged with murdering white prison guard John Vincent Mills.[146] The cover of the issue features Williams in the foreground, sitting in a chair and looking stoically off into the distance. The space behind her is populated with the faces of black activists and revolutionaries, the visages of the Soledad Brothers and Angela Davis among them. The image is black and white, except for two elements in color: Williams's sweater and the title of the article. Emblazoned in fuchsia, the title of the article floats over the image of Williams and the sea of black faces, all flanked by a series of vertical bars.

In the accompanying article, the newspaper editors framed Williams as a militant crusader and revolutionary warrior. They noted that through her "tireless activity on behalf of the Soledad Brothers, she became involved in

THE BLACK PANTHER

INTERCOMMUNAL NEWS SERVICE 25 cents

VOL. VII NO. 25   Copyright © 1971 by Huey P. Newton   SATURDAY, FEBRUARY 12, 1972

PUBLISHED WEEKLY   THE BLACK PANTHER PARTY   MINISTRY OF INFORMATION BOX 2967, CUSTOM HOUSE SAN FRANCISCO, CA 94126

ANOTHER MOTHER FOR STRUGGLE

MOTHER OF BROTHER FLEETA DRUMGO IS FIGHTING TO FREE ALL POLITICAL PRIRSONERS

Cover of the *Black Panther*, February 12, 1972.

the larger movement to free all political prisoners" and that these events "brought Sister Inez Williams to another, a higher level in understanding our oppression, and, thereby working to end it." Williams, they wrote, struggled for "[Drumgo's] and her survival and right to live in dignity as human beings, expanded. Her direct experiences with this ruthless power structure had not defeated her. The murderous and racist tactics of the State ha[d], in fact, served to contribute another fearless fighter for the basic human rights of all people."[147]

Images featuring women like Williams reflected how Panther women provocatively recast the Black Revolutionary Woman during the party's intercommunal phase. During a period in which the organization actively worked to demilitarize its image, the newspaper editors foregrounded black women's everyday acts of militancy. The placement of the components of the cover image featuring Drumgo's mother underscores this point. Williams dominates the frame, and, seated in a chair, she is the only figure staving off the encroaching vertical lines—arranged in the same array as prison bars—from obscuring the collection of faces of activists and revolutionaries. This framing simultaneously cast Williams as an emancipator, holding the carceral state at bay so that the revolutionaries behind her can escape, and as the last line of defense protecting black activists and community members from long arm of the state. Foregrounded against a sea of mostly male faces, Williams's position as a protector and redeemer shifted the party's visual markers of revolutionary symbolism. The cover image gives the reader the sense that Williams should be considered a revolutionary just like the radical black men behind her and that both Panther- and public-sanctioned revolutionaries literally and metaphorically supported her struggle and depended on her leadership. The editors also used the cover to rhetorically redraw the boundaries of the Panthers' revolutionary identity. The choice to label Williams as a "mother" in struggle, and to visually link her to the term through the limited use of color, suggested that black motherhood and revolutionary womanhood were not mutually exclusive concepts. Throughout the 1970s, Panther women inserted a broader range of black women into the party's revolutionary canon. They also proffered an ideal of the Black Revolutionary Woman as a community-based, anti-imperialist mother or actor who carried on the Panthers' revolutionary struggles.

The accompanying article about Williams's politics further legitimized her revolutionary potential. The party maintained that the prison system was one of the most ardent manifestations of state-sponsored race, class, and gender oppression in America and across the globe. As inter-communalists, the Panthers' goal was to identify oppressive mechanisms of the state and work to free all people from their grasp. Williams exemplified this revolutionary ethos. Far from being an uneducated, marginal, and apolitical black woman, the Panthers cast her as a political theorist with a "higher understanding" of the machinations of the state and viewed freeing her son as a critical part of building a larger prison abolition movement. In the process, Panther women expanded the definitions of who could be a radical or revolutionary actor and of what constituted a revolutionary act. They also framed the party as a space that welcomed women of all walks of life and one in which black mothers became Black Revolutionary Women through their ardent expressions of intercommunal politics.

The Panthers also established their intercommunal identity through Revolutionary Art. In the early 1970s, Gayle Dickson became one of the primary artists for the paper. Dickson was originally a member of and an artist for the Seattle chapter, where she drew signs for the local free medical clinics under the pen name Asali.[148] When the Central Committee consolidated the organization in 1972, Dickson relocated to Oakland. Like other women, she picked up where she left off, creating Revolutionary Art for the newspaper in Oakland. According to other rank-and-file activists, Dickson had a profound impact on the party's artistic culture. Fellow artist Reginald "Malik" Edwards recalled that she was known for a "distinct application of a traditional form to capture 'Panther ideology.'"[149] Dickson's artwork often featured black women from all stages and walks of life, frequently participating in and advocating for the Panthers' survival programs. Her artwork foregrounded black women's collective feelings of oppression and joy, their relationship with the party, and their efforts to eradicate racism.

For the June 3, 1972, edition of the paper, Dickson created a mixed-media image of an older black woman carrying a bag filled with food from the Free Food Program. On the bag is an endorsement of Seale for mayor of Oakland. The woman, sporting a button promoting Elaine Brown for Oakland City councilwoman, wears a green beret with a pin stating, "Vote for Survival," and carries a flyer announcing the candidacy of Shirley Chisholm for president. The woman's eyes are closed, her head tilted back, and she is wearing a broad smile, rejoicing over the goods that she has received from the Panthers. Above the image, "Let It Shine, Let It Shine! Let the Power of the People Shine!" appears.[150]

Mixed-media image by Gayle Dickson from the *Black Panther*, June 3, 1972.

Mirroring the articles in the *Intercommunal News Service*, Dickson centered and then transformed traditional images of black womanhood by visually uniting them with symbols of the Panthers' revolutionary ethos. Although the subject of the June 3 image is an older black woman—a figure not typically included in the black revolutionary imaginary—Dickson uses color, scale, and shading to cast her as part of the Panthers' revolutionary community. The artist reserved her use of color for the older woman's clothes, a hat and overcoat that cover most of her body. The representation plays on the Panthers' symbolism, as the woman's hat and coat are reminiscent of the Panthers' signature black berets and leather jackets. Dickson's use of green, rather than a sharper color like blue or fuchsia, reflected the Panthers' goal of demilitarizing their image without completely distancing themselves from their revolutionary imagery during their intercommunal phase. Viewed against the stark black background, and the caption that included the phrase "power of the people" above, the older woman's clothing simultaneously conveys a sense of power, warmth, and community, while connecting the woman to the Panthers' earlier emblems and rhetoric.

Dickson solidifies this relationship between black womanhood and the Panthers' intercommunal ethos by inserting paraphernalia featuring women into the image. These elements invite the viewer to reimagine the scope of the party, revolution, and women's roles within it. The "Vote for Survival" and "Elaine Brown [for] Council Woman" buttons on the woman's beret and coat connect the symbols of past Panther militancy to its present programming, affirming the party's electoral politics as part of the organization's revolutionary canon. The bag full of groceries that she carries champions the Panthers' Free Food Program. However, the inclusion of the "Shirley Chisholm for President" flyer transforms the grocery bag into a political statement about the potential of black women's leadership. Viewed alongside and in the same frame as the empowered older black woman and the endorsement of Elaine Brown's political leadership, the image invites a new vision of black revolution and freedom—one in which black women lead the party, the community, and the nation.

In other drawings, such as the one on the back page of the July 1, 1972, issue, Dickson used black women to personify the Panthers' internationalist politics. Published a month after the Panthers' Anti-war, African Liberation, Voter-Registration Conference, her image of a middle-aged black woman conveyed the Panthers' intercommunal ethos (see the image in introduction). The woman in the image is wearing a blue shirt tucked into her apron and is standing barefoot. Like the drawing of the older woman, she carries a bag of goods from the Free Food Program: eggs, milk, and other groceries, which the artist represents through mixed-media cutouts. Foregrounded as a black, white, and color figure against an all-black background, this woman also wears a "Bobby Seale for Mayor" button. Framing the image is a caption that represents her politics: "Yes, I'm Against the War in Vietnam, I'm for African Liberation, Voter Registration and the People's Survival!"[151]

Here again, Dickson relies on color and scale to convey black women's radical politics and empowerment. Her use of blue to accentuate the woman's shirt tucked into her black skirt and white apron conjures up images of domesticity and domestic workers, more akin to Mildred or Mallory than women in the Panther Party. Yet, this does not mean that Dickson relinquished her commitment to conveying black women as political and powerful. The stark blue shirt against the all-black background accentuates the woman's positioning and arms. The arm closest to the viewer is held at an angle, with the hand in a fist, defiantly placed on her hip. Her other arm effortlessly supports the goods from the Panthers' Free Food Program and contributes to her resistive and empowered stance. The result is an image that fuses ideals of domesticity and empowerment, creating an image of a middle-aged black female woman who, like Inez Williams, may have been a maid or a mother but was also powerful, strong in her own right, and a participant in the Panthers' community programs.

Dickson's illustrations conveyed Panther women's arguments about the power and potential of everyday black women. She both challenged and expanded prototypical visual representations of the black revolutionary by drawing the woman in rollers, barefoot, and in an apron. Not only did this suggest that black women need not present themselves in archetypal revolutionary paraphernalia, such as an Afro, leather jacket, and arms, it also implied that black women from all segments of the black community had the potential to be empowered, radical political actors. Dickson accentuated this point with the scale and positioning of the figure. The woman dominates and literally defies the image frame, her hair and feet exuding beyond the center square in which she rests, her angled body conveying a sense of motion reminiscent of figures in Lewis's drawings.

Such artwork resolved lingering debates over the revolutionary potential of the Panthers' intercommunal programs. Long after the intraparty schism, remaining members faced lingering accusations that the survival programs were reformist instead of radical. Artistic representations like this one challenged this dichotomy through strategic placement of images and captioning. The artist juxtaposed survival program paraphernalia, such as the "Bobby Seale for Mayor" button, with a caption that conveyed the featured woman's anti-imperialist, nationalist politics. Taken together, the caption and image simultaneously presented black women as nuanced political actors and affirmed the Panthers' intercommunalist position as the natural evolution of, rather than a break from, their previous political stances. The woman's personal support of these politics, coupled with her undeniably strong stance, reinforced the Panthers' intercommunal politics and the black women who adopted this political position.

Dickson's artwork represented black women's ability to analyze, synthesize, and proselytize progressive and radical black politics and, similar to her postwar foremothers, showed how black maids and mothers could lay claim to the Panthers' radical personas and politics. Through her artwork, she literally and metaphorically redrew the boundaries of the Panthers' revolutionary ideal to be more inclusive of a broader range of black women. She also added depth and complexity to depictions of black women as caregivers, parents, and domestic workers, illustrating how, through intercommunalism and survival programs, they could adopt a radical political identity as part of their daily lives. Dickson argued that everyday women became revolutionaries by being empowered leaders of their families and communities, politically engaged citizens, anti-imperialists, and ardent internationalists. She broadened the Panther readership's and leadership's political frame, illustrating a more inclusive conception of the revolutionary figure—one that could account for the myriad ways in which women engaged in the Panthers' community politics. Her artwork countered contemporaneous characterizations of black women in the domestic sphere as docile and apolitical. It also extended the Panthers' shifting imagery by drawing on their revolutionary systems, symbols, and rubrics in order to define the black revolutionary as an undeniably feminine political actor.

With women at the helm of the organization, its programs, and its political literature, the party offered diverse representations of gender roles and revolutionary identifications during its intercommunal phase. The Black Revolutionary Woman could be a mother, like Inez Williams, or a domestic or grandmother, like those featured in Dickson's artwork. She articulated a radical, democratic, and intercommunal political platform, made legible through her physical and visual support of Panther programs and electoral politics. The Black Revolutionary Woman was also a political actor and figure in her own right, no longer needing to measure up to men or receive their endorsement. Amid long-standing discussions over the role of women in the party and Black Power, Panther women boldly asserted that black women from all walks of life were revolutionary leaders.

This new vision of revolutionary womanhood reflected the party's female leadership and organizational base. In 1973, while fleeing to Cuba to avoid facing another murder charge, Newton expelled Seale from the party and appointed Brown chairman of the organization.[152] Under Brown's leadership, the party flourished as an Oakland-based democratic organization.[153] Although their numbers had dwindled significantly, members spent the remaining years of the decade building a local base for the party through a combination of survival programs, women-centered political and organizational alliances, and electoral politics. Panther women also revitalized and revolutionized public education through initiatives such as the Oakland Community School, an alternative educational center that Ericka Huggins and Donna Howell ran from 1974 to 1982.[154] With women at the helm, the Panthers ushered in a period of growing black electoral participation, unprecedented minority coalitions, and progressive education reform in Oakland.[155]

Panther women made significant inroads in raising black voter registration, community education, and urban development throughout the 1970s. However, their extensive community mobilization was not enough to stymie the organization's decline. By 1974, the *Intercommunal News Service*, a major source of revenue and arguably the most influential aspect of the party, decreased in frequency of publication and circulation.[156] Three years later, Newton returned from Cuba and resumed control over the party. Brown had always considered her leadership of the organization to be temporary; however, she found it impossible to organize amid Newton's increasingly erratic behavior and the sexism that she and other women in the party faced. She resigned in November 1977, after Newton ordered the beating of a female Panther. Her departure was a significant blow to the party's image and political power.[157] A small cadre of women, including Abron and Huggins, continued to work for the organization throughout the 1970s, lending the Panther name and support to African liberation struggles, including the Zimbabwe African National Union, and causes closer to home, including the Black Veteran Association.[158] The last edition of the paper appeared in October 1980. The party officially closed its last office in 1982.[159]

The Black Panther Party propelled Black Power from a local phenomenon to an international movement and, in the process, injected new ideas about manhood and womanhood into the black political imagination. Two important factors help to explain the Panthers' success: an ideology that evolved in concert with the political climate, and their construction of the black revolutionary as a political identity. Black women were critical to both of these ventures. They developed the Black Revolutionary Woman as a way to redefine their roles in American society. They also used this political identity to push the party to formally endorse a gender-inclusive ideology and organizational culture.

For Panther women, the Black Revolutionary Woman was a unifying rather than a static identity. Their definitions of the female revolutionary figure evolved in concert with party ideology as well as surrounding political and social movements. Although they theorized this persona from multiple vantage points and political moments, they were dedicated to reimagining black women as politically conscious, militant, ideologically engaged revolutionaries. Women in the party were not able to completely eradicate sexism from the daily work of political organizing. However, they did expand their male counterparts' perceptions of their political, social, and cultural roles.

Their success in reshaping the party's gender dynamics shows that the Panthers' record on gender roles was more progressive and complex than is commonly acknowledged. What began as an armed brotherhood that equated power with patriarchy became, in theory and, many times, in practice, a gender-inclusive organization, largely because of women's rhetorical and imagistic projections of womanhood. Statements of support for gender equality from leaders such as Eldridge Cleaver and Huey Newton reflected the effects of Panther women's efforts at redefining gender roles. They also punctuated the organization's larger evolution from a male-dominated group to one of the first Black Power organizations to formally support women's liberation and actively work toward a gender-inclusive organizing structure and ethos.

Panther women's evolving image of the Black Revolutionary Woman circulated the globe through the *Black Panther* newspaper, demonstrating the appeal of this ideal for both the party and the general public. Readers encountered the ideas and images that women such as Lewis, Greene, Bird, and Robinson promoted and registered them as direct challenges to dominant ideas about black women that white society and movement men endorsed. Provocative, accessible, and idealistic, the gendered ideal that the party put forth offered black women a conduit through which to practice individual and collective oppositional politics and through which to reject limiting ideas of their power and potential. For many women inside and outside the party, Black Revolutionary Womanhood was a new way to publicly assert power and empower others.

Panther women simultaneously sustained and reinvigorated debates over the potential of black women to transform radical and nationalist organizing. Like their postwar predecessors, they understood that idealized models of black womanhood had the potential to unify women around a set of ideals and spur them toward political action. By the mid-1960s, party women weren't the only ones engaged in these debates. Their contemporaries also formulated new definitions of black womanhood that circulated in the public sphere. Women in cultural nationalist organizations, for example, developed the ideal of the African Woman, a model that also gained significant traction among black female activists in the late 1960s and early 1970s.

CHAPTER THREE

The African Woman, 1965–1975

While the Panthers focused on making the West Coast an epicenter of revolutionary activism, other organizers transformed Black Power on the Eastern Seaboard. On Labor Day weekend 1970, thousands of activists gathered in Atlanta for the first meeting of the Congress of African People (CAP). At the end of this four-day gathering, participants voted to form a united federation of organizations under the same name, guided by the principle of "operational unity." They also announced their goal to realize the "four ends of Black Power"—self-determination, self-sufficiency, self-respect, and self-defense—for "Africans on the American continent" and "Africans all over the world."[1]

Newark-based poet, actress, and organizer Amina Baraka presided over the "Social Organization" workshop, one of several sessions designed to decipher women's roles within CAP members' expanding Black Power vision.[2] Baraka led a diverse group of activists—including young Newark organizer Nettie Rogers and Black Power elder Audley Moore—in debating their "fundamental roles and relationships among African people."[3] At the close of the conference, these workshop participants had created a set of resolutions detailing the responsibilities of black women in the home, family, and community. These guidelines were a critical step in their efforts to reimagine black women as African Women and as activists prepared to realize CAP's Black Power "ends" on a global scale.

The Congress of African People, and the African Woman ideal, had its roots in the cultural nationalist ideology of Kawaida, an ideology guided by the idea that culture is the "crucible in which black liberation takes form."[4] Activist and theorist Maulana Karenga (Ronald Everett) created the doctrine in 1965 and developed its practices and rituals through the Us Organization, a Los Angeles–based cultural nationalist group. Karenga shared his ideas about the importance of cultivating a distinct, black-centered cultural and political worldview with Newark organizers Amina and Amiri Baraka, who adopted and practiced the philosophy in their organization, the Committee for Unified Newark (CFUN). By 1970, Us and CFUN had popularized Kawaida and cultural nationalism across the country, fostering activists' interest in forming a united, culturally conscious political front.

Kawaidists maintained that black cultural autonomy was a prerequisite to political revolution. To that end, Us and CFUN members developed a set of programs and rituals designed to "re-Africanize" black Americans and transform their relationship with black identity and culture.[5] Armed with this new, African-centered perspective, practitioners would be better prepared to reject Western political, economic, and cultural hegemony. They would also be uniquely positioned to advance and enact black cultural and political sovereignty.

Reimagining black manhood and womanhood was at the core of this cultural project. Like their counterparts in other organizations, cultural nationalists contended that redefining gender roles was the basis of social and political transformation. Organizational leaders created new definitions of manhood and womanhood based on Kawaidists' interpretations of social relationships in ancient African societies. Steeped in idealism, and the prevailing patriarchy of the day, they originally defined the African Woman as an activist who induced cultural revolution through child rearing, education, and homemaking. Mirroring rather than redefining dominant Eurocentric constructs, initially, cultural nationalists' gendered ideals had more in common with American values than African ones.

Kawaidist women quickly developed their own definitions of the African Woman that challenged patriarchal interpretations of the doctrine and their organizational roles. In their publications, speeches, and position papers, they reenvisioned the African Woman as an activist who advocated for black women's equal participation in black liberation as a critical step in the cultural emancipation of African peoples all over the world.[6] As in the Panther Party, Kawaidist women's political self-conception evolved in a dialectical relationship with the ideological and organizational progressions of Us, CFUN, and CAP. Women produced new iterations of the African Woman ideal based on their gender-specific interpretations of Kawaida. In turn, leaders revised their interpretations of Kawaida and its rituals based on female members' expansive interpretations of this ideology. This reciprocal process transformed cultural nationalist organizing between 1965 and 1975, causing activists to adopt more equitable interpretations of gender roles and the Kawaida philosophy.

Us, Watts, and Them: The Foundations of
Modern Cultural Nationalism

Kawaida gained traction in the mid-1960s amid a shifting black activist milieu. Los Angeles, the birthplace of the philosophy, epitomized these various political strains. By 1965, several streams of black organizing coursed through the City of Angels, making it an epicenter of black thought and activism. The metropolis had a thriving civil rights movement that included local chapters of the Congress of Racial Equality (CORE), the Student Non-violent Coordinating Committee (SNCC), and the National Association for the Advancement of Colored People (NAACP) that were populated with area residents and students from local universities. Inspired by the surge of protests across the country, students established chapters of national civil rights groups that served as operational bases for fighting campus and community racism.[7] Other young local activists became Freedom Riders, connecting with activists in Southern cities like Monroe, North Carolina, who shook up the nation by challenging segregation on interstate buses. When they returned from the South battered and bruised from racist attacks, they brought news of the Southern black freedom struggles to college campuses and community centers.[8]

While student organizing invigorated local interest in civil rights activism, groups like the Nation of Islam (NOI) ignited a new wave of black nationalist militancy. Frequent visits by their leading minister, Malcolm X, who established Temple No. 27 in Los Angeles in 1957, solidified the organization's stronghold in the city in the early 1960s.[9] The NOI's critique of white culture, reverence for black heritage, and promotion of black self-determination drew in thousands of black Angelenos looking for organizational, cultural, and spiritual responses to white cultural and political hegemony. Support for the group also reflected nationalist and Pan-Africanist sentiment across the city. NOI allies, including local press moguls Sanford and Patricia Alexander, created like-minded secular organizations such as Africa House. Billed as a space for "Black Americans, Africans and Blacks of African descent ... to join hands culturally, socially, economically, and historically," members hosted African bazaars, lecture series, and African-language courses designed to counter cultural oppression and connect black residents with their African heritage.[10] The NOI and other nationalist-leaning secular organizations fostered black identity and cultural and political consciousness in the City of Angels.

Groups such as Donald Warden's Afro-American Association wedded student activism and black nationalism. In Northern California, where the association originated, the lawyer and radio-host-turned-activist attracted burgeoning young radicals such as Panther leaders Huey Newton and Bobby Seale to his group. In Los Angeles, Karenga joined and led the local chapter of the group.[11] The future Panther leaders found Warden's attention to cultural reclamation and capitalism limiting in its ability to address black political and economic ills.[12] Karenga was more convinced. For the Los Angeles organizer, Warden's emphasis on reclaiming black culture was in line with similar arguments advanced by a range of black radicals from Alice Childress to Malcolm X.[13] Furthermore, Warden's extensive study of African history and languages at the University of California, Los Angeles, lent support to his calls for culturally based activism.[14] In late 1964, Karenga left Warden's group and formed a nationalist study group with similar ideals called the Circle of Seven.[15] Local events would soon transform this study circle into the city's leading black nationalist organization.

On August 11, 1965, Watts, a largely black neighborhood in Los Angeles, erupted in violence. That evening, two Los Angeles policemen stopped Marquette Frye, a young black man, on the suspicion that he was driving under the influence. What began as a traffic stop turned into a full-scale revolt after an argument between Frye, his mother, and the police turned violent. Word of the altercation spread throughout the city, and, by nightfall, Watts was in the midst of a revolt.[16] Erupting only five days after President Lyndon B. Johnson signed the Voting Rights Act into law, the uprising foregrounded the limitations of civil rights legislation as a solution to America's intractable race problem. Civil rights luminaries such as Dr. Martin Luther King Jr. "minimize[d] the racial significance" of the rebellion and framed the violence as "the rumblings of discontent from the 'have nots.'"[17] Los Angeles activists—including members of the Circle of Seven—interpreted the riot as Watts residents' unequivocal embrace of black nationalism and their insistence on "unconditional community control, self-definition, and self-determination."[18]

The Us Organization developed out of the haze of the Watts rebellion. On September 7, 1965, Karenga, along with local activists Dorothy Jamal, Brenda Haiba Karenga, Tommy Halifu, Sanamu Nyeusi, and Hakim Jamal, transformed the Circle of Seven into the cultural nationalist organization.[19] "Us" referred to both the organization and the black community and implied their opposition to "them," or their white oppressors.[20] Members framed the group as the ideological successor of the recently slain Malcolm

X and the logical organizational response to Watts residents' calls for black self-determination. Hakim Jamal, a close associate of Malcolm X, briefly headed the group. Shortly thereafter, Karenga became the primary leader of the organization.[21]

The Us Organization's goal was to bringing about revolution through cultural education and political coalition building.[22] In contrast to other collectives, members (or advocates, as they were called) were not interested in building a mass organization. Instead, the group functioned as a small band of organizers intent on reorienting black Americans' cultural compass through the Kawaida doctrine. The philosophy called for the reclamation of black Americans' African past and identity through a set of cultural, social, and political practices based in the African value system, or the Nguzo Saba. Us Organization advocates changed their names, dressed in African clothing, and developed organizational practices and community protests based on the seven pillars of the Nguzo Saba: Umoja (unity), Kujichagulia (self-determination), Ujima (collective work and responsibility), Ujamaa (cooperative economics), Nia (purpose), Kuumba (creativity), and Imani (faith).[23] Both advocates and local residents embraced and articulated these principles through Us-driven rituals and holidays such as Kwanzaa, a secular synthesis of African and African American cultural traditions that they celebrated during the traditional Christmas holiday season; Kuzaliwa, a celebration of Malcolm X's birthday; and Uhuru, a commemoration of the Watts uprising.[24]

Events like its annual Uhuru celebration epitomized Us's ability to unite Black Power organizations under the banners of cultural reorientation and political mobilization. The 1967 ceremony brought thousands of local residents to Us's headquarters to hear then-SNCC chairman H. Rap Brown and Panther leader Huey Newton speak about the need for black self-determination and political mobilization.[25] If the Watts commemoration showcased Us's ability to garner support for black-centered cultural celebrations, then its participation in the Temporary Alliance of Local Organizations (TALO) reflected its cross-organizational political engagement. The TALO coalition included the regional chapters of SNCC, CORE, the NAACP, and the black nationalist group Self-Leadership for All Nationalities Today. The collective engaged in several citywide initiatives, the most successful of which was its police-monitoring program, the Community Alert Patrol. Not only did the program help curb police brutality in Watts, it also predated and precipitated the Panthers' armed police patrols in Oakland.[26]

After TALO, Us joined the Black Congress. Billed as the "latest amalgamation of militants and civil rights groups in the city," the group included black student unions, the LA County Welfare Rights Organization, Self-Leadership for All Nationalities Today, Donald Warden's Afro-American Association, and local activists including future Panther leader Elaine Brown.[27] Us played a central role in the coalition, moving its headquarters to the congress's building and transforming its newspaper, *Harambee*, into the congress's official publication. Karenga served as the vice chair of the federation of groups, and Us advocates worked with other organizations on local issues to formulate collective responses to the black community's local and national concerns. Through the Black Congress, Us helped build political "unity without uniformity" and fostered local consensus on national and international issues such as the community's response to April 1968 assassination of Dr. Martin Luther King Jr. and the Vietnam War.[28]

While male advocates headlined protests and cultural events, Us women developed the organizational infrastructure advocates needed to lead the community in their goal of cultural education. Female advocates organized as part of two subunits within Us: the Malaika and the Muminina. The former was composed of all women in the organization, while the latter was a smaller circle of higher-ranking women who represented their interests within the administration. The Muminina reported to the group's executive committee, the Circle of Administrators. They also had representation on the board itself.[29] Women served in a variety of roles within Us. For example, Tiamoyo Tosheleza Karenga was chair of the legal committee, and Maisha Abunuwas served as a counselor and adviser to members of the organization. Female advocates also belonged to the youth educational committee and the cultural activities committee and engaged in fund-raising efforts.[30]

The most visible example of Us women's activism was the Us School of Afroamerican Culture, an independent community education center in Los Angeles. Advocates viewed study as a key component of cultural nationalist activism. Accordingly, they developed a school to teach children about their culture, heritage, and struggle. Brenda Haiba Karenga served as the chair of education and the principal of the school. Other advocates, such as Regina Damu, Sanamu Nyeusi, Hasani Heshimu, and Ahera Msemaji, taught black children about African history and culture.[31] The school curriculum consisted of classes in history, music, Swahili, dance, and "issues of struggle." Tiamoyo Tosheleza Karenga taught a travelogue class in which she took "the children around the world in pictures, introducing them to the customs, dress, and language ... of different African peoples."[32] Through the school curriculum, these women created empowering songs and activities for children that taught them black history, an appreciation of their culture, and tools to combat white cultural hegemony. They also codified organizational doctrine by integrating the Nguzo Saba into every lesson.[33]

The teachers at the Us Afroamerican School epitomized the Kawaidist ideal of the African Woman. When developing the doctrine, male leaders determined that the primary roles of a woman were to "inspire her man, educate her children, and participate in social development." To achieve these goals, she was to "minimize [each man's] weaknesses and maximize his strengths," "educate the children in accord with the beliefs of the organization," and "participate in social development by developing alternative social customs for the black community."[34] At the Afroamerican School, Us women inspired men and boys to become leaders in the community; educated children in new, black-centered traditions; and played an integral role in the social development of the next generation of black Angelenos. Female advocates also developed and shaped alternative social practices such as the Kawaida-inspired wedding ceremony and promoted Us-created holidays, including Kwanzaa.

Us leaders' patriarchal approach to cultural reinvention also extended to the private sphere. According to the original Kawaida doctrine, the African Woman was to openly accept and participate in polygamous relationships. Us leadership argued that taking on a subjugated or submissive role within the family was a way to "inspire" or support black men. They also postulated that adopting polygamous practices was a medium through which black men and women could refute white, Eurocentric familial constructs and mirror household structures found in African societies. However, as E. Frances White has noted, Us members based their doctrine and social practices on an inaccurate and ahistorical model of Africa that collapsed the cultural, economic, and social differences among past and present African societies, countries, and cultures.[35] Instead of exemplifying African practices, the organization's original gender mandates reinforced dominant constructions found in Western societies and fortified the Moynihan-inspired argument that black families suffered from a shortage of black men.[36]

Other activists openly questioned the Us advocates' ideas about men's and women's roles. SNCC member Gwendolyn Patton pointed out that the group's conservative gender hierarchies were more analogous to a white, "Victorian philosophy" of gender roles than an African one.[37] Patton's fellow SNCC member Frances Beal argued that "assigning women the role of housekeeper and mother . . . [was] a highly questionable doctrine for a revolutionary to maintain."[38] Patton's and Beal's criticisms were not simply critiques of the Us Organization, they were also responses to a larger trend within the Black Power movement in which an increasing number of male activists insisted that a black woman's greatest contribution to black liberation was "having babies for the revolution." However, Us garnered increased scrutiny because many of their catechisms—including male leaders' insistence on the "natural" superiority of men—represented some of the most extreme articulations of this viewpoint.[39] Recognizing these ideological contradictions, some women resigned from Us in protest.[40] Others chose to transform the organization's conservative gender constructs from within the group.

Contemporaneous events accelerated Us women's reconceptualization of the African Woman ideal. Several factors—including negative media portrayals of Karenga and police targeting of the organization—precipitated significant changes to the group's operating procedures.[41] Fearing its growing influence, the FBI and local law enforcement tried to dismantle Us through raids of its facilities and arrests of individual members.[42] The bureau also bred animosity between Us and the Black Panther Party, which culminated in the January 1969 confrontation that killed Panthers John Huggins and "Bunchy" Carter and imprisoned the Stiner brothers.[43] This deadly altercation took a toll on Us as well. In the months following the incident, members grew fearful of retaliation from the Panthers, withdrew from community organizing, and developed a paramilitary structure in an attempt to prevent future attacks.[44]

In the midst of these organizational changes, women emerged as leaders within Us. Previously, female advocates held positions on many committees and leadership roles in the Afroamerican School. After 1969, they began to take on roles in the organization's administrative and security sectors. Their new responsibilities included tasks such as intelligence gathering and security detailing, jobs that Us members previously considered to be the purview of men.[45] This new division of labor meant that women worked alongside men and, at times, headed segments of the organization. It also created opportunities for female advocates to reshape the Kawaidist gendered imaginary in favor of more equitable perceptions of gender roles.[46]

Us Organization women introduced their progressive conceptualization of the African Woman through newspaper articles like "View from the Womans' [sic] Side of the Circle" (1969), published in *Harambee*. In the essay, the Malaika defined the African Woman as an activist who was committed to the gendered directives of Kawaida but not circumscribed by them. Us Organization women based their new conceptualization of African Womanhood in the Kawaidist principle Ujima, or collective work and responsibility. The women contended that, by 1969, men and women in Us were practicing the principle of Ujima "together in a oneness that verge[d] on symbiosis." They credited this organizational and ideological unity to advocates' adherence to the Kawaida doctrine. However, the Malaika also argued that the group had achieved a higher level of consciousness and organizing because women had moved from a "minimum" to a "maximum practice" of gender-specific cultural nationalist tenets and objectives.[47]

The Malaika envisioned the African Woman as an activist who engaged in the most expansive practice of the doctrine's directives for women: inspiration, education, and social development. Us leadership's interpretations of inspiration were often predicated on male support and community education. The Malaika broadened this definition of inspiration to include women's independent, public acts of political struggle. "We inspired our men in the past and we are still continuing to inspire them in those same ways today, but we have also found new ways to inspire them," they explained. Us leadership stated that "Black Men [were] inspired by Black women who are capable of carrying on the revolution in their absence." The Malaika argued that black men were "inspired even more by Black women who can carry on the revolution in their presence." Female advocates, they noted, did "not have to wait for the future in order to make a positive contribution" to political struggle. Instead, the African Woman could and should be an inspiration to her entire community through her public political activism alongside and, if needed, in lieu of black men.[48]

Us Organization women also challenged limiting interpretations of women's roles in education and social development. According to the Malaika, in 1969, "the revolution being fought" was a "revolution to win the minds of [their] people." Given the urgency of the political moment, the African Woman could no longer limit herself to educating children in the home or the schoolhouse. She had a responsibility to reach beyond traditional spheres of domestic influence and "educate the people by forming an unbroken circle between [their] education and the social development of [their] community." This reciprocal relationship between education and social development meant that women also had to reconceptualize their roles in community organizing and move beyond archetypal spaces of women's work. The Malaika advanced a vision of the African Woman in which she enhanced the cultural growth of the black community by setting an example of "complementarity" in the public sphere by "attend[ing] community meetings," teaching about "Black Cultural nationalism," and appearing at and leading public events alongside black men.[49]

The Malaika concluded the article with their resolute vision of the African Woman. They declared that through practicing Ujima, the "US organization ha[d] produced the first truly revolutionary woman" of the Black Power movement, a woman who was "submissive yet vocal, who [was] revolutionary yet feminine, who [was] complimentary [*sic*] not equal." The African Woman did not seek independence but rather a more balanced interdependence with her male counterpart. She contributed to the struggle not by "changing [her] role, but by broadening the scope of [her] role."[50]

More than simply a product of political exigency, the Malaika's article reflected women's critical engagement with the intersection of black womanhood, contemporary political struggle, and the Kawaida doctrine. Us Organization women claimed that the quotidian practice of cultural nationalism required a complete commitment to the Nguzo Saba—especially the principle of collective work and responsibility. Engaging in this practice at the highest level necessitated more porous definitions of gender roles and an expanded conceptualization of the gender-specific directives for women embedded in Kawaida. It also required Us members to engage in a collective redefinition of the African Woman ideal. Accordingly, the Malaika envisioned the African Woman as an activist who found parity with her male counterpart in her inspirational and educational work and who took on a leading role in shaping cultural nationalists' political projects through Kawaidist directives. Their reformulation of this political identity advanced a progressive and politically responsive interpretation of Kawaida. It also challenged the ideological basis on which male-female relationships within Us rested by suggesting that advocates' conceptions of gendered political organizing could be more flexible than their fellow activists' previous philosophical interpretations had initially indicated.

In theorizing their version of the African Woman, the Us Malaika bent the gender-specific pillars of Kawaida to fit their needs but did not break with dominant conceptions of the ideology. Kawaida doctrine held that equality between men and women was a false concept.[51] The Malaika reinforced this point. In their political literature, they sought to broaden the definition of what constituted "women's work." However, they remained invested in a gendered division of labor and distinctly masculine and feminine political identities. This approach to redefining black womanhood set women in Us apart from their activist contemporaries. Many female organizers disputed Black Power sexism by challenging conventional binaries between masculine and feminine organizational acts or traits. Us Organization women maintained that the African Woman did not have to mimic the dress or actions of men—she did "not have to wear overhauls [sic] and combat boots in order to play an active role in the black revolution."[52] For the Malaika, the radicalizing aspect of their gendered theorizing and organizing lay in their rejection of Eurocentric cultural and political models and their progressive interpretation of the gendered directives of the Kawaida doctrine.

Us Organization women's "broadened" conceptualization of the African Woman's roles was also a manifestation of their ideological acuity and political acumen. The Malaika were committed to cultural nationalism. They also astutely discerned that their male counterparts would be more accepting of their expansive vision of their roles if they formulated their arguments using the central directives of the Kawaida doctrine. By employing the principle of Ujima as their point of departure, and reinforcing the pillars of the African Woman ideal, the Malaika were able to frame their vision of African Womanhood as an extension of the core elements of the philosophy. Moreover, in defining the African Woman as an activist who "maximized" the quotidian practice of the doctrine, they positioned their interpretation of the philosophy as the most advanced and accurate understanding of Kawaidist practice. This challenged male advocates to adopt their analysis of women's roles, lest they appear to be less committed to cultural revolution. They were successful. In the ensuing years, Karenga renounced his sexist positions and called on other male practitioners to "stop denying [African] women their full and heroic role in the history and development of [black] struggle."[53]

The Malaika had little time to enact their vision of African Womanhood or expand on their ideas about it in organizational publications. The years following the 1969 UCLA shootout brought about a breakdown in organizational leadership and the decline of Us's local and national prominence. During this "crisis" period, there was an exodus of advocates from the Us Circle of Administrators and the paramilitary subunits.[54] Some advocates abandoned the organization completely. Others joined the ranks of the Kawaidist-inspired CFUN in Newark, New Jersey.[55] Nevertheless, Us made an indelible impact on Black Power organizing and the era's gendered imaginary. Moreover, the Us Malaika began the process of redefining the

African Woman as the political companion rather than the private consort of men, a trend that female advocates in Newark would continue to develop.

From Us to CFUN: Cultural Nationalism Goes National

Us Organization advocates who ventured to the east found a thriving activist community that developed concurrently, and at times in conjunction, with Black Power organizing in Los Angeles. In Newark, as in many other cities, black activists created a dynamic local organizing culture that included political protests, independent black community schools, and a vibrant black arts and culture scene.[56] Events such as the 1966 Afro-American Festival of Arts encapsulated Newark's brand of Black Power. Billed as a "celebration of the emergence of the urban Afro-American ... as an independent and self-determining group," the festival, spearheaded by Newark native, artist, and activist Amiri Baraka, brought together cultural critics like Harold Cruse and Black Power brokers like Stokely Carmichael in an effort to encourage black residents to repudiate white paternalism and seize black political and cultural power.[57]

Local institutions such as the Barakas' Spirit House carried on this combination of cultural and political mobilization. A cultural and community center for Newark's black community, Spirit House was the ideological and organizational legacy of the Harlem-based Black Arts Repertory Theatre and School (BART/S). Beat-poet-turned-activist Amiri Baraka had founded BART/S in 1965 in the aftermath of Malcolm X's assassination. He envisioned it as community-driven artistic center that articulated the guiding principles of Black Power through plays, music, and other forms of creative production. Although short-lived, BART/S attracted cultural luminaries like Sonia Sanchez and Larry Neal and ignited the Black Arts movement, now considered the artistic corollary to Black Power.[58] After BART/S collapsed, Baraka returned to Newark intent on creating "art that would reach the people."[59] Spirit House was his next attempt at building the cultural wing of black militancy. Located on Sterling Street in Newark's predominantly black Central Ward, the center served several functions: it was a production space for the Baraka-led theater group (the Spirit House Players), a location for community meetings, and, eventually, the site of an independent black elementary school.[60]

Spirit House quickly became a staple within Newark's burgeoning Black Arts scene. Local artists like Sylvia Robinson (Amina Baraka) and Nettie

Rogers fostered black cultural production at clubs like the Cellar, where they would perform dances and read poetry that reflected young artists' collective goal of developing a black cultural aesthetic in the late 1960s.[61] Robinson, familiar with Baraka's plays from her time as a trained artist, actress, and dancer, found herself personally and politically drawn to Baraka and his vision. The two eventually married and began to build Spirit House as "another edition of the Black Arts."[62]

Spirit House fostered the relationship between Karenga and the Barakas and the spread of Kawaida in Newark. When the Us leader came to Newark to formalize plans for the upcoming 1967 Black Power Conference, he visited the Barakas' cultural center. Several months later, the couple temporarily relocated to the West Coast while Amiri Baraka was a visiting professor at San Francisco State University. In June 1967, the couple went to Los Angeles for CORE's annual convention, an event that featured Karenga, his former mentor and organizer Donald Warden, and sports icons such as Muhammad Ali.[63] At Karenga's invitation, the Newark activists visited Us headquarters and attended a Kawaida wedding ceremony. The LA leader's ideology and group impressed Amiri Baraka. He found Us advocates' discipline and dedication to cultural reorientation to be a "higher stage" of cultural and political organizing than the work taking place in Newark. The Barakas returned to Newark in June 1967, armed with Karenga's doctrine and prepared to implement it at Spirit House.[64]

The Newark couple arrived home as the city was on the brink of rebellion. On July 12, 1967, black residents in the Central Ward saw police carry badly beaten taxi driver John Smith into the Fourth Precinct police station. By nightfall, a crowd had gathered outside the station, demanding to see Smith and confirm his safety. Police ignored the angry crowd, prompting Newark CORE leaders to mobilize residents in peaceful protests the next day. After these protests yielded no results, residents adopted a more direct approach: throwing bricks and Molotov cocktails at the police station. In response, officers stormed out of the station dressed in full riot gear, attacked demonstrators, and ignited a rebellion in Newark that resulted in six days of rioting and millions of dollars in property damage.[65]

Eight days later, Newark hosted the Second Black Power Conference. The meeting was one of four international Black Power conferences that took place across North America between 1966 and 1969. One of several summits that composed what historian Komozi Woodard has called the Modern Black Convention Movement, the 1967 conference anointed a new generation of black leadership and ignited ideological debates over the

Kawaida wedding ceremony, Us Organization, Los Angeles.
Courtesy of Getty Images.

principles and direction of Black Power.[66] Thousands of activists gathered
in the city, which was still smoldering from the cinders of rebellion, to discuss black self-determination and political independence.[67] Jessie Jackson
and Maulana Karenga opened the conference by calling on black activists
to develop a united front of Black Power organizations.[68] Other prominent
attendees included Audley Moore and black feminist leader Florynce "Flo"
Kennedy, who voiced their support for armed self-defense and black-
produced media and cultural programming.[69]

The Second Black Power Conference transformed black organizing in Newark. The gathering exceeded the planners' expectations, drawing in activists from across the political spectrum and fostering lively debates about the merits of reform and radicalism. Still reeling from the beating he endured at the hands of riot police the week before, Amiri Baraka featured prominently at the meeting, maintaining that the Newark rebellion was a sign of local residents' categorical support for self-determination. His sentiments resonated with local activists, and, by the conference's end, they had begun to develop local organizations dedicated to achieving local black political independence. Baraka emerged from the conference as a potential leader of this new wave of local organizing—making Newark's crystallizing "Black Power experiment" a Kawaidist-inspired enterprise.[70]

Women were also key organizers in Newark's postconference Black Power scene. Amina Baraka created the United Sisters, a nationalist women's study group that analyzed their roles in education, community control, and African culture.[71] The United Sisters also established the African Free School, a community education center where they paired traditional academic training with lessons in Swahili, hieroglyphics, and Zulu folklore.[72] Other women joined the Sisters of Black Culture, a group dedicated to helping black women "understand [their] role as women in Black revolution."[73] These women's groups became part of a burgeoning organizational network that fostered Black Power and cultural nationalism in Newark. They also began vital conversations about alternative definitions of black womanhood within Kawaidist organizing.

The United Sisters and the Sisters of Black Culture helped build a black political front in Newark. At Karenga's suggestion, in 1968, both women's collectives joined forces with three other local groups—the United Brothers, Spirit House, and the Black Community Defense and Development (BCD)—to create the Committee for Unified Newark.[74] The United Sisters and United Brothers functioned as CFUN's political arm, while the Spirit House Players oversaw the Kawaidist cultural production for the group. The BCD styled itself after the Us Organization's paramilitary wing, the Simba Wachanga. The Sisters of Black Culture functioned in a similar capacity as the Malaika in Karenga's Los Angeles group.[75]

CFUN's first venture was to develop a citywide unity platform and bid for black political control. With Karenga's help and guidance, activists developed the "Peace and Power" campaign, an ambitious crusade for Black Power and community control through local electoral politics. Initially, organizers set out to elect two black men, Ted Pickney and Donald Tucker, to seats on the Newark City Council in the November 1968 election. In addition to increasing black political representation, the electoral race would also function as a trial run for future political campaigns, including the 1970 mayoral election.[76] Peace and Power organizers lost their bid for the two city council seats. However, CFUN members successfully infused Black Power and cultural nationalism into the local consciousness through their citywide political organizing.

Despite the partial success of the Peace and Power campaign, ideological and organizational differences threatened to derail CFUN's progress the following year. The fallout from the UCLA shooting consumed Us and Karenga, damaging his relationship with Baraka and other CFUN members. When the Us leader returned to Los Angeles, CFUN activists lost their ideological and organizational mentor. Karenga's departure augmented clashes among CFUN's leadership. A trio of men—Amiri Baraka, Balozi Zayd, and Mfrundishi Maasi—originally headed the conglomerate of Newark collectives. After the failure of the campaign, Baraka suggested that the group focus on political education and consolidate the multiple organizations into one collective to mount another political challenge. Leaders of the BCD and the Sisters of Black Culture disagreed with his proposed restructuring and left the group. In the waning months of 1969, CFUN had lost its political and ideological mentor as well as a significant segment of its organizational base.[77]

Women emerged as key organizers and leaders following this organizational split. Amina Baraka converted the United Sisters into the Women's Division of CFUN and began standardizing operating procedures within the group. The Women's Division organized, developed, and managed CFUN's growing number of programs and publications, including Spirit House; day care centers; a publishing house, Jihad Productions; and a grocery cooperative, Duka Ujamaa.[78] In keeping with Kawaida directives for women to educate children and participate in social development, CFUN women, like their Us counterparts, also continued to lead and staff the African Free School. The school flourished under Amina Baraka's leadership, becoming an extensive preschool and elementary education center.[79] Through the school and the myriad other programs that CFUN women maintained, female advocates developed practical ways to implement the core principles of Kawaida and translate the ideology into tangible community-building initiatives.

The Muminina, a small circle of high-ranking women, further extended women's reach and influence in CFUN. This subset of women was responsible for overseeing the social and cultural programs within the organization. The cadre, which included Amina Baraka, Jaribu Hill, Salimu (Nettie) Rogers, Jalia Woods, and Staarabisha Barrett, developed organizational practices such as the Kawaida wedding, birth, and funeral ceremonies.[80] They served as teachers at the African Free School and at CFUN's Political School of Kawaida.[81] The Muminina also developed organizational literature aimed at codifying the doctrine, helping black women develop an "African personality," and delineating the traits of the African Woman. With these and other women at the helm, the Women's Division became the largest and most diverse subunit within CFUN. It was also responsible for devising the innovations that increased the functionality and reach of the cultural nationalist group.[82]

As the Women's Division helped transform CFUN into an exemplar of Black Power organizing, Amiri Baraka became convinced that the Newark model could be actualized on a larger scale. In 1970, he called together activists to develop an organizational apparatus "whose function would be to struggle for Black Power wherever black people were in the world."[83] In September of that year, organizers from across the political spectrum met in Atlanta to create the Congress of African People, a federation of organizations designed to operationalize activists' many interpretations of Black Power at the international level.

The capacious conference participant roster bespoke the potential of the new group. Organizers and movement figureheads such as Betty Shabazz joined forces with Pan-Africanists such as Owusu Sadaukai (Howard Fuller; head of the grassroots, black-led Malcolm X Liberation University), elected officials such as Julian Bond, and representatives from African anticolonial struggles such as Evelyn Kwanza, who came from Zimbabwe to help develop a "Black Agenda" for the impending decade.[84] Along with thousands of other participants, these organizers engaged in eleven workshops designed to unite the many factions of the black freedom movement in order to achieve black liberation. The unprecedented cooperation among movement factions helped foster participants' excitement about returning home to develop concrete programs to liberate their communities. Given the widespread support and symbolic performances of unity at the conference, it was no wonder that the slogan for the meeting and the organization became "It's Nation Time."[85]

CAP's formation inaugurated a new approach to intramovement organizing and augmented the visibility and popularity of cultural nationalism. Departing from previous Black Power meetings, organizers called on activists to create coalitions among black nationalists, mitigating intragroup feuding over leadership. This conjoining of organizations under CAP's banner of black liberation ushered in a period of unprecedented unity among black nationalist, civil rights, and other black leftist groups.[86] In the months following the conference, CAP had organizational branches in over twenty-five cities, including Boston, Chicago, Houston, San Diego, and Washington, D.C. CFUN became the program office and the headquarters for the group, injecting cultural nationalism into Black Power organizing at the national level.[87]

If CFUN functioned as CAP's ideological steward, then its Women's Division was CAP's second in command. Women in the Newark chapter of CAP used this position to their advantage, working to reformulate CAP members' perceptions of gender roles and hierarchies. At the local level, CFUN's Muminina and Malaika units encouraged Amiri Baraka to denounce ideological and organizational sexism and use his influence to eradicate it within CAP's ranks.[88] They also developed a body of literature aimed at reconceptualizing the African Woman ideal across CAP chapters. Through their handbooks and advice columns, the Malaika and Muminina challenged male advocates' patriarchal interpretations of women's roles and asserted their primacy in cultural nationalist organizing. Their reconfiguration of the African Woman pushed organizational leaders to adopt more equitable organizing frameworks and more expansive interpretations of the Kawaida doctrine.

From African Woman to Afrikan Woman

Women across CAP's multiple chapters dedicated the 1970s to "dealing with the topic" of the African Woman.[89] The current political climate made their focus timely. By the early 1970s, black women in many different organizations—including the Black Panther Party and SNCC—openly denounced sexism within the movement. CAP also blossomed amid the growing women's liberation movement. Discussions of gender equality, sexism, and reproductive rights infiltrated the mainstream political and social discourse as women poured into civil rights, Black Power, and New Left organizations.[90] These debates fostered a proliferation of black and white women-centered and feminist collectives dedicated to achieving women's equality in the workplace, politics, and society.[91] Like their counterparts in other Black Power organizations, women in CFUN and CAP maintained that mainstream women's groups were only interested in addressing white women's concerns. They distanced themselves from the contemporaneous women's liberation movement both rhetorically and organizationally, opting to promote progressive gender politics from within their organizations.

CFUN women inaugurated these efforts with the "Mwanamke Mwanachi," or the "Nationalist Woman" handbook. A CAP-distributed publication made available for members in 1971, the Muminina designed the manual as "an outline for sisters to pick up and use" or as a guide for women's daily practice of Kawaida.[92] Akin to Us women's publications, the handbook reinforced the central tenets of Kawaida and leaders' gender-specific prescriptions for the African Woman. CFUN women broke new ground, however, by using the handbook to directly challenge organizational hierarchies and redefine the axis on which activists measured the African Woman's political and ideological legitimacy.

In the first section of the handbook, the Muminina combined praise for the Kawaida doctrine with criticism of practitioners' patriarchal interpretations of its principles. They began by recapitulating Kawaida's catechisms on the "natural" roles of women and men. Members of the Women's Division affirmed that "women can not [sic] do the same things as men ... they are made by nature to function differently." They also confirmed that men's and women's "natural" differences manifested in different responsibilities in day-to-day political organizing. Yet, the Muminina were unwilling to accept that these "natural" differences justified gendered hierarchies within the cultural nationalist community. Departing from traditional interpretations of the philosophy, they asserted, "Nature has made women [sic] submissive—she must submit to man's creation in order for it to exist. This does not mean that she has to follow for the sake of following or to be subservient to him." Instead, CFUN's leading women framed men's and women's roles as equal components of a holistic emancipatory political practice: "To speak of roles is to be concerned with completion—the balance of nature. . . . Roles do not mean that one is superior or inferior to the other but necessary—complementary to the whole."[93]

The Muminina brought this same perspective to bear on their assessment of doctrinal directives for women's roles: inspiration, education, and social development. They reaffirmed that these arenas were the pillars of the African Woman's activism. However, they reconceptualized the ways in which women could and should enact these principles. Male leaders and advocates defined inspiration primarily as women's submission to the will and word of men. The Muminina redefined this tenet based on black women's personal, political, and ideological interests. "By *being* African (color, culture, consciousness) woman is inspirational," they wrote. "By having an emotional commitment to Nationalism the Black Woman is inspirational.... By having a sincere undying faith in our leaders, our people and our righteousness and victory of our struggle is inspirational."[94] Their conceptualization of women's roles in education and social development followed a similar pattern, emphasizing how women could embody and execute these principles through self-referential political and emotional acts. If Us women envisioned the African Woman as an activist who "broadened" her practice of Kawaida-sanctioned roles, then women in CFUN argued that her practice of these principles need not rely on gender hierarchies or center black men.

In the second half of the handbook, the Muminina established a new dimension of African Womanhood: necessary roles. In the section titled "The Two Aspects of the Woman's Role," the Newark women explained that "the African woman has a natural and necessary role to play in the building of [the] nation." She had "natural" roles in the inspiration, education, and social development of the community that she "would have to perform . . . even if [she was] free." Necessary roles were the functions that African Women performed because black Americans were still oppressed, or "still slaves—a nation without political, institutional or coercive power."[95] The Muminina argued that political struggle required black women to be active members in all aspects of organizing. They maintained that African Women had "to learn such things as secretarial skills, weaponry, first aid, driving, [and] administrative skills," in addition to, and sometimes in lieu of, performing their "natural," or gender-specific, tasks. They warned readers that "it might be 'nice' (but harmful) to think that women should just sit at home—sewing, cooking, taking care of the house and children." However, female advocates needed to face the fact that they were part of a "BLACK AND POWERLESS PEOPLE" who needed to do all they could to attain "self-determination, self-respect, self defense." The Muminina summarized this section by stressing the futility of gendered divisions of labor in the political trenches: "All who can work will have to *work hard* until we have liberated ourselves, then and only then—when we are free can we again decide whatever new roles women must have."[96]

The "Nationalist Woman" handbook revealed CFUN women's preoccupation with creating a viable model of African Womanhood rooted in cultural nationalist ideology and their lived experiences as activists in the black liberation struggle. Writing in the midst of a rapidly changing movement, the Muminina argued that the contours of African Womanhood had to be predicated on concomitant political struggle instead of antiquated and ahistorical ideas about men's and women's roles. Rather than completely rejecting the Kawaida doctrine, the Muminina developed a new axis on which to measure black women's cultural nationalist organizing. Taking their cue from their Us predecessors, who called for women to move from a "minimum" to a "maximum" role, CFUN women redefined the African Woman as an activist who fulfilled her "natural" roles by enacting her "necessary" ones. Ultimately, the Muminina reimagined the African Woman as an organizer who practiced a gender-inclusive form of cultural nationalism and tailored her activism to fit the needs of the political moment. She was also an activist who renounced ideological rigidity in favor of an evolving view of cultural revolution and women's roles within it.

The handbook was as much a guide for reconceptualizing Kawaida as it was a manual for women's organizing. According to the Muminina, the African Woman could exclusively perform her "natural" roles if, and only if, black Americans were free. Absent the realization of black liberation, both men and women needed to take on whatever "natural" and "necessary" roles the struggle demanded. To relegate the African Woman solely to her "natural" roles was to fundamentally misunderstand the current state of the black liberation struggle. It was also to proffer a static conception of revolution. As CFUN women explained, the African Woman's "necessary roles will change as the needs of the nation change," and she should "be conscious enough to know what skills are needed at the particular time—what to do and when and where to do it."[97] The Muminina's emphasis on the necessity of a malleable understanding of African Womanhood reflected their claims that a black-centered cultural and political ideology could not be divorced from the present struggle in Africa or the Americas; that the practice of Kawaida was context dependent, and, as a result, advocates' ideas about men's and women's roles must be responsive to the environments in which they organize. Indeed, in redefining women's roles, the Muminina engendered a new interpretation of Kawaida, one that used the doctrine's culturally restorative and diasporically minded qualities in service of developing a dynamic and constantly evolving political praxis.

As CFUN women pushed against the boundaries of the cultural nationalist gendered imaginary, they bumped up against ideological walls. The "Nationalist Woman" Handbook was among the most progressive documents that Kawaidist women had produced. Yet the heteronormative gender roles on which the ideology rested caused female advocates to express their ideas about the African Woman in hierarchical terms in order to reconcile their fidelity to CAP and their lived experiences as activists. CFUN women's claims about the "natural" roles and submissiveness of women reflected these ideological confines. Although the Muminina qualified these claims by challenging male advocates' tendency to equate biological differences with social hierarchies, they could not completely disrupt this masculinist approach. The handbook simultaneously reinforced and defied Black Power masculinism and reflected the complexities and limitations of the gendered imaginary as a subversive space for women.

CAP leadership would take up female advocates' call for greater doctrinal specificity and more equitable organizing structures in the following year. At their 1972 conference held in San Diego, members elected Amiri Baraka to the chairmanship. Baraka used this opportunity to develop a more nuanced conception of Kawaida that was responsive to the needs of women and men within the organization. The leader's pursuit of greater ideological specificity was the product of female advocates' critiques and CAP's organizational growth and influence. Meetings such as the 1972 Gary Convention foregrounded the need for a more malleable ideological framework. Over eight thousand black activists and intellectuals participated in the March 1972 National Black Political Conference in Gary, Indiana. Designed to set a national black agenda and create a unified political front, the largely CAP-organized event fostered political and ideological diversity, injected radical black activism into mainstream political debates, and offered activists a space to debate how to best respond to the contemporaneous conservative Nixon administration and its antiblack policies.[98] The meeting foregrounded the potential of a cohesive national black agenda. However, the ideological and organizational cleavages that developed among activists revealed the limitations of the "unity without uniformity" approach that CAP used to organize.

Faced with the very real difficulties of developing a unified political ideology and agenda, CAP members increasingly looked abroad. Congress activists began to study African liberation groups like Sékou Touré's Democratic Party of Guinea and Julius Nyerere's Tanganyika African National Union, which further highlighted the importance of theoretical pliability.[99] Participation in international conferences also refined CAP members' approach to black liberation. Attending events like the 1972 All-Africa Women's Conference and the Sixth Pan-African Congress in 1974 broadened these activists' perceptions of their roles in national and international liberation struggles. Members brought these ideas to bear on their

CAP-sponsored activism, prompting changes in how they conceptualized their roles within cultural nationalist organizing.[100]

Baraka began to reformulate Kawaida by pairing women's organizational strategies with the philosophical teachings of African liberation leaders.[101] The CAP leader noted how CFUN women's "variations on [CAP's] Pan-Afrikan or neotraditional social organization" advanced and modernized cultural nationalist organizing.[102] He also recognized the potential in following the approaches of successful African anticolonial struggles. Combining these influences, Baraka announced a new ideological direction for the organization in 1972. CAP would now focus on three interrelated and evolving stages of black liberation: nationalism, Pan-Africanism, and Ujamaa (practiced by modeling African scientific socialism).[103] This new ideological phase placed CAP at the epicenter of multiple ideological currents. Members did not abandon their commitment to cultural liberation. However, they began to adhere to a broader conceptualization of cultural nationalism that rejected the rigidity of traditional interpretations of Kawaida in favor of a multifaceted, internationalist, and class-conscious politics.[104] Within this approach, cultural nationalism became the launching point of a more expansive political frame. As former member Michael Simanga explains, members began to conceive "Nationalism (domestic focus), Pan-Africanism (global African focus), and Socialism (global oppressed people's focus)" as "interrelated concepts" that were "closely aligned to other African and Third World liberation movements."[105]

Women members developed new ideas about African Womanhood in tandem with CAP's shifting ideological frame. They articulated their increasingly progressive and global conceptions of gender roles through Amina Baraka's "Social Organization" articles and the CFUN Malaika's "Social Development" column in *Black NewArk* and *Unity and Struggle*—CFUN's and CAP's newspapers. Like the Panthers' "Sisters' Section," these print spaces began as mediums through which women in these groups reinforced conservative conceptions of the African Woman.[106] As the organization evolved, however, women used these gender-specific arenas to promote more progressive ideas about black womanhood that both codified and challenged CAP's new ideological ethos. Between 1972 and 1975, they projected a version of the African Woman that was steeped in CAP's expanding, Pan-African perspective and driven by the idea that black liberation could only be achieved if black women realized their full political and ideological potential.

In the August 1973 edition of her "Social Organization" column, Amina Baraka envisioned the African Woman as the vanguard of cultural nationalist, Pan-African, and socialist liberation. The Women's Division leader opened the article, "On Afrikan Women," by emphasizing the importance of female advocates' educational, cultural, and inspirational role in developing a black-centered political movement. "All of our children are being miseducated or uneducated, especially where we Afrikan women have not found it necessary to struggle to help create alternative institutions for ourselves," she told readers. "We must take an active role in the National and World Liberation of Afrikan people. We must become skilled in all areas, it will take all skills to struggle toward victory.... We must work and study without complaint ... push and support and develop Afrikan Culture based on tradition and reason. Let our lives and ways inspire all Afrikan People to reject European culture and values."[107]

In the second half of the article, Baraka diverged from CAP's standard characterizations of women's roles by encouraging her female readership to envision themselves as consummate political thinkers. As "Afrikan Women," she told them, "we must seek political clarity and educate ourselves, so we can support and help make revolution for Afrikan people all over this World." The leader called on women in CAP to "begin to study the scientific politics of revolutionaries so that [they could] understand the revolutionary nature of [their] work" and "provide the world of Afrikan children with an identity, purpose, direction."[108]

In this and other "Social Organization" entries, Amina Baraka presented a version of African Womanhood that reified and reconfigured CAP's cultural nationalist gendered imaginary. Reflecting the lingering influence of Kawaida, she located the crux of the African Woman's activism in the spheres of inspiration, education, and social development. She also situated the African Woman's gender-specific work in the global context, mirroring CAP's increasingly Pan-Africanist orientation. The Women's Division leader departed from traditional Kawaidist discourses, however, in her framing of black women as studied political activists. She envisioned the African Woman as an organizer who inspired and educated men, women, and children through an ideologically grounded political agenda rather than philosophical abstraction. To be sure, her emphasis on social scientific reasoning reflected a broader trend within CAP in which leadership encouraged members to study the political theories of African leaders and socialists. Yet Amina Baraka's emphasis on women's political study had important implications for gender constructs within the cultural nationalist group. Previous

The Malaika, women in Newark Congress of African People.
Copyright 1972 by Sura Wa Taifa.

iterations of Kawaida maintained that political theory was the purview of men. Baraka not only challenged anti-intellectual characterizations of female advocates, she also asserted that women's ideological acuity was a prerequisite for the realization of CAP's Pan-Africanist and socialist vision.

Amina Baraka's characterization of the African Woman as a studied revolutionary was also a response to continuing ideological debates within CAP. By 1973, congress members had begun to de-emphasize what they deemed to be the "mystical" or unscientific elements of cultural nationalism, including its religious elements and its lionization of male leadership. Yet the old model of mysticism and masculinism still lingered.[109] In calling on CAP women to develop an African-inspired political identity based on the "scientific politics of revolutionaries" rather than the hermetic interpretations of black men, the Women's Division leader charged black women with eradicating the remaining vestiges of Kawaidist conservatism. She also cast them as the progenitors of new forms of cultural nationalist thought and practice.

Malaika-authored articles for the "Social Development" section of *Black NewArk* and *Unity and Struggle* reinforced this shifting perception of the

African Woman. As with Baraka's column, in the 1970s, the authors of these articles deftly navigated female advocates' fidelity to CAP's philosophies and political goals and their own efforts to challenge conservative interpretations of their roles. In their September 1973 edition of the column, for example, the Malaika published an untitled piece that promoted women as the keepers and promoters of black culture. In response to concerns about the negative portrayal of black Americans in film, television, and popular culture, CFUN women argued that the African Woman should "educate [her] children as to who [they] are—Afrikan people, what [they] must do—build black institutions, and how will [they] do it—armed with the proper ideology."[110] Encapsulating their previous writings, the Malaika suggested that women were the ideal culture bearers and educators precisely because they were well versed in alternative institution building and the "correct" understanding of Kawaida doctrine and its philosophical tenets.

The Newark women paired entries establishing women as cultural keepers with other pieces in which they asserted their centrality to political and economic organizing. In their February 1974 edition of the column, "How Do We Get Out of This Mess?," the women's group framed the African Woman as a politically engaged activist who enacted expansive interpretations of Kawaidist principles in order to advance black liberation. The Malaika opened the article by recapitulating claims from the "Nationalist Woman" handbook, reminding readers that "Black people in America (and around the world) [were] a people without power" and that the African Woman would need to take on whatever tasks or roles were necessary in order to achieve black liberation. They then built on this premise to assert their primacy in political and economic organizing. "Politics control our lives (To think otherwise is to be totally unrealistic)," they told their readership; politics "determines how wealth is distributed and this determines how people will live." To remedy this powerlessness and lack of black wealth, the Malaika encouraged their female readership to adopt "the rational and scientific approach to distributing wealth" that was "known traditionally as Ujamaa in Afrikan society." "We need to take this traditional attitude of mind and apply it, with scientific reasoning, to our own situation in America in 1974," they claimed. In closing, they reminded readers, "So when we find ourselves trying to figure out what we need to get ourselves out of this mess that we are caught up in . . . we must remember that we need unity, we need to move to be united, we need a 'Unity Movement'—and we need that unity to be under an Ujamaa system."[111] Rather than looking to men or inspiring them to become politically active, the Malaika framed the African Woman as a politically advanced and ideologically adept organizer who rooted her political organizing in an African-centered worldview.

By the mid-1970s, Malaika and Muminina members were using organizational spaces to transform patriarchal framings of their organizational and ideological contributions. Their columns showcased how female advocates proffered more expansive ideas of women's roles without undermining their theoretical and ideological commitments. Women's Division leaders still charged women with Kawaidist-inspired responsibilities like social development and education. However, they argued that black women were uniquely suited for these tasks because of their institution-building knowledge and ideological acumen rather than their inspirational abilities. Their column entries are notable for their lack of references to domesticity, the adoption of marginal roles, or the support or inspiration of men. Indeed, CFUN women's response to the question of how black Americans could get out of the oppressive "mess" of American society was to rely on the expertise of women organizers who were uniquely positioned to lead the black community due to their nuanced understanding of politics, ideology, and global black struggle rather than their supposed innate ability to inspire or educate men and children.

CAP women's sustained efforts to renegotiate their roles simultaneously reflected and advanced cultural nationalists' ideas about manhood and womanhood. The organization emerged during a period of heightened debates about the role of women in political organizing. Recognizing the demands of the political moment, Kawaidist women developed a body of literature aimed at reshaping members' real and imagined understandings of gender roles. From 1968 to 1972, when CFUN's and CAP's organizing structures still largely rested on traditional Kawaidist views, they appropriated the tactics of their Us predecessors: reaffirming the central values of the philosophy while also expanding the parameters of women's doctrinally assigned roles. After 1972, when CAP adopted a more expansive, Pan-African approach to nation building and liberation, they promoted a progressive, culturally grounded, and diasporically minded vision of the African Woman in their women's columns and editorials. A key component of this latter phase was female advocates' insistence that the African Woman, whether participating in education, child-rearing, politics, or economics, was armed with the "proper ideology" and a "scientific approach" to addressing the problems facing the black community. Irrespective of the ideological or organizational moment in which they theorized, however, female advocates consistently imagined the African Woman activist as a conscious organizer and political actor in addition, rather than in opposition, to her traditional or "natural" roles as a mother, caregiver, and educator.

It was the persistent inclusion of traditional gender roles that continued to set CFUN and CAP apart from their contemporaries. Members of these groups certainly proffered more progressive ideas about women's rights and roles than their male counterparts. Yet their debates and discussions about black womanhood lacked the outright disavowal of conservative gender roles and the critique of prevailing ideological and organizational systems that their contemporaries produced. It was not that CFUN women were uninterested in women-centered or feminist principles. Rather, their fidelity to the Kawaida doctrine—an ideology predicated on gender conservatism—limited their ability to fully incorporate a feminist critique into their projection of gender roles. Despite these ideological and organizational barriers, female advocates' formulations of the African Woman still advanced the Black Power–era goal of remaking black identity and transformed conversations about women's roles within this faction of political organizing.

In July 1974, CAP women moved these conversations from print to the public when they announced the creation of the CAP Afrikan Women's Conference. Organizers billed the meeting as "an important step toward heightening the political awareness and educational development of Afrikan Women in order that [they] may more effectively strive for the unification of all Afrikan People." The multiday meeting consisted of workshops dedicated to traditional forms of women's organizing, including education, health, and social organization. The agenda also included seminars in politics, communications, and institutional development, as well as lectures from "Afrikan women from America's liberation movements, West Indies, and progressive Afrikan countries."[112]

In the months leading up to the conference, women across CAP chapters published their views about how a woman could become a "high-level revolutionary" in *Unity and Struggle*. In "The Role of the Black Woman in the Revolution," CAP Pittsburg members established their approach to defining the ideal female activist. They explained, "We as Revolutionary Afrikan women must be the creators and builders of a new revolutionary way of living. Our attitudes must be of the re-creation of the Afrikan Personality.... Our roles must be twofold, that of natural and necessary roles for the total liberation of Afrikan peoples. The Afrikan Nationalist Woman must inspire the family to be committed revolutionaries, educate the children to be committed revolutionaries, and participate in revolutionary social development."[113] Like their Newark counterparts, they reminded readers that the black struggle required that the African Woman be involved in "all aspects of the struggle" and that she must be "aggressive as if [black Americans] REALLY were a POWERLESS people!" The Steel City group also asserted that "women of the struggle have minute limitations—just as the men have minute limitations," but they also noted that this should not prevent women from "political participation, economic participation, physical and military participation, etc." The best way for the African Woman to "contribute to the strength and growth and development of [her organizations]" was to maintain her commitment to African-centered paradigms and be involved in all areas of political, intellectual, and cultural struggle.[114]

The prevalence of this and other like-minded articles in *Unity and Struggle* demonstrated women's widespread debate over the contours of African Womanhood and their rising influence within CAP's print and political culture. "The Role of the Black Woman" showcased CAP women's efforts to codify the progressive vision of African Womanhood that the Muminina articulated in the "Nationalist Woman" handbook. It also foregrounded their insistence on black women's rightful place at the forefront of CAP's ideological and organizational evolution. The publication of female advocates' articles indicated that CAP leadership supported their efforts and made concrete attempts to change public perceptions of the organization's patriarchal ethos—even as the group remained tethered to traditional ideas about men's and women's roles. In the waning years of the 1970s, CAP members were actively searching for ways to transform global black nationalist paradigms into tangible political formations. Female advocates compelled leaders to acknowledge that they could only achieve this goal if they endorsed an antipatriarchal interpretation of Kawaida and insisted on women's full participation and emancipation in global black political and cultural struggle.

More than seven hundred men and women gathered at Rutgers University's law school to discuss how to actualize the ideal of the African Woman that female advocates envisioned. The three-day Afrikan Women's Conference included women from multiple chapters of CAP and representatives from CORE and the Socialist Workers Party. The conference also attracted international attention. Students from Ethiopia and female ambassadors from Guinea attended the event.[115] Throughout the conference, organizers foregrounded black women's oppression and emphasized the integral role they could play in bringing about unification and self-determination throughout the diaspora.[116] The politics workshop dealt with "the question of women's oppression and generally agreed that women suffer triple oppression[:] that of . . . race, class, and sex," while social organization workshop attendees focused on "the total development of healthy, revolutionary relationships." Hundreds of women debated the merits of "the creation of free and independent public schools" in the education meeting, and health and wellness workshop participants focused on "the protracted struggles to minimize the exploitation and discrimination of [black] people." By the end of the event, attendees were in "unanimous agreement that [they] should put forth an anticapitalist, anti-imperialist, and anti-neo-colonialist position" that advanced black women's liberation.[117]

The Afrikan Women's Conference, and the anti-imperialist position that participants produced, hastened key ideological shifts within CAP. In the months following the meeting, Amiri Baraka formally rejected traditional interpretations of Kawaida and its masculinist maxims. He instead encouraged CAP members to adopt Revolutionary Kawaida, a political position that combined the best practices from Karenga's philosophy with principles and frameworks put forth by African state leaders. This new ideological position employed CAP members' long-term investment in black culture, nationalist politics, and Pan-African solidarity in service of bringing about self-determining black communities and nations.[118]

A central pillar of Revolutionary Kawaida was the disavowal of the patriarchal practices embedded in the traditional doctrine. Baraka asserted that CAP now adamantly "rejected the interpretation of Kawaida as a form of reactionary chauvinism either racial or sexual." He also called on members to repudiate the practice of "extended famil[ies]," or polygamy, and "the feudalism which sought to make [their] women beautiful African objects."[119] Finally, the CAP leader argued that the group's investment in patriarchy was counterrevolutionary. "Part of our failure to become revolutionary is our continuing need to subjugate our women under contemporary feudalism," Baraka remarked. "It was not uncommon 2 or 3 years ago for brothers from nationalist organizations to be skeptical about women even learning doctrine because they thought the sisters might apply themselves to learning more of the doctrine than they, and, hence, they would be shown up as the unserious advocates they were."[120]

Amiri Baraka's stance mirrored that of Maulana Karenga, who, by 1974, had also rejected sexist interpretations of cultural nationalism. The Us leader published tracts in which he revised his statements about women's roles, arguing that black Americans would "never liberate [themselves] as a people" until they rid themselves of the "behavioral patterns like sexism, male chauvinism, and parasitic and perverse pimpism in [their] relations with each other."[121] Baraka's and Karenga's evolving perspectives on gender roles were the product of female advocates' public and private renegotiations of those roles. Indeed, Baraka maintained that CFUN and CAP women "fought [men] tooth and nail about [their] chauvinism," forcing male advocates to "see women as equals in struggle."[122]

Organizational leaders also credited women with accelerating CAP's leftward ideological turn. Baraka contended that the Afrikan Women's Conference in July 1974 was a "concrete step onward and upward in the ideological development of the Black Liberation movement here in North America." Specifically, the CAP leader argued that the conference showcased the "need to draw Black Women not only into that liberation movement, but directly into the struggle against capitalism and imperialism."[123] In that same spirit, the following year, he formally rejected the remaining ideological tenets of Kawaida and formally endorsed a gender-inclusive, anticapitalist, anti-imperialist, and socialist platform.

In 1975, CAP shifted into its third ideological period: Marxism. Baraka reconceptualized CAP as "a Black Liberation Party" that waged "a National Liberation Struggle in North America, and this Black liberation Struggle is Key to Socialism!" He envisioned it as "a Marxist influenced party in that it utilize[d] political-economic analysis critical of capitalism"; "a Leninist influenced party in that it emphasize[d] practice as well as theory"; and a Maoist party in that it use[d] world revolutionary theory ... to create an indigenous ideology of National Liberation and Socialist revolution."[124] Before this point, CAP members' interest in anticapitalism and socialism had been tempered by their ongoing belief in black cultural particularity. Subsequently, Baraka and other leaders outlined an ideological platform that elevated class above cultural nationalism.

Women in the organization found CAP's Marxist turn productive. No longer tethered to cultural nationalist mandates, they developed new ideological and organizational spaces in which to articulate and enact more radical definitions of black womanhood. In January 1975, they founded the Black Women's United Front (BWUF), an "anti-racist, anti-imperialist, and anti-capitalist" group dedicated to ending the "triple oppression" of black women."[125] The BWUF functioned as a collective within CAP, with members hosting a series of meetings and assemblies to develop a women-centered, socialist agenda.[126] Local chapters carried out the groups' antiracist, anti-imperialist platform by holding rallies in support of Joan Little, a North Carolina woman accused of killing a white prison guard who tried to rape her, and bringing together unions and industry leaders to develop "work incentive programs, hospital and pharmaceutical benefits, and day care facilities" for black women.[127]

CAP's Marxist turn marked the end of female members' investment in reshaping the African Woman ideal. Instead, BWUF members focused on developing a political identity predicated on antiracist and anticapitalist mandates. In their founding position papers, leaders framed their original ideas about womanhood as undertheorized understandings of gender roles, labeling their previous conceptions of the African Woman as "idealist" and a product of their incomplete "understanding of Capitalism and its relationship to oppression, nations, workers, and the family."[128] This position deviated from their previous writings, in which CAP women privileged the ideal of a singular, race-conscious African Woman at the expense of acknowledging the class and cultural differences among black women within and outside the organization. BWUF members' evolving position on black womanhood was certainly reflective of the larger political milieu out of which the collective arose; however, it was also indicative of CAP women's ongoing interest in developing new understandings of black womanhood based in their present realities rather than imagined ideas about their African pasts. Both CAP and the BWUF dissolved before members could fully develop this new political position and self-conception. Nevertheless, the formation of the BWUF not only represented black women's organizational impact, it also showed how black women adopted, transformed, and applied CAP's "Black Power ends" to their gender-specific needs and goals.

CAP women's ongoing efforts to reimagine black womanhood were a testament to the importance of cultural nationalist ideology and organizing during the Black Power era. Activists across the political spectrum often lamented the detrimental effects of white cultural hegemony, but few organizations offered tangible frameworks for rebuilding black cultural heritage. The Kawaida doctrine, and the ceremonies and rituals that cultural nationalists developed, provided black Americans with a conduit through which to repair real and imagined connections to their African homeland, foster new forms of Black Power, and develop counterhegemonic models of manhood and womanhood. Accordingly, Kawaida had mass appeal, even as it reproduced the white, heteropatriarchal gender constructs and practices that advocates sought to counter. The holiday Kwanzaa is one example of Kawaida and cultural nationalism's lasting influence, as it has been appropriated by black Americans outside the black nationalist community and is still practiced today.[129]

Black women's interpretations and applications of Kawaida were a key impetus behind the ideology's popularity and evolution. As members of the Us Organization, CFUN, and CAP, they transformed, modernized, and popularized cultural nationalist organizing. The Women's Divisions of these groups continually developed useful and accessible ways to implement the core principles of Kawaida. They also fundamentally redefined the African Woman ideal, transforming it from a conservative, patriarchal concept into a political identity rooted in their gender-specific interpretations of cultural nationalism and their lived experiences as activists. Armed with this more expansive understanding of their political and cultural roles, black women became leading organizers of grassroots Black Power initiatives in Los Angeles and Newark. After the formation of CAP in 1970, they expanded their reach and influence, helping to transform the federation of organizations into a dominant black nationalist group.

Women's reshaping of the gendered imaginary influenced the ideological and organizational direction of cultural nationalist groups. Us Organization and CFUN members found ways to assert their own gender-specific political priorities while remaining committed to Kawaida ideology. They created an evolving definition of African Womanhood that was steeped in the goals of cultural revolution, yet also critiqued the practice of separate spheres of political work. Their strategy was not always one of blatant accusation and criticism; rather, it was one that challenged practitioners of the philosophy to adhere to its most emancipatory elements and work toward the liberation of *all* black Americans. This methodology allowed them to shape the debate in favor of more egalitarian interpretations of Kawaida; influence the organizational and ideological trajectories of Us, CFUN, and CAP; and, in the words of a former male member, inaugurate "period[s] of tremendous transformation in the consciousness of the men of the organization."[130] Karenga and Baraka may have been the spokesmen of cultural nationalism, but black women were important theorists of this tradition, refining and advancing the philosophy by reimagining their political and social roles.

CAP women also engaged in this process of self-definition on the international stage, working with women outside of the organization to rethink their roles in global black liberation. By the mid-1970s, the domestic Black Power movement was ablaze with protests, conferences, and groups dedicated to ending capitalist and imperialist oppression at home and abroad and to developing a global black political community united in its goal of bringing about Pan-African liberation and black sovereignty.

This Pan-African sentiment permeated through new and established domestic Black Power organizations, causing activists to reconsider the meaning of black manhood and womanhood on a global scale. Female advocates were among the many black women who participated in these protests and international meetings designed to develop a unified Pan-African agenda. They also engaged in debates about black American women's roles in international liberation struggles. The documents and speeches black women produced for these meetings reflected their efforts to establish and redefine their role in Pan-African organizing. These texts also helped developed the ideal of the Pan-African Woman—a political identity that championed black women as the vanguard of a gender-conscious, diasporic emancipatory struggle.

CHAPTER FOUR

The Pan-African Woman, 1972–1976

Alberta Hill was one of the many women in the Congress of African People (CAP) interested in redefining black women's roles on a global scale. Hill was a member of The East, a Brooklyn-based Kawaidist organization and CAP affiliate.[1] Looking to foster relationships with African women abroad, the East Sisterhood—the women's division of the organization—engaged in an ambitious fund-raising campaign to send Hill as their representative to the July 1972 All-Africa Women's Conference (AAWC) in Dar es Salaam, Tanzania. Sisterhood members viewed Hill's participation in the AAWC as a way to strengthen black American women's Pan-African consciousness, as well as their personal and political ties with the diaspora.[2]

Hill's journey to Africa represented one of the many ways in which U.S.-based black women practiced Pan-Africanism during the Black Power movement. In the 1960s, a record number of African countries gained their independence from European colonial powers. In the subsequent decade, self-governing countries including Tanzania and Ghana became paragons of Black Power's potential.[3] Animated by the idea that they were witnessing the "unparalleled degeneration" of "white power," Black Power activists increasingly situated their domestic organizing within the global context.[4] They participated in a range of Pan-African-inspired protests and meetings, including African Liberation Day (ALD), the AAWC, and the Sixth Pan-African Congress (Sixth PAC). Not only did these protests and summits bolster ties between domestic and international movements, they also served as conduits through which U.S.-based activists articulated their real and imagined identification with Africa and as Africans.

This swell of Pan-African activism presented new opportunities for female organizers to reshape ideas about black womanhood within Black Power organizing. Although they had long been active in diasporically oriented struggles, male-centered ideas about Pan-African liberation and leadership had dominated popular and political conversations about global black liberation. Moreover, Black Power organizers' ideas about the role of women in worldwide liberation were often predicated on American-centered conceptions of Pan-Africanism circulating in the public sphere. In the late 1960s, many activists espoused a form of the ideology that was influenced by, if not directly associated with, the cultural nationalist philosophy of Kawaida.[5] This diasporic outlook initially reflected a cultural nationalist–inspired concept of a masculine, universal, and undifferentiated Pan-African polity. It also originally relegated women to the sidelines in global liberation endeavors.

Black women organizers reinvigorated their efforts to assert their primacy in diasporic projects in the 1970s. Activists across organizations and ideologies attended international meetings where they collectively developed working papers, speeches, and conference referenda aimed at developing a new concept of women's roles in Pan-African organizing—one that was more ideologically malleable and nuanced than that of their cultural nationalist counterparts. Increasingly, these organizers and theorists insisted that the ideal female Pan-Africanist had a realistic grasp on the present state of global black oppression and on the variegation of women's experiences across the diaspora. They also asserted that the Pan-African Woman should mobilize with a clear understanding of how the potential for international black unification and liberation rested on women's accurate analysis of the interrelated effects of racism and capitalism across the world.

Black women's efforts to reshape ideas about their roles in Pan-African organizing had appreciable effects on the national and international stage. Not only did their conference papers and political resolutions challenge monolithic, masculinist characterizations of the Pan-African actor and diasporic community, they also often proffered more holistic approaches to theorizing Pan-African ideologies and organizing strategies. Their attempts to situate women at the forefront of Pan-African organizing did not wholly excise conservative characterizations of diasporic liberation. However, their speeches, working papers, and resolutions proffered intersectional approaches to Pan-Africanist mobilization that Black Power activists in the United States embraced.

Pan-Africanism in the Black Power Era

Activists' 1970s Pan-African organizing was the latest iteration of black activists' long and concerted interest in championing nationalism and self-determination on the African continent and among people of African descent. Since the eighteenth century black Americans had practiced Pan-Africanism—a fluid concept that included articulations of the awareness of the linked oppression and fate of peoples of African descent, expressions of affinity and kinship with Africa, and concrete organizing strategies aimed at achieving global black liberation.[6] By the early twentieth century, activists and intellectuals had developed a global network of grassroots and elite organizations dedicated to reconceptualizing black Americans' relationship to the African continent. Amy Jacques Garvey's unapologetic embrace of African heritage and continental redemption led thousands of black Americans to practice Pan-Africanism through the worldwide Universal Negro Improvement Association.[7] At the same time, theorists and activists like W. E. B. Du Bois worked to secure the "political and civil rights for Africans and their descendants throughout the world" through a series of Pan-African congresses, the first five of which took place between 1900 and 1945 in Europe and North America.[8] Through Garveyism, the Pan-African congresses, and myriad other forms of Pan-African expression, black activists developed a multilayered approach to rebuilding their homeland and their cultural and political connections to it.

Midcentury African decolonization struggles transformed Pan-African organizing on African and American soil. The precipitous rise of independent African countries and territories after World War II transformed the geography of the continent and the political orientation of activists. Spurred on by shifting geopolitical alliances, activists reinstated major diasporic summits such as the Pan-African congresses after a wartime hiatus. They also abandoned their gradualist approach to liberation and located the nucleus of Pan-African struggles in the working class. The Fifth Pan-African Congress (Fifth PAC), held in Manchester, England, in 1945, exemplified this new political direction.[9] The Manchester meeting was the first time that representatives from Africa and the West Indies attended the congresses. The meeting also marked a changing of the guard in global black leadership. Previously, a small circle of middle-class British and black American elites had controlled the meetings. Fifth PAC delegates and leaders included unionists, politicians, and future African state leaders such as Kwame Nkrumah and Jomo Kenyatta. This new generation of activists supported more radical political and economic agendas and called for the "complete and absolute independence" of West African countries, universal suffrage, and self-government for African peoples across multiple colonized territories.[10]

Stimulated by Fifth PAC resolutions, and the period of decolonization of African nations that followed, U.S.-based Black Power activists framed their organizing as a link in the chain of global black uprisings. Although they did not always explicitly identify as Pan-Africanists, their belief in a global African "family" framed their organizing efforts. Postwar activists such as Mae Mallory intertwined Black Power and Pan-Africanism through the February 1961 protest of Patrice Lumumba's assassination at the UN. In that same year, the Student Nonviolent Coordinating Committee (SNCC) linked the fates of black students in Alabama and Africa through liberation schools and its International Affairs Commission, a policy wing designed to shift American perceptions and policies toward the African continent.[11] Black Panther Party members continually asserted their support for anticolonial liberation struggles taking place in South Africa, Zimbabwe, Mozambique, and Guinea-Bissau. Meanwhile, the Us Organization and the Committee for Unified Newark (CFUN) practiced Kawaida, a cultural nationalist ideology aimed at repairing black Americans' cultural connection to Africa.[12] These protests, organizations, and political orientations ensured that Black Power–era projects were internationalist in scope and helped fuel the surge of Pan-Africanist activism that characterized the movement in the early 1970s.

Student movements further fostered this internationalist impulse. Quoting from their backpacks full of books by intellectuals like Martiniquan psychiatrist and philosopher Frantz Fanon, black co-eds shouted down university administrators and boycotted American companies with imperialist interests in Africa. In April 1972, hundreds of students occupied a library at Cornell University and demanded that the school divest from the Gulf Oil Corporation. Withdrawing the university's monetary support, they argued, would "force the company out of Portugal's African colonies."[13] Students at Lincoln University picketed Foote Mineral Company in Exton, Pennsylvania. They charged that the company violated UN sanctions by importing chrome from Rhodesia, a country in which the white majority ruled and terrorized the indigenous African minority.[14] The Youth Organization for Black Unity, a coalition of student and grassroots organizations, provided infrastructure for many student-led, globally conscious political protests. Under the stewardship of activists like Sandra Neely and Joyce Nelson, the collective lent financial and media support to collegiate Pan-African protests and fostered co-eds' global political consciousness through their newspaper, the *African World*.[15]

Events like ALD united students, black nationalists, and other leftist activists together under the banners of Pan-Africanism and anticolonialism. A daylong series of coordinated protests designed to call attention to American imperialism and African liberation struggles, ALD transformed black American activists' perceptions of African independence, global politics, and U.S. imperialist intervention in African countries. The seeds of ALD germinated throughout the 1960s by way of globally minded protests, activist envoys to Africa, and Black Power organizers' increased contact with African leaders. Durham-based activist Owusu Sadaukai (Howard Fuller) took the initial steps to bring the idea to fruition. Sadaukai had a long history of supporting global black liberation, most notably through the Malcolm X Liberation University, an independent black community school in North Carolina. In 1971, Sadaukai witnessed African liberation struggles firsthand when he visited the liberated territories of Mozambique. Living amid members of the Mozambique Liberation Front (FRELIMO) deromanticized his ideas about Africa and African liberation. The activist's monthlong trek through the Mozambican countryside offered sobering lessons on everything from the futility of empty revolutionary rhetoric to the importance of gender equality in liberation struggles. The trip also highlighted the importance of disrupting black Americans' complicity with American imperialism in Africa.[16] When he returned, Sadaukai suggested that black American activists hold a day of coordinated demonstrations in support of African independence and liberation struggles. In the waning months of 1971, activists announced plans for the first ALD.[17]

Black women activists across the country played a critical role in bringing the first ALD protest to fruition. Black Power icons and figureheads including Angela Davis and Malcolm X's widow, Betty Shabazz, were part of the ALD steering committee.[18] As officers on the ALD Coordinating Committee, other women, such as former SNCC and Congress of Racial Equality member Florence Tate, helped coordinate the day of multicity protests.[19] These and other women were among the organizers who, in early 1972, announced that marches would take place in multiple cities in "support of liberation efforts in Africa and in demonstration of solidarity between Africans born in the United States and Africans born on the continent."[20] Washington, D.C., was to be the epicenter of the ALD protests, with additional demonstrations taking place in San Francisco, Toronto, Dominica, Antigua, Grenada, and other North American cities.[21]

On May 27, 1972, thousands demonstrated in support of African liberation, decolonization, and black self-determination. Dressed in outfits adorned with African symbols and carrying signs declaring, "Africa for the Africans," the majority of ALD participants took part in the Washington, D.C., march through "Embassy Row where the governments of the United States, Portugal, Rhodesia and South Africa were denounced."[22] On the way, Sister Inez Reid from Chicago's United Africans for One Motherhood International stopped at the Rhodesian Information Center to accuse the country of "perpetuating chemical, biological, and conventional warfare," while the Women's Division of CFUN implored bystanders to make their "contributions for the liberation of African People."[23] Audley Moore led the D.C. marchers to their rallying point at the Washington Monument, which activists renamed Lumumba Square for the day.[24] On monument grounds, overlooking a sea of black, green, and red flags, Black Panther leader Elaine Brown gave a rousing speech in which she called the demonstration the "most beautiful thing [she'd] ever seen in [her] life."[25] Moore also addressed the crowd, framing the march as a welcome realization of her fifty-four years of Pan-African organizing.[26] The Washington, D.C., march reached its zenith when thousands of participants, led by Sadaukai, chanted in unison, "We are an African People."[27]

A resounding success, the first ALD protest was a pivotal and promising moment in Black Power–era Pan-African consciousness and organizing. One of the largest and most diverse protests on American soil, the daylong demonstration countered claims of black Americans' domestic-centered perspectives and foregrounded the potential of Pan-Africanism to unite groups and factions across the Black Power movement. Widespread participation in the event reflected black Americans' growing embrace of Pan-Africanism as a political ideology, while protest speeches, flyers, and position papers distributed at the event raised participants' awareness about African politics and liberation struggles. Armed with this information, protesters showed their willingness to move beyond "Back-to-Africa" ideas of Pan-Africanism and embrace more holistic understandings of global liberation that accounted for black peoples' common experiences of oppression under racist and capitalist regimes.[28]

As protests like ALD generated Pan-Africanist sentiment, they also engendered questions about black women's role in Pan-African organizing. Historically, black women often composed the infrastructure of grassroots and elite Pan-African organizations and events. However, their participation rarely translated into adequate recognition of their ideas and perspectives about diasporic liberation. Organizers and intellectuals often framed the path to African redemption and liberation as one requiring the restoration of black manhood, casting women as "propagations of male mythology," or as mothers and molders of the African nation or continent and its people.[29] This patriarchal perspective produced discourses and iconography replete with rhetoric of black men "emancipating" and "redeeming" "Mother Africa" in the first half of the twentieth century.[30] In the latter half, activists continued to conceive of Pan-Africanism and African liberation in masculinist terms. Black Power activists and intellectuals designated theorists such as Kwame Nkrumah, Julius Nyerere, and Walter Rodney as the intellectual and organizational leaders of Pan-African movements, unwittingly relegating women to traditional roles as rank-and-file organizers, nurturers, educators, and caregivers. This male-centered perspective on diasporic organizing often conceptualized the Pan-African community and its leaders in patriarchal terms and lacked a clear recognition of women's specific needs within and perspectives on global black liberation.

ALD organizing and symbolism were two of many manifestations of the complicated and, at times, contradictory debates over the role of women in Pan-African organizing. As Fanon Che Wilkins explains, the ALD Coordinating Committee used the image of an African woman in indigenous clothing, with a baby in her arms and rifle on her back, as a symbol and advertisement for the protest. On the one hand, such imagery—a nod to the female liberation fighters Sadaukai encountered in Mozambique—framed women as vital figures on the front lines of liberation struggles.[31] On the other hand, these representations suggested that women should remain tethered to traditional roles such as child-rearing and motherhood. Similarly, black women played critical organizational and ceremonial roles in the initial daylong protest; however, their participation and visibility did not result in an interrogation of the complicated gender politics embedded in the event or Pan-African organizing writ large.[32] As activists' globally minded organizing increased in size and scope, black women examined this approach. At international summits and conferences, they developed more capacious ideas about Pan-Africanism and women's roles within it, challenging masculine approaches to global liberation.

The All-Africa Women's Conference

Two months after ALD, black women from the United States joined activists from across Africa at the AAWC in Dar es Salaam. Founded in 1962 in Kenya, the Pan-African women's conference was part of a growing network of African women's organizations dedicated to women's full social, cultural, and political equality across the continent. By the time the organization marked its tenth anniversary at the Dar es Salaam meeting, it had become one of the premier women's organizations on the African continent.[33] The 1972 AAWC participant roster included women in delegations from Zambia, Algeria, Egypt, Congo, Mali, and Zaire, as well as delegations from outside Africa, including participants from Cuba and Korea.[34] It also marked the first time that organizers invited women from the United States to participate.[35] From July 24 to July 31, women like Audley Moore and Alberta Hill represented black women in America, joining with activists from all over the world to discuss the conference theme: "The Role of the African Woman in Liberation Struggles."[36]

AAWC organizers invited Moore to give a keynote address. She used this opportunity to cast the conference, and black American women's inclusion in it, as a constitutive moment in the formation of a new Pan-African identity and agenda for women. Moore began by remarking on the significance of the conference committee's invitation. "I have the honor to convey sisterly greetings to you from thousands of your sisters in the United States of America who are conscious of their African heritage and are here with you today in love and spirit," she noted. "We feel greatly honored by this opportunity to be here with you in this All Africa Women's Conference held in Dar es Salaam." The seasoned activist insisted that the meeting was a seminal step in forging a unified, progressive model of Pan-African Womanhood. She noted that the committee's "invitation to [U.S. women] across the Atlantic" had the potential to unite women across the diaspora "more than any occurrence since the terrible days of slavery" and that their unification could reinvigorate Pan-African organizing and help black women around the world defeat their "common enemies, United States imperialism, and racism, the most deadly enemies of the liberation forces in Africa today."[37]

In order to mobilize her diverse audience around a unified concept of Pan-African Womanhood, Moore had to minimize their differences and amplify their shared history. To achieve this goal, she relied on the cultural nationalist–driven narrative of a universal African past. The keynote speaker dedicated the first part of her speech to developing a matrilineal history of African heritage and redemption as evidence of the need for black women throughout the world to unite around common identifications and goals. "The African woman can rightly be called the mother of civilization as she is known for her creativity, her humanity, her productivity, her valor, and her great beauty," she explained. "From the earliest historical times, records show African women as queens and rulers of great dynasties, as warriors, and as merchants." Moore also credited women with laying the "foundation for the organization of all subsequent societies" and for developing the family unit structure before "western imperialist nations began to trade in the black bodies of [their] glorious ancestors" in the early sixteenth century. She charged her audience with reclaiming this history, and their rightful place as the leaders and progenitors of culture and community, by mobilizing around a shared Pan-African identity and organizing agenda.[38]

Moore then used this narrative of a unified African past to proffer a progressive model of black women's future activism. She encouraged her audience to adopt an identity and political outlook based on their shared African heritage rather than their national identifications or individual concerns. Moore warned that black women the world over could not "rely on the morality of the world to give [them] any type of solution for [their] struggle." She argued that "what [was] necessary [was] a total mental revolution." The activist called on the women in her audience to "move to a position of consciousness of the fact that liberation [would be] won when and only when [they could] formulate a concept of [their] struggle around a common cause." She implored them to "turn [their] attention inward and remove all distracting social practices and eliminate all tendencies towards internal divisiveness" and "rebuild [their] social, political and economic culture in such a way that black people will know and feel that it was worth all [their] years of suffering and racial degradation to be once again a part of [their] great African ancestral tradition."[39]

The elder activist argued that global transformation required her audience to do more than simply identify as a collective group; black women had to mobilize around a globally conscious political platform. Moore postulated that women should play a leading role in developing and enacting an antiracist, anti-imperialist Pan-African agenda. Throughout her address, Moore stressed the interrelated nature of her audience's racist and imperialist oppression and the need for women to collectively mobilize against American and European domination. She also delineated a political platform for women that was focused in its anti-imperialist and antiracist aims but elastic enough for her audience members to adapt it to fit their lived conditions. She encouraged AAWC participants to engage in protests and organizations designed to reclaim land, wealth, and natural resources in the Americas and Africa and demand "reparations for all these years of inhuman treatment inflicted upon [them]." She also urged them to engage in politics and organizing aimed at raising the "health standards of [their] people." This was the only way to rid the black world of the "scourge of colonialism and neo-colonialism" and develop independent black nations and liberated national groups.[40]

As her time at the podium drew to a close, Moore assured her audience of black American women's identification with and investment in the Pan-African project she espoused. She explained that in 1972, "as never before, there [was] a large degree of conscious development toward Africanization on the part of black people in the United States." Underscoring this point, she noted, "We want you to know that when your great leaders and statesmen speak, they are speaking to and for us, also. . . . For we are Africans, too, regardless of being born in the U.S.A." The keynote speaker closed her speech with a rousing statement of gendered Pan-African unity: "Long live the unity of African People! Long live African Women wherever they are! Long live the All-African [sic] Women's Conference! Long live our Motherland, Africa!"[41]

Moore's AAWC address illustrated one facet of black American women's efforts to reconcile existing interpretations of Pan-Africanism with their progressive visions of women's roles in global black political organizing. Throughout the speech, she reinforced narratives of a universal African heritage and black Americans' "re-Africanization" akin to those cultural nationalists espoused. Moore also continued to "take for granted the gendering at work" in contemporaneous Pan-Africanist formulations, adopting masculinist language when speaking about Africa as an undifferentiated territory and as an ancestral "motherland."[42]

Even as she rehearsed these essentialist formulations, Moore challenged activists' reflexive associations of manhood and African redemption. Her activist contemporaries often linked African-descended peoples together through a patrilineal African origin narrative; the keynote speaker proffered a women-centered version of the fall and redemption of the African continent. She replaced masculine symbols with feminine ones, conjuring visions of African women as queens, merchants, and rulers and asserting the importance of women in restoring the continent to its former glory. This recounting of an undifferentiated African past was deeply flawed. Yet Moore used it as evidence of women's ability to adopt identities and roles besides those dictated by racist, imperialist, and patriarchal regimes.

Moore also peppered her speech with progressive ideas about Pan-Africanism and women's organizing. Embedded in the keynote address were calls for her audience members to identify with a global black community and mobilize around a political agenda that accounted for the international effects of the interrelationship between racism and imperialism. This was a departure from her contemporaries' calls for women to adopt ahistorical, "African" roles in order to demonstrate their Pan-African consciousness. Her divergent approach was apparent in her calls for black women to undergo a "total mental revolution." To be sure, this suggestion was an effort to convince her audience to reject Eurocentric and imperialistic ideals and identifications. However, it was also a call for women across the diaspora to rethink their fidelity to the patriarchal and parochial dimensions of contemporaneous Pan-African organizing. Moore underscored this point by providing a list of causes that women should address and organizing strategies that they could and should enact. The agenda she enumerated— everything from land and wealth reclamation to reparations, health care, and cultural rehabilitation—delineated a central and indispensable role for women, irrespective of their national, ideological, or ethnic affiliations.[43] Ultimately, Moore projected an idea of Pan-African Womanhood that maintained its fidelity to U.S.-centric, culturally driven doctrines while also framing women as meaningful and autonomous organizers invested in more rigorous practices of globally minded activism.

The vision of womanhood that Moore promoted shared commonalities with other gendered models that Black Power activists produced. Akin to organizers in the Us Organization, CFUN, and CAP, she expressed her abiding investment in developing an African-centered definition of womanhood as a conduit through which to restore the ruptures of the Middle Passage and to assert women's Pan-African consciousness. Influenced by cultural nationalism but not beholden to it, however, the AAWC speaker's vision of the Pan-African Woman did not rehearse the same fidelity to the doctrine's prescriptions of the "natural" roles of women. She framed women as vital Pan-African activists who redeemed Africa and liberated the diaspora by taking on a leading role in shaping contemporary anti-imperialist struggles and constructing a united, gender-conscious Pan-African subjectivity and political front.

Black American women's participation in international summits like the AAWC catalyzed their interest in developing nuanced, progressive conceptualizations of women's roles in global black liberation. As Russell Rickford has noted, these exchanges were often also moments in which black American activists endured quick "lesson[s] in realpolitik."[44] Women like Moore and Hill found these gatherings to be instances in which they were forced to reconcile their political imaginings of the diaspora with black women's lived experiences in other countries and political systems. The Pan-African summits of the 1970s allowed black women to redefine their roles in U.S.-centered organizing and experiment with new ideas about black women's self-development and identification outside of male-led and male-centered spaces. Through their participation in events like the AAWC, these activists forged real and imagined Pan-African communities and gendered political identities, using new ideas about black womanhood as a lingua franca to unite women across the diaspora.

The final resolutions of the 1972 AAWC echoed Moore's calls for women to adopt Pan-African identifications and prominent organizing roles. As they closed the proceedings, participants from the United States, Latin America, and a range of African countries vowed to return to their home countries and "drop ancient prejudices they had about themselves," "take their rightful place as liberators and moulders of the future of Africa," and "march forward as one people, with one identity."[45] News of the Pan-African women's conference, and reprints of Moore's speech, reached audiences in America through the black press throughout the fall of 1972.[46] By the end of that year, other black women activists had already initiated plans for another Pan-African summit in Dar es Salaam.

Black Women and the Sixth Pan-African Congress

Audley Moore and Alberta Hill returned to the United States as Pan-African organizing was proliferating within black organizing circles. Building on the success of the first ALD protest, organizers created the African Liberation Support Committee (ALSC), a national organization designed to "effectively fight for the independence of Africa and African peoples all over the world."[47] ALSC members promoted Pan-Africanism through educational seminars; literature on imperialism, racism, and colonialism; and subsequent annual ALD protests. Other organizing efforts included the SNCC-staffed Center for Black Education (CBE) and Drum and Spear Bookstore in Washington, D.C. The former functioned as a grassroots education center, the latter as an "alternative source of communication" across the Atlantic, publishing and selling texts that promoted Tanzanian-inspired Pan-Africanist principles.[48] While some black activists championed global black unity through U.S.-based organizations, others cultivated it firsthand. A handful of activists participated in programs like the Pan-African Skills Project, an organization that placed black Americans with "technical and scientific skills" in African nations. Headed by former SNCC organizer Irving Davis, the group recruited several hundred black Americans to work in countries such as Tanzania, Zambia, and Guyana. Their efforts promoted transatlantic linkages and attempted to expedite African development and nation building.[49]

The idea to hold another Pan-African congress had been germinating within international Black Power circles since the late 1960s. The uptick in

Pan-African organizing confirmed the potential of such an event. According to James Garrett, a D.C.-based SNCC organizer, plans for the Sixth PAC accelerated at the 1969 International Black Power Conference in Bermuda, when Roosevelt Brown, a Bermudan parliament member and conference organizer, shared Kwame Nkrumah's proposal for a "meeting of Black people to take place on the African continent."[50] After the success of ALD, and numerous meetings within Africa, U.S.-based activists became increasingly convinced of the possibility and promise of such a gathering. They envisioned the summit as a space in which to chart a course for the future of the decolonized black world.

In 1971, a small collective of U.S.- and Caribbean-based organizers took concrete steps to make the next congress a reality, traveling around the world to meet with African heads of state and liberation leaders. Garrett, Brown, writer Liz Gant, and others began meeting with black organizations in Europe to garner interest and support of the congress. Once Garrett returned to D.C., the group of organizers expanded and they made plans to establish a headquarters or secretariat. In the latter half of 1972, activists connected with the D.C.-based CBE became the primary congress coordinators.[51] Former SNCC activists and CBE members—including Geri (Stark) Augusto, Judy Richardson, and Jennifer Lawson—spearheaded this early phase of Sixth PAC organizing. These women helped develop the organizational infrastructure for the congress, managed the initial logistics of the meeting, established domestic and international offices for the event, and composed the meeting's guiding documents.[52]

In the fall of 1972, Augusto drafted the Sixth PAC "Call to Congress."[53] Heeding the advice of her mentor, Trinidadian intellectual C. L. R. James, she framed the twentieth century as the "Century of Black Power," defined by "a unified conception of all peoples who have been colonized" and the "unparalleled degeneration" of "white power." According to Augusto and other early congress organizers, African and African-descended peoples, "whether inside or outside of Africa," were taking it upon themselves to "solve the problems that threaten to overwhelm human society." The Sixth PAC would bring these groups together and channel their efforts into collective programs to promote self-determination, political freedom, economic self-reliance, and anti-Western modes of social, political, and cultural organization. Augusto announced organizers' plans to "pursue the development of a Pan-African Science and Technology Centre . . . designed to serve the vast array of needs of African people in the scientific and technological fields." She also reiterated the coordinators' call for "Africans everywhere, whatever [their] political attitudes ... to come to the Congress, give it [their] support, and spread the news about it." The Sixth PAC could only be a success, organizers argued, if all people from across the African diaspora attended and took "complete part in shaping the forces that touch Africa and its people."[54]

Black women from across the United States answered the call. Sylvia Hill, then a professor at Macalester College in Minnesota, became the secretary-general for the North American region, which included the United States and Canada. Hill volunteered to help organize the event because she felt that the time was ripe for the diaspora to "contribute to the transformation of Africa in terms of its fight against colonialism and apartheid, but also in the sharing of [its] science and technology skills for development."[55] As secretary-general, she organized and led the series of planning meetings designed to select members of the North American Delegation and establish its platform. Hill served as the primary contact and correspondent for the delegation's ten regional districts: New England, Mid-Atlantic, South, Midwest, West, Southwest, and four Canadian territories. She was also responsible for working with other national planning committee members to select delegates and observers based on a given applicant's previous movement work, involvement in congress organizing, "commitment to the betterment of African People," and their potential to engage in Pan-African organizing after the congress's end. Delegates had voting privileges at the congress, while observers could raise issues and questions through petition. Once more than two hundred participants from the United States and Canada had been selected, Hill coordinated travel for them.[56]

Other women took part in the discussions that shaped the positions that their region and, eventually, the North American Delegation would put forth at the congress. The North America Region Planning Conference was the first step in this process. Nearly two hundred activists from more than forty organizations met May 11–13, 1973, at the Institute for African Affairs at Kent State University in Ohio to hear information about the Sixth PAC, address different viewpoints about the congress, and develop procedures for selecting who would represent their regions. Attendees heard speeches from C. L. R. James, Sixth PAC secretary-general Courtland Cox, Owusu Sadaukai, and others. They then branched off into workshops to produce reports on liberation movements, health and nutrition, and political and educational mobilization. Scholars and organizers like Dr. Frances C. Welsing and Barbara Kamara chaired the health and nutrition workshop, while other women, including Hill, debated delegate-selection procedures and financial support.[57]

A central point of contention at the Kent State meeting was whether racism or imperialism was the primary animator of global white supremacy and the driving force of black oppression. Black Marxists and nationalists had been waging this "two-line struggle," or the race versus class debate, for the better part of the twentieth century.[58] During the 1970s, this ideological argument manifested most prominently among members of CAP and the ALSC. After ALD, ALSC leaders began to openly embrace class-first approaches to black liberation. Conversely, black nationalists within and outside CAP continued to insist on the particularity and pervasiveness of racist systems. In the year and a half leading up to the Sixth PAC, these theoretical disagreements evolved into factional fissures, hung over precongress talks, and accelerated intraorganizational disputes.[59]

Black women activists refused to let their political participation and priorities become mired in these debates. They applied to be delegates, special guests, and observers at the conference and emphasized their interest in having their gender-specific concerns reflected in delegation documents. Lois L. Johnson, a lawyer living in Palo Alto, California, submitted an application to be a member of the North American Delegation to the congress. Johnson, who had already cut her organizing teeth in groups like the Us Organization–led Black Congress and CAP, indicated that her legal and finance experience made her qualified to assist the delegation in the areas of education and social science, political organizing, and international banking and finance.[60] Dara Abubakari (Virginia Y. Collins), a grassroots activist from New Orleans and a lifelong Pan-Africanist, also applied to be a member of the group traveling to Tanzania. Abubakari wanted to travel to Dar es Salaam in order to share her expertise in political organizing, youth organizing, and health and nutrition. Drawing on her long history of organizing in women-centered Pan-African groups like the Audley Moore–led Universal Association of Ethiopian Women, Abubakari also indicated that she was expressly interested in focusing on "women's issues" at the congress.[61]

Female activists also figured prominently at regional meetings, insisting on their inclusion in delegate-selection lists and inserting their priorities in regional position papers. Beatrice Waiss and Jo Anne Favors were among the activists who participated in the Midwest District meetings in fall 1973. In these gatherings, they analyzed the position papers put forth at the Kent

State meeting and presented others foregrounding what they viewed to be the most pressing issues facing the Pan-African world. Along with other members from this district, they insisted that education should be a central feature of the North American Delegation's platform. They produced position papers to undergird their claims, framing "education as a process of developing self-reliance and self-determination among African people."[62]

Audley Moore and Sister Ebun Adelona were part of the steering committee of the New England District, a group that included members from The East, academics from Yale and Stony Brook University, and staff from independent black publications such as *African Progress*. Reflecting the deep-seated nationalist leanings of the communities of the New York area, participants from this region developed a platform that emphasized the adoption of an "African personality" and the importance of repairing the ruptured ties between Africans and black Americans. New England–based activists insisted on the importance of using the congress to forge ties among Africans and the diaspora. They called on the national delegation to encourage African leaders to recognize black Americans' heritage and roots by "giving African Americans the opportunity to choose between assuming American citizenship, returning to Africa, or establishing a nation state" and by creating an embassy system to foster communication and solidarity among people of African descent.[63]

New England District members also made strong recommendations on how the North American Delegation and the congress should view the "role of women." They asserted that black women could not "conduct a struggle in isolation from the struggle that [they were] waging for African Liberation" and that "a progressive policy toward the liberation of African women [was] a viable instrument in [the] struggle against capitalist exploitation, imperialism, and neo-colonialism."[64] Their claims reflected black women's ongoing insistence on their centrality to black liberation, as well as their interest in redefining women's roles as part of the planning, execution, and goals of the event. They also indicated how black women integrated their priorities into Sixth PAC organizing and contributed to their districts' efforts to "define and offer a concept of the 'World African community'" that was gender inclusive.[65]

Hill expressed support for regional participants' interest in redefining their roles in the Pan-African world. In her published reports on congress organizing, the Sixth PAC secretary-general reminded readers that the "totality of the black race and the many dimensions of our problems as a people necessitate us viewing our problem in a world context." She encouraged readers, activists, and potential delegates to "move to view the problems of [their] specific localities as an extension of European and American aggression" and to "create new methods of mobilization and organization" that used their communal assets "to [their] benefit as African people."[66] Hill also implored black activists and community members to support the Sixth PAC, as it was an opportunity to develop a Pan-African agenda based on the diaspora's shared goal of ending "euro-american" domination and dependency across the world.[67] These organizing reports became one of several conduits through which black women shaped debates about the contours of Pan-Africanism within the United States. Hill and other national organizers reinforced the importance of situating the black American struggle in the global context and encouraged activists to mobilize around a shared, inclusive understanding of the devastating global effects of racism and imperialism.

While women like Hill and Moore helped hammer out the North American Delegation's positions, others continued to plan the meeting at home and abroad. Judy Claude, Jo Anne Favors, Edie Wilson, Kathy Flewellen, and Geri Augusto formed a powerful organizing cohort that helped bring the congress to fruition. Claude, who was an experienced organizer with SNCC in Nashville, participated in the early Sixth PAC planning meetings in Washington, D.C., before joining the national organizing team.[68] Favors worked alongside Hill in the North American Delegation coordinating office in Saint Paul, Minnesota.[69] Wilson, who began organizing with the CBE as a college student, traveled with Sixth PAC secretary-general Courtland Cox to West Africa to represent the congress in the early planning stages.[70] Later on, she joined Flewellen and Augusto in setting up the Sixth PAC International Secretariat in Dar es Salaam, established in November 1973. Augusto became an information officer and the official liaison with the anticolonial African nationalist organizations headquartered in Dar es Salaam.[71] Collectively, Flewellen, Augusto, and Wilson were in charge of "practically everything from protocol to passports" in Tanzania. They also worked with the Tanzanian government to coordinate logistics while garnering media coverage of the event, spearheading fund-raising initiatives, and heading the collection and distribution of delegation position papers.[72]

If women like Hill stressed the potential of the Sixth PAC to address racism and imperialism, then others like Augusto heralded its promise to tackle patriarchy. In a May 1974 interview, she explained that, at the Sixth PAC, the "position of sisters throughout the African world [was] sure to be discussed." Augusto contextualized the relevance of this discussion within contemporaneous liberation struggles and nation-building schemas. She explained, "Some liberation movements use the term 'National Reconstruction.' Within that term is great significance because it implies a reconstruction of the nation physically, and a reconstruction of attitudes, values, systems of economic [sic] and politics, and culture. . . . One of the facets of this kind of national reconstruction is [the] position of women." Referencing the gender parity policies of African liberation groups like FRELIMO, Augusto argued that the "rest of the African World" was "behind the [African] liberation movements" in developing a gender-inclusive vision of Pan-Africanism. She predicted that the Sixth PAC, in large part due to the participation of women across the diaspora, was to be a constitutive moment for reshaping Pan-Africanist perceptions of gender roles and womanhood.[73]

By spring 1974, Augusto, Hill, and other organizers continued to plan and promote the Sixth PAC amid mounting ideological and logistical tensions. Hill and Claude strategically maneuvered around activists' egos and misgivings about the timing and purpose of the congress. They also navigated a fraught delegate-selection process, contentious in part because of the intensifying ideological divisions among activists and participants' accusations of congress organizers' elitism.[74] Diplomatic tensions compounded procedural ones. Sixth PAC organizers had conceived of the meeting as a nongovernmental affair with limited representation from heads of state. However, just weeks before the conference was scheduled to take place, the governing party of Tanzania, Tanganyika African National Union, announced that delegates had to be appointed by their respective countries in order to participate. The American and Canadian governments were not officially involved in the congress, exempting delegates from these countries from adhering to this protocol. However, the policy barred militants, activists, and opposition groups from Antigua, Trinidad, Barbados, and other countries whose governments were key sponsors of the event.[75] The exclusion of certain activists, intellectuals, and nations shifted the character and political ethos of the meeting, transforming it into a state-sanctioned event rather than a people's convention.[76] The decision cost the congress key supporters, including Walter Rodney and C. L. R. James, both of whom had played a pivotal role in legitimizing and developing the summit. James abstained from participating in the meeting in protest of the decision, while Rodney, a widely respected Guyanese intellectual, denounced the elitist orientation of the congress.[77]

Despite complications, the Sixth PAC, held June 19–27, 1974, attracted delegates from across the globe.[78] Participants heard opening speeches by

Tanzanian president Julius Nyerere and Guinean president Sékou Touré. CAP leader Amiri Baraka and ALD founder Owusu Sadaukai followed with oratories that emphasized the importance of scientific reasoning and class struggle in Pan-Africanist projects.[79] As the gathering continued, delegates and observers engaged in a range of workshops including "Political and Material Support for Liberation Movements" and "African Youth and Development." In the afternoons, they convened in smaller workshops, organized around central themes such as "Economic Development through Self-Reliance," "The Organization and the Use of Pan-African Technical Skills," "The Use of African Resources in the Struggle for Liberation," and "Technology and the Development of Natural Resources."[80] After a week of debate, each delegation produced a set of general declarations replete with their positions and prognostications on economics, politics, science and technology, and gender roles.

The North American Delegation was the largest contingent at the conference, with women from across the United States and Canada composing a significant portion of the group.[81] Activists such as Joan Saunders and Florence Tate attended workshops and committee sessions, while experienced organizers such as Audley Moore and Mae Mallory were special guests and observers at the meeting. Muriel Snowden, a progressive civil rights activist from Boston, was in attendance, as was Brenda Paris, the secretary of the ALSC.[82] Other delegates included Barbara Huell, a leader at Atlanta's Martin Luther King Jr. Community School; Dorothy Dewberry, a well-known SNCC activist; and Monica Steward, a student at Vassar College.[83] Alyce Gullat, a professor at Howard University, thought that President Nyerere's opening speech "was an excellent motivational tool for those interested in total freedom," while Bernetta Bush of the Midwest American Delegation supported the Sixth PAC because she believed that it "provided a vehicle which allow[ed] for significant interaction between African[s] and those of African descent around aspects of their struggle throughout the world."[84]

As Augusto and other women predicted, the question of women's roles in Pan-African organizing was a topic of debate. Organizers designated two workshop sessions to the subject: "Cultural Revolution and the Future of Pan-African Culture" and "Women's Contribution to the Pan-African Struggle."[85] Workshop conversations generated position papers aimed at reorienting participants' ideas about women's rights and roles. On June 24, Grenadian delegation representative Carl Buxe read "The Role of Women in the Struggle for Liberation," a statement summarizing his contingent's

Mae Mallory and Amiri Baraka at the Sixth Pan-African Congress, Dar es Salaam, Tanzania, 1974. Hoyt William Fuller Collection, Atlanta University Center, Robert W. Woodruff Library.

stance on gender equality within Pan-African liberation. In the position paper, women from the delegation foregrounded the vital role they played in their country's independence struggle and lauded female freedom fighters in African liberation movements. They also stressed the importance of developing regionally and historically specific interpretations of Pan-Africanism, warning that the "wholesale transplantation" of independence models across the diaspora would have negative implications for newly freed black nations and the women within them.[86] Other women, such as those in the Sierra Leone Delegation, firmly proclaimed in their congress documents that "the world is basically a patriarchal society" and argued that activists' complicity with this oppressive system hampered black liberation as a whole. They called for a united effort in fighting sexism "through attitude formation, education, legislation, research and studies, seminars, and international conferences," starting with the Sixth PAC.[87]

Women in the North American Delegation also engaged in these conversations about how to redefine their roles in Pan-African organizing. Like their counterparts from other countries and constituencies, they developed position papers documenting the "question of women in the struggle" in congress workshops and meetings.[88] Their Sixth PAC documents captured the dialectic between their experiences as black women in the United States and their identification as members of a global black activist community, as well as their interest in reshaping political struggle. Participants also emphasized the indisputable nature of black women's past and present contributions to Pan-African struggle, the need for reorienting black American activists' attitudes about gender hierarchies in political organizing, and the importance of developing a diasporically minded ideology that could account for black women's gender-specific experiences with racist and imperialist oppression. Activists circulated and published many of these papers and resolutions after the Sixth PAC, broadening the event's impact and foregrounding the potential of these meetings to foster new ideas about black womanhood within Pan-African organizing.[89]

In an untitled working paper, delegation members offered their insights into how to reshape popular ideas about women's roles in Pan-African organizing. The Sixth PAC participants framed the document as an examination of "political activists in North America" and the racial, gendered, and economic "conditions peculiar to North America." Although their focus was largely U.S. based, workshop members indicated that they were looking to develop new, multifaceted ideas about black women's "community involvement." They argued that retheorizing their roles within the American context could help broaden their struggle and align it with those of women across the diaspora.[90]

From the outset, the group indicated that the goal of the paper was not simply to justify the importance of women to Pan-African organizing; it was to identify some of the primary ways in which conservative gender politics had hindered their participation in Pan-African liberation struggles. They based their commentary on the claim that "the question of women in the struggle [was] not a question of creating a role for women"; rather, the "question [was] the nature of the role of women in the struggle in the *minds* of women, men, and children" (emphasis in the original). The Sixth PAC participants argued that the real issue at stake within the North American context was "that the 'freedom' of women [was] dependent upon men, children, and women casting aside the mind sets and lifestyles which perpetuate the practice that women are caretakers, sex objects, and clerics, only."[91] With this goal in mind, participants documented how activists could disrupt patriarchal attitudes and practices and foster more gender-inclusive understandings of Pan-Africanism and women's roles within it.

Chief among their suggestions was a collective reorientation of activists' conceptions of Pan-African organizing and political work. Delegation members emphasized that no group could "improve world system[s]" if they did not consider the ways in which "work must be organized so that women can actively participate." They argued that there was a "deliberate need for support systems," including childcare and political education programs for men, women, and children, to "make a woman's work meaningful and productive toward the liberation of African people."[92] Their solution: a different model of mobilizing. Participants called on activists to eschew top-down approaches to movement building in favor of a small-cell or cadre model of political organizing. Not only would this method ensure that women's needs and emancipatory visions were integrated into political organizing, it would also help reshape traditional attitudes and mind-sets about women's political and intellectual work.

Delegation members also postulated that anti-intellectual characterizations of women impeded the development of the Pan-African ideologies that undergirded their political work. The group maintained that "women's brains [were] able to conceptualize struggle as well as men's" and that they could discuss "ideology to a mixed audience just as easily as they [could] discuss ideology on a panel for [a] women's workshop or conference." They asserted that U.S.-based activists needed to fundamentally rethink their lionization of male leaders as the preeminent Pan-African theorists and recognize that black women were equally capable of interpreting and formulating global black liberation theories. To neglect to do so, they argued, was "to deny [their] people and [the] cause of half of its capacity for struggle."[93] It was also to run the risk, as women from other delegations noted, of adopting Pan-African schemas without interrogating their applicability to particular geopolitical and gender-specific frames. Viewing ideological debate and development as a central component of the Pan-African Woman's role would aid organizers in their goal of developing nuanced understandings of diasporic struggle and liberation. Accordingly, U.S. Sixth PAC participants insisted on black women's theoretical acuity and cast them as capable ideologues poised to develop a "correct" analysis of racism, imperialism, and black struggle.

Changing attitudes about women's ideological acumen also meant challenging beliefs about black manhood. Participants argued that healthy debate about black Americans' relationship and potential contributions to diasporic struggles was a prerequisite for creating new theories of Pan-African liberation. Such consensus could only be achieved, they reasoned, if activists relinquished American-centered, Moynihan-inspired ideas about black male emasculation. As they did in their other organizations, the female delegates asserted the importance of intragender support. However, they rejected conceptions of black manhood that rested on men's unquestioned monopoly on political and ideological leadership. Here again they argued that this approach to gender roles had important implications for the study and practice of Pan-Africanism, noting, "If a man cannot be disagreed with for his manhood's sake, and our womanhood's sake, we develop paper tigers unable to engage in the realities of revolution. Everyone loses when [women] do not question, demand and have input into the ideology espoused as the correct line for our people to follow."[94] Workshop participants suggested that existing ideas about black manhood and gender hierarchies crippled the larger Pan-African liberation project. Just as black women needed to re-define their worldview and priorities in order to advance global black libera-tion, so too did Pan-African emancipation depend on men's reorientation of their gendered political self-conception.

If Moore's AAWC speech established black American women's contri-butions to the Pan-African past, then Sixth PAC delegates charted their role in the future of it. Female delegates and observers used Sixth PAC workshops to engage in discussions about how to change traditional and apolitical char-acterizations of their roles, confront gender hierarchies within Pan-African organizing, and develop inclusive and experientially minded theories of the relationship between U.S.-based liberation struggles and those taking place around the world. Theorizing in this heterogeneous context also caused them to develop ideas about gender roles grounded in their geopolitical context. The North American Delegation continued to assert the linked fate of black peoples worldwide. However, a concern with American-based attitudes about gender roles and Pan-African organizing ran throughout this and other congress documents. They were interested in developing a new conception of women's roles that, like Moore's, laid claim to their Afri-can heritage while also asserting the specificity of their contemporaneous conditions.

Their efforts coalesced into a different understanding of Pan-Africanism and women's roles within it. Sixth PAC participants' calls for women to de-velop and engage in "meaningful and productive" work not only centered black women in Pan-African projects, they also countered largely symbolic and ahistorical characterizations of their roles and work. Workshop mem-bers' emphasis on gender-inclusive ideological debates cast women as cru-cial Pan-Africanist ideologues and asserted that any theory of global black liberation that did not include women's perspectives was inadequate and incomplete. Their insistence on changing the attitudes of men not only framed women as equally powerful Pan-African actors, it also belied conceptual frameworks that equated Pan-African liberation with the restoration of black manhood. In their efforts to hammer out women's historically and culturally specific roles in Pan-African organizing, women at the Sixth PAC made concrete steps in developing a nuanced and materially grounded conception of women's roles in diasporic organizing. They also laid the groundwork for delegation members to develop more rigorous and inclusive definitions of Pan-Africanism at home and abroad.

Some of these ideas and themes would make their way into the North American Delegation's official position on women presented at the end of the congress. "Women's Contribution to Pan-African Struggle," a paper included in the "General Summary of Positions" of the North American Delegation, summarized American delegates' perspectives put forth before and throughout the event. A three-part document in which delegates enumerated black women's "ancient," "modern," and "future" contributions to Pan-African organizing, the resolution functioned as a critique of women's historical and contemporaneous exclusion within congress documents and debate. It also served as an index of the delegation's shifting perceptions on women's roles in global black liberation efforts.

The delegation opened the resolution by recapitulating the history of black advancement through the lens of black women's activism and leadership. Echoing Moore's AAWC speech, they framed the diaspora as emerging from a single African lineage that the "ancient African woman" advanced and refined. Delegates noted that historically, this woman "took her place as an equal in society in which she made many valid contributions to her family, as the mother of civilizations . . . to warfare as an inventive tactician . . . to economics as the mistress of the marketplace and the inventor of agriculture." These contributions, they argued, positioned women of African descent at the vanguard of the Pan-African liberation struggle.[95]

Delegation leaders offered a litany of examples attesting to women's "modern" efforts at sustaining and liberating the diaspora. They emphasized how black women had made their mark in the "area of politics," citing the activism of women such as "Fannie Lou Hamer, Rosa Parks, Madame Cissie, Queen Mother Moore, [and] Shirley Dubois," as well as "the many African women who are soldiers in the liberation armies of Guinea Bissau and Mozambique." Such women, they noted, had fought to maintain their homes and families in the face of "highly oppressive system[s]." They had also developed alternative, Pan-African-inspired community schools such as Gertrude Wilks's Nairobi School in East Palo Alto, California.[96] The delegation credited women with being important "preserver[s] of health and ... curer[s] of illness" and with playing a "vital role in the economic management of the community." Summarizing black women's activism, they concluded that the black woman's role had "always been one of continuous contribution whenever and wherever the need arose. Her traditional role, as a functional contributor to society as a whole, has reasserted itself even after 400 years of limitations, blunting of spirit and overt oppression."[97]

The delegation then used this history of black women's activism as the basis for their pronouncements about black women in prospective Pan-African organizing. Going forward, they argued, "there should be a strong emphasis on the 'harmonious dualism' of pre-colonial African societies" or a "recreation of unity between men and women, a unity in which the African woman stands beside, not behind, not ahead of, the African man." Sixth PAC participants envisioned this gendered unity as "characterized by [women's] mutual support and leadership in all spheres—home, battlefield, workforce, and community." They also suggested that black women reaffirm their solidarity with "African women, and men, toward the end of self-determination and a strong united Africa" by strengthening their "commitment to and participation in the Pan-African liberation struggle" and by making "concrete moves to eliminate racism, capitalism, imperialism, and neo-colonialism, through boycotts etc."[98]

This final position paper reflected delegates' preoccupation with redefining black women's roles in Pan-African organizing and the limitations of this exercise within an American-centered Pan-African framework. The first half of the resolution indicated their interest in centering and acknowledging black women as critical members of the historical and contemporary Pan-African community. The "ancient" contributions section notably recapitulated traditional narratives of a universal African past, while the "modern" contributions section framed black American women as Pan-African Women by rhetorically fusing their "modern" contributions with those of other women across the diaspora, blurring the boundaries between their activism, goals, and identities and those of women in other regions. This promoted a unified but falsely inscribed understanding of Pan-African identification and community among black women. It also situated U.S.-based black women as leaders in the diaspora's ongoing quest for cultural reidentification and self-determination.

In the "future recommendations" section, delegates once again attempted to reconcile their U.S.-centered view of Pan-Africanism with a more nuanced idea of women's and men's roles. On the one hand, they promulgated an idea of the Pan-African Woman as an activist who ascribed to the Kawaida-derived "African Value System" and an idealized understanding of "pre-colonial societies." Such frameworks, often promoted by cultural nationalist groups such as CFUN and CAP, offered the promise of "re-Africanization" without attending to the temporal, regional, and ethnic heterogeneity of African histories and cultures.[99] On the other hand, the document included statements that eschewed cultural and political abstraction and gestured toward a more nuanced interpretation of Pan-African identification based on political analysis and coalition building. Delegates' prescriptions for women to invest their energies in "Pan-African solidarities" and "concrete" efforts to eliminate racism created openings for women to develop new definitions of black womanhood rooted in their lived experiences with racism and imperialism.

Other aspects of delegates' prognostications for the future of the Pan-African Woman were more progressive. The statement directly countered hierarchical concepts of gender roles imbedded in existing Pan-African frameworks. Participants' assertion that the Pan-African Woman stood "beside, not behind or ahead" of, her male counterpart was an unequivocal statement of support for women's equality. Furthermore, their contention that women were leaders in "all spheres" of work challenged claims—most notably put forth by Kawaida practitioners—that women's "natural" roles were in the areas of child-rearing and education.[100] Reporters covering the event for the Tanzania *Daily News* noted that, throughout the congress, there was a consistent call for the Pan-African world to "do something about its womenfolk."[101] By the end of the congress, the North American Delegation members had responded, rhetorically disavowing hegemonic gender hierarchies and gesturing toward more inclusive models of Pan-African organizing.

These final resolutions reflected black women activists' concerted efforts to center and challenge debates about black womanhood from the planning stages of the congress until its end. Soon after Augusto drafted the "Call to Congress," women across organizations and ideological affiliations responded, offering their support and labor to make the meeting a success. More than simply providing the organizational infrastructure for the event, they used the meeting to reimagine their roles in Pan-African organizing in their respective activist circles. They also brought this perspective to bear on their congress activism. In regional and national meetings, workshops, working papers, and formal resolutions, U.S.-based women asserted their centrality to past and present Pan-African projects and their investment in reformulating the intersection of black womanhood and Pan-African praxis. They also emphasized the importance of developing a holistic and inclusive concept of global black liberation.

Similar to the women who redeveloped the African Woman ideal, women at the Sixth PAC simultaneously relied on and eschewed the dominant theories of Pan-Africanism that circulated among members of the American delegation. Many in the largely male contingent proffered a model of Pan-Africanism that positioned black women as the symbolic mothers and molders of the nation. Women at the Dar es Salaam meeting used aspects of this discourse to their advantage, employing similar rhetoric and ideas to emphasize their centrality to Pan-African projects and to center their personal and political needs. They then concurrently challenged the conservative gender constructs that undergirded U.S.-centric ideas about African liberation and offered astute analyses of how women's unique position within racialized imperialist schemas could be the genesis of more nuanced Pan-African liberation projects. In the end, the North American Delegation proffered an idea of a Pan-African female organizer who, like the African Woman, was immersed in an undifferentiated Pan-African framework yet simultaneously dedicated to vanquishing the conservative gender hierarchies on which this framework so often rested. Their progressive approaches were not enough to completely overturn the masculinist impulses of the delegation. Nevertheless, female delegates' workshop papers and resolutions—along with the North American Delegation's final pronouncements about the Pan-African Woman—reveal black women activists' investment and influence in developing a model of womanhood that was more progressive and intersectional than their Kawaidist counterparts or male activists had initially projected. At a moment when activists the world over were rethinking the meaning and substance of global black liberation, female participants used these openings to encourage their fellow organizers to develop more precise analyses of Pan-Africanism and women's roles within it.

The Sixth PAC ended with a series of declarations rather than concrete political or social actions. As Sylvia Hill noted in her post hoc analysis of the meeting, one of the "most striking features of the Congress discussions and speeches was how little [participants] were able to develop a program as a people." In her estimation, they were bogged down with "verbalizing the problem" and were therefore unable to develop concrete programs for Pan-African liberation.[102] The final Sixth PAC resolutions and outcomes confirmed Hill's assessment. By the end of the meeting, participants had vowed to "completely restore the dignity of African people through the building of socialism" and to "exclude all racial, tribal, ethnic, and religious considerations in the development of Pan Africanism."[103] This statement in support of the class side of the two-line struggle led many to conclude that the "Marxists were in command" of the event.[104] Participants' emphasis on race and class orthodoxies led most analysts to characterize the Sixth PAC as a moment of political possibility undercut by ideological factionalism. The lack of concrete results from the meeting further undergirded these negative assessments. By the close of the congress, delegates did not make provisions to create a permanent Pan-African secretariat, nor did they establish a date and place for the next congress. Accordingly, many viewed the meeting as a tactical failure.[105]

Nevertheless, the Sixth PAC did strengthen ties among black activists and organizers across the Atlantic. The meeting offered the opportunity for women and men from North America to solidify real and imagined bonds with African countries and cultures and offer tangible support to African liberation groups. The North American Delegation brought three hundred pounds of medicine for and donated blood to anticolonial liberation fighters. As Hill pointed out, "this was concrete support that did not just happen"; it was the result of coordinated efforts among black peoples across the globe, and the gesture fostered a shared sense of solidarity across ideological and factional lines. Organizers also noted that leaders of African countries and communities welcomed members of the North American Delegation, allowing them to "reaffirm [their] relations to [their] homeland" and fostering their interest in further linking their movements for freedom throughout the black world.[106] Although the Sixth PAC highlighted the impossibility of uniting the diaspora under a single, consolidated Pan-African agenda, it played an important role in cultivating global black political consciousness through the creation and circulation of documents aimed at redefining and refining the future of Pan-African advocacy.[107]

Congress participants' final "Resolution on Black Women," was an overlooked outcome of the event. The collective statement was both an affirmation of women's activism and a challenge to male-centered conceptions of Pan-Africanism. The document unfolded in two sections: a series of considerations followed by a statement of resolutions for participants to adopt. Leaders opened by asking activists and readers to consider that black women were "playing a key role in the revolutionary struggles against imperialism and racism"; that they "have historically suffered a triple oppression of race, class, and sex"; that black women "in capitalist countries serve[d] as workers and [were] an integral part of production"; and that "black women [had] too often been relegated to secondary, perfunctory positions with mechanical functions in our organisations and have not been allowed to develop to their fullest political and social consciousness." They also suggested that organizers take note of the fact that "women are equal to man [*sic*] in all respects and they should be looked upon as sisters and comrades-in-the-struggle."[108]

In line with this analysis, delegates ended the resolution with resounding statements of support for women's equality and inclusion in Pan-African organizing. They announced their intent to give their "full support of the political struggles being waged by Black women" and called on "states and organisations represented at the Congress to address themselves to the question of women's oppression in a more thorough manner."[109] Although the issue of women's equality was not a central point of discussion at the congress, female participants transformed the Sixth PAC into an event in which delegates from across the globe acknowledged their equality to men and indispensability to Pan-African liberation.

If the goal of the Sixth PAC was to chart a new course for Pan-African organizing, then this final resolution reflected the inroads women had made in showing that masculinist conceptions of Pan-African identity and community were insufficient for the task at hand. They maintained that global liberation required all members of the Pan-African community to change their "attitudes" about womanhood, manhood, and women's work. Black women activists also argued that their intersectional oppression made them the ideal activists to develop new holistic emancipatory practices. The "Resolution on Women" reflected these points, discursively linking Pan-African liberation and black women's liberation rather than subsuming the latter in the former. The resolution also identified and named the intersecting racist, imperialist, and sexist forces at work in black women's oppression and the importance of viewing women as political actors in their own right. Ultimately, the document echoed female participants' efforts to problematize conventional constructions of diasporic publics, as well as their interest in forging new models of womanhood that did not rely on masculinist and essentialist interpretations of Pan-African identity or community.

For many women, discussions and experiences at the Sixth PAC transformed their identification with Africa and their subsequent internationalist activism. As organizer Judy Claude recalled, "there was an idealism about Africa in general, [and] Tanzania in particular" that "drove a lot of folk" before they attended the international meeting. Afterward, she noted, "that idealism remained or it died."[110] Audley Moore was one of the women for whom the optimism endured. She viewed the Sixth PAC as the culmination of years of Pan-African organizing that included ALD and the AAWC. While in Tanzania, she remarked, "This is the most historic occasion that has happened in the world thus far as the African people are concerned. To me it is rewarding, for I have lived to see the fruits of our efforts.... Africans tell us, this is your home—Come live with us."[111]

For others, the Sixth PAC spurred their interest in conducting globally conscious political work at home. Sylvia Hill recalled that her "commitments" to antiapartheid work stemmed from participation in the Sixth PAC.[112] After the conference, she relocated to Washington, D.C., and founded the Southern Africa News Collective. This group evolved into the Southern Africa Support Project, an organization that raised funds on behalf of liberation struggles in Zimbabwe, Namibia, and South Africa. Hill, Cecelie Counts, Sandra Hill, and other members of the organization provided material assistance to these countries and organized solidarity protests, particularly at the South African embassy, that catalyzed the Free South Africa Movement.[113]

Africa, and, in particular, Tanzania, continued to be an epicenter of organizing for other black women activists.[114] After the Sixth PAC, Geri Augusto remained in Tanzania and worked as an editor at the Tanzania Publishing House. She helped edit congress documents and produce *Resolutions and Selected Speeches from the Sixth Pan-African Congress*, one of several anthologies of Sixth PAC proceedings and resolutions.[115] Claude also stayed in Tanzania after the congress to study its transition from a former British colony to an independent socialist state.[116] Edie Wilson completed her doctorate in the United States and returned to Tanzania in 1976.[117]

As ALSC secretary Brenda Paris noted, international events such as the AAWC and Sixth PAC were "instrumental in giving [black American women] a worldview."[118] Indeed, the rise of Pan-African-inspired international events and meetings in the 1970s offered black American women new opportunities to advance their African identifications and self-determination on a global scale. These activists brought this perspective to bear on their Black Power–era goal of racial and gendered redefinition. They experimented with creating new concepts of black womanhood guided by a Pan-African rather than an American political frame. In striving to develop a new understanding of Pan-Africanism that could meet their needs, they intervened in male-dominated conversations about the contours of Pan-Africanism and men's and women's roles in diasporic struggle. Although they may have fallen short of completely upending the prevailing Pan-Africanist frameworks, their speeches, position papers, and documents gestured toward dynamic alternatives to the static ideas of African unity that many leaders on both sides of the Atlantic espoused. Analyses of Pan-Africanism and international Black Power organizing have often overlooked the importance of black women's participation in international proceedings. Yet through their engagement at these events, they refined Pan-African ideologies and redoubled their efforts to cast themselves as vital political actors in the international arena.

Chief among their claims was the idea that contemporaneous conceptualizations of Pan-Africanism suffered from more than just oversimplified ideas about race and class; they were also hampered by patriarchal outlooks. By the time delegates gathered for the Sixth PAC, U.S.-based activists were deeply entrenched in debates over the primacy of race or class in global liberation schemas. Black women activists challenged this dichotomy at international meetings and events. Whether in their speeches to the AAWC or in working groups at the Sixth PAC, they refused to assert the primacy of one form of oppression over the other, instead insisting that female Pan-Africanists should take a leading role in addressing the simultaneous manifestations of white domination. Moreover, they consistently foregrounded instances in which black women were the victims not only of racism and imperialism but also of the white, heteronormative gender constructs that these systems supported. Sixth PAC participants also proffered an idea of Pan-Africanism and diasporic activism that implicitly or explicitly eschewed patriarchy and argued that the ideal female activist rejected all of these forms of oppression. Not only did their political writings challenge the binary of the two-line struggle, they also injected an intersectional ethos into conversations about the contours of late twentieth-century Pan-Africanism.

Black American women's ideas about Pan-African Womanhood also challenged dominant, male-centered discourses about Pan-African subjectivity and liberation. In their speeches and working papers, these organizers disputed black male leadership's claim to ideological and organizational authority and framed the ideal female Pan-Africanist as a capable political actor and theorist. In the process, they disrupted historical and contemporary associations among nationalism, masculinity, and Pan-Africanism and highlighted the impossibility of subordinating the "woman question" when charting the future of global black revolt. Their debates over women's roles in organizing underlined the stakes of Pan-African ideology and clarified the importance of integrating a gender critique into the "correct analysis" of global black struggle. In the 1970s, Black Power activists embraced Pan-Africanism as a higher and more rigorous emancipatory framework than their earlier nationalist formulations. Black women argued that Pan-African liberation schemas had to incorporate a more equitable and nuanced conception of women's roles and goals in order to reach the next plane of ideological and political struggle.

The drive to integrate Pan-Africanism and their gender-specific concerns galvanized women across the Black Power political spectrum. Spurred on by international liberation struggles, they actively pursued some form of Pan-Africanism that combined their desires for international black liberation and an end to women's "special oppression." Many of these women looked to African liberation struggles and African countries to find examples of how to integrate their race and gender identities. Others drew inspiration from women in Latin American and Asian countries. While women such as Audley Moore and Alberta Hill visited Tanzania, other activists, including Gwendolyn Patton and Frances Beal, traveled to Cuba and Chile, interacting with activists there whom they found to be fruitful models of women's radical political activism. Encouraged by the anticolonial struggles and collectives they witnessed, they theorized new forms of black womanhood with these Third World liberation models in mind.

CHAPTER FIVE

The Third World Black Woman, 1970–1979

Summits like the Sixth Pan-African Congress heightened Black Power activists' expectations for liberation on the African continent. They also stimulated their real and imagined connections with men and women in the Third World. While women in the Congress of African People (CAP) expressed their global consciousness through Pan-African-inspired organizing, other activists developed separate groups aimed at forging a black and Third World political front. The Third World Women's Alliance (TWWA), a multiracial coalition created and led by black women, spearheaded this facet of Black Power organizing. By the early 1970s, the women's group became a critical part of the U.S. Third World Left, a collection of activists who created material and ideological links with people of color in African, Asian, and Latin American countries in order to critique the U.S. social and political order.[1]

The roots of the TWWA lay in the Student Nonviolent Coordinating Committee (SNCC), which, by the late 1960s, championed a globally minded, anti-imperialist position expressed through Black Power politics and rhetoric. As the organization evolved, female members created an ad hoc group—the Black Women's Liberation Committee (BWLC)—to address black women's roles and goals within SNCC's increasingly nationalist and internationalist agenda. Eventually, the BWLC evolved into the TWWA. From 1970 to 1979, the alliance functioned as a separate women's group with the goal of achieving black liberation, self-determination, and self-sufficiency through an antisexist, antiracist, and anti-imperialist agenda.

TWWA leaders envisioned the organization as a collection of "black and other third world women" working together to fight "all forms of racist, sexist, and economic exploitation."[2] They developed a body of literature aimed at redefining black womanhood with this Third World perspective in mind. Whereas their contemporaries emphasized black women's domestic and diasporic identifications, TWWA members were expressly interested in developing a political identity that was predicated on their commonalities with other women of color around the world. As the multiethnic coalition evolved, leading members further refined their approach. They cast black women as distinct political actors within the group and insisted that defining black womanhood through a Third World frame bolstered rather than abated their efforts to restructure gender hierarchies and advance Black Power organizing.

Through a sophisticated combination of editorials, articles, interviews, and illustrations in their newspaper, *Triple Jeopardy*, TWWA members rhetorically and imagistically blurred the lines between the identities and problematics of black women and other women of color. What emerged was the concept of the Third World Black Woman: an activist who recognized the commonalities of oppression among women of color and the potential of a multivalent ideological approach to eradicating them. Alliance members championed the ideal of a radical black female activist who infused feminist and socialist principles into her race-based political organizing and who approached her political activism from an anti-imperialist, internationalist perspective. Equipped with this expansive ideal, TWWA members challenged contemporaneous concepts of black women's roles in Black Power organizing and advocated for the emancipatory potential of reimagining black womanhood with black women's race, class, and gender oppression and liberation in mind.

A robust and rigorous ideological framework undergirded the alliance's elastic conception of black womanhood. Composed of organizers who had also been active in civil rights, Black Power, antiwar, and women's rights organizations, the TWWA rejected dogmatic theoretical approaches and adopted a political philosophy that appreciated the simultaneity of black women's subjugation and emancipatory potential. Its members consistently articulated a multifaceted political ideology that hewed elements from socialism, black nationalism, and feminism. They also insisted on the impossibility and ineffectiveness of distinguishing between these ideological commitments in pursuing black women's liberation.

The TWWA's intersectional approach extended and expanded movement principles and thought throughout the 1970s, and past the point that many consider to be the heyday of Black Power.[3] The organization was established within Black Power organizing circles and guided by members' interest in developing a model of black womanhood that could account for their liberatory goals. Organizers reconciled these commitments through the Third World Black Woman, proffering a political identity and an organizing agenda that deployed central Black Power tenets and resolved movement problematics in gender- and class-specific ways. Not only did this generate rhetorical and tangible spaces in which black women could promote and practice core Black Power principles, members' expansive interpretations of the era's central ideas and goals also garnered a broader base of support for movement causes. Using the Third World Black Woman ideal, TWWA members reshaped contemporaneous debates about black womanhood and movement organizing. They also reinforced and bolstered Black Power projects, popularized them among black women and other women of color, and formalized black women activists' long-standing commitment to intersectional theorizing and activism.

Black Power, Anti-imperialism, and the Third World

Insurgent political movements at home and abroad accelerated the appeal of a Third World–focused women's organization. TWWA members came of age in the midst of the 1950s Cold War division of the globe, in which First World nations attempted to use African, Latin American, and Asian countries as chess pieces, aiming to collect them for their communist and anticommunist empires. Postwar-era activists voiced their unequivocal support of the African and Asian nations that refused to be pawns in this game. Whether through their participation in the meeting of Third World nations at the 1955 Asian-African Conference in Bandung, Indonesia; their championing of African states and state leaders; or their support of Latin American anticolonial liberation struggles, many activists agreed with Alice Childress's domestic worker character, Mildred: First World governments should stop their "pussyfootin' pretense" and recognize Third World nations' right to be free.[4]

Postwar activists' cultural and political critiques paved the way for the evolution of the U.S.-based Third World leftist front of the 1960s. Inspired by their predecessors—and leaders such as Fidel Castro in Cuba, Kwame Nkrumah in Ghana, and Mao Zedong in the People's Republic of China— Black Power organizers formulated the next phase of black internationalist organizing by forging real and imagined connections between the experiences of "U.S. minorities and Third World majorities in a moment of global decolonization."[5] Across organizations and ideological perspectives, activists drew parallels between the American government's treatment of black Americans at home and the treatment of people of color abroad fighting the crushing weight of colonial regimes. Linking their social justice struggles with those of people in Latin America, Africa, and Asia, Black Power activists became vital supporters of the global anti-imperialist insurgency that characterized late 1960s and early 1970s.

Founding TWWA members were originally organizers in SNCC, a group that, by 1967, was becoming an integral part of the U.S. Third World front. Organized and mentored by globally minded activist Ella Baker, SNCC organizers were well aware of the long tradition of transnationalism and anticolonialism imbedded in the black organizing tradition.[6] From its beginning, the student-led organization took a "concerted interest in anti-colonialism and nationalism on the African continent and throughout the Third World," championing this position before it gained widespread popularity in the early 1970s.[7] Whether through their formal statements of support for African liberation struggles or members' treks to West African countries, the organization was at the forefront of challenging antiapartheid struggles in Africa and the United States.[8]

Initially, SNCC workers balanced their internationalist inclinations with a concentrated effort to win civil rights at home. Through a decentralized, grassroots voting and civil rights campaign, members successfully expanded the black American electorate, challenged systemic white supremacy, and expedited the passage of federal civil rights legislation.[9] The group of interracial student organizers found that integrating political parties was not enough to dismantle white political and economic supremacy. Despite their concerted national efforts to level the racial playing field, by the late 1960s, the majority of black Americans remained trapped in low-paying jobs, shut out of political offices, and barred from most educational and cultural spaces.

SNCC activists formally adopted Black Power strategies—including separatist organizing and support of self-defense—in an attempt to subvert white political hegemony. Many in the group were well aware of black activists' long tradition of armed, black-centered organizing, particularly in the South.[10] Since SNCC's founding in 1960, black volunteers endorsed these principles more as a "pragmatic judgment" than as an "absolute principle."[11] After member Stokely Carmichael's famous June 1966 call for "Black Power," members codified this position as the organization's official doctrine. Between 1966 and 1968, SNCC workers created independent black political parties, expelled white members from the group, and formed a short-lived alliance with the Black Panther Party in Oakland, California.[12]

The student organizers also began to foreground their Third World–inspired, anti-imperialist critique of U.S. policies and practices. They voiced their support for a host of international causes ranging from anti-apartheid protests to Caribbean liberation movements.[13] Their public opposition to the Vietnam War garnered the most attention. In January 1966, SNCC organizers published a statement detailing their opposition to the conflict. In it, members denounced the American government's intervention into Vietnam and linked the treatment of the Vietnamese people with the oppression of people of color in Africa, Latin America, and, most notably, the United States. In the following months, members engaged in antiwar and antidraft demonstrations and traveled to Vietnam to report on the effects of American imperialism firsthand.[14] SNCC's leftward turn—manifested in its stalwart critique of U.S. foreign policy, expulsion of white liberals, and endorsement of separatist organizing—caused the group to lose critical financial support. It also drew the ire of the Johnson administration and cost the collective valuable allies within the local and federal government.[15]

If the loss of outside support handicapped SNCC, then internal ideological fissures hastened its dissolution. By 1968, SNCC activists, centralized in collectives in cities such as Atlanta, New York, and Washington, D.C., were pursuing increasingly divergent paths to black liberation. Some organizers continued to push for separatism and black nationalism, a stance that Carmichael made famous but that Atlanta volunteers such as Gwendolyn Robinson had originally postulated and supported. In early 1966, Georgia-based members argued that white participation hindered black organizing and that black Americans should organize themselves in their own communities. To achieve this, SNCC should "cut [itself] off from white people" and form its "own institutions, credit unions, co-ops."[16] In the following years, the city continued to be the epicenter of SNCC's Black Power thrust. Other members, such as Geri Augusto, Judy Richardson, and Jennifer Lawson, congregated in the nation's capital, intent on integrating a Pan-African perspective into their grassroots activism. These organizers helped create and staff the Center for Black Education and the Drum and Spear Bookstore, institutions that fostered Pan-African education and protest.[17] Another collection of activists ran SNCC's International Affairs Commission in New York City. Headed by James Forman, and staffed by Mae Jackson and Frances Beal, among others, the commission worked to integrate SNCC's Black Power and anti-imperialist politics, most notably through their position papers on the Vietnam War and South African apartheid.[18] According to Forman, the collective was expressly interested in "inject[ing] an anti-imperialist position" into SNCC and into the movement as a whole.[19]

SNCC workers were not the only ones thinking in global terms. The Vietnam War—and the wide-ranging antiwar movement that developed to counter it—brought activists' debates about imperialism, globalization, and self-determination to the fore. Innovations in print culture helped bridge experiential and theoretical gaps among activists around the globe, while the desegregation and modernization of travel collapsed geographical divides among people of color worldwide.[20] Black educators, activists, and students learned about Third World independence struggles through Black Power organizations' vibrant print culture, which included periodicals such as the *Black Panther* and the Youth Organization for Black Unity's paper, *African World*. Organizers such as SNCC workers Ruby Doris Smith Robinson and Fannie Lou Hamer now trekked through Africa and Asia in an effort to witness independence struggles and decolonized African nations firsthand.[21] Other young activists—including several future members of the TWWA—participated in international exchanges such as the Venceremos Brigade, a program that offered American students the opportunity to live and work in postrevolution, Castro-led Cuba.[22] By the late 1960s, black activists across the movement were becoming increasingly convinced of the need to align their domestic battles with Third World liberation movements abroad.

Exposure to women abroad also refined black women's ideas about gender equality at home. Images, firsthand accounts, and news reports of women fighting on the front lines in liberation struggles in Africa and Vietnam contrasted sharply with black male leaders' calls for black women to remain on the margins of political activity within the United States. SNCC was at the epicenter of these debates about gender roles within liberatory organizing. During its 1964 "Freedom Summer" voter registration initiative, female volunteers began to raise questions about sexism within the movement. When organizers met the following November in Waveland, Mississippi, veteran white activists Casey Hayden and Mary King were among a group of women who circulated a then-anonymous memo in which they claimed that "competent, qualified, and experienced" women in the group were "automatically assigned to the 'female' kinds of jobs" due to gender bias.[23] Black women framed their experiences differently. Cynthia Washington, for example, found that black women's "skills and abilities were recognized and respected." However, she also noted that their black male counterparts often failed to recognize how sexism and patriarchy mediated other aspects of their political organizing and organizational culture.[24] SNCC women's divergent viewpoints were emblematic of, and part of, the impetus behind the surge in feminist organizing in this period. By the late 1960s, parallel white and black feminist movements developed, replete with separate organizations, publications, and strategies aimed at ending sexism and racist patriarchal structures.[25]

These issues of sexism plagued SNCC as it evolved into a Black Power organization. Despite its democratic ethos, the organization did not escape the contemporaneous Moynihan-inspired rhetoric that framed black women leaders as "castrators" and endorsed the marginalization of women in political organizing. Black women in SNCC recognized the paradox of this patriarchal position. As New York–based member Frances Beal wrote, "Since the advent of Black power, the Black male has exerted a more prominent leadership role in our struggle for justice in this country. He sees the system for what it really is for the most part, but where he rejects its values and mores on many issues, when it comes to women, he seems to take his guidelines from the pages of the *Ladies Home Journal*."[26] Beal's statement epitomized the perspective of many black women in SNCC. They supported Black Power, black manhood, and black male empowerment. Yet these activists questioned how their male contemporaries could champion the demise of racism and capitalism but be content to keep patriarchy intact.

Beal was one of the many women in the group who began to raise questions about the gender dynamics within the organization. Emboldened by the burgeoning feminist movements unfolding around her in New York City, she and other SNCC women started to assert the importance of gender equality, reproductive rights, and black women's race, class, and gender oppression in gatherings. In 1968, she presented a paper on the interrelationship of forced sterilization, class discrimination, and reproductive rights at a local SNCC meeting. This paper fostered conversations that would eventually become the basis for her groundbreaking polemic, "Double Jeopardy: To Be Black and Female." In this 1969 essay, Beal offered a searing critique of the oppressive elements of nationalist organizing; foregrounded the interrelationship of black women's race, gender, and class oppression; and politicized gender-specific issues such as sterilization and birth control.[27] Beal and other New York SNCC women's statements and essays sparked new ideological debates within the group and foregrounded the need for a distinct political identity and agenda for black women within the organization.

Other women in the group, including Gwendolyn Patton, approached these same issues from an anti-imperialist frame. Born in Detroit and raised in Montgomery, Alabama, amid the insurgency of local civil rights boycotts, Patton was swept up in grassroots black activism at an early age. As a student at the local, historically black Tuskegee University, she became a campus leader and a member of what she called a "close-knit, intellectual student movement." Her organizing led to her election as the first female student government president. She also joined SNCC and became an organizer with the original Black Panther Party in Lowndes County.[28]

The January 1966 murder of Patton's fellow Tuskegee student and SNCC organizer Sammy Younge fostered her black-centered, anti-imperialist outlook. Younge was one of the many black men drafted into the U.S. Navy to fight for democracy abroad only to find that neither their service nor their lives were valued at home. He returned to Alabama after two years in the armed service and organized with Patton at Tuskegee and within SNCC before he was shot to death for using a "white only" bathroom at a local gas station.[29] The young sailor's brutal murder catalyzed SNCC's antiwar position, in which activists like Patton compared his death to those of "peasants in Vietnam" gunned down by American troops.[30]

If Younge's death illustrated the importance of adopting an anti-imperialist position for Patton, then living and working among other SNCC women emphasized the indispensability of women to political struggle. As their contemporaries negotiated ideals like the Black Revolutionary Woman and the African Woman, Patton engaged in private conversations with activists including Faye Bellamy, Cynthia Washington, and Gwendolyn Robinson about the role of women in Black Power organizing.[31] In their correspondence, they recounted how they had "been doing a lot of things, reading, thinking, about the black woman's role in the revolution" and had come to the conclusion that "no revolution[, no matter] . . . where it is being fought, can be fought between men alone or by men alone." Citing examples from Africa, Algeria, Vietnam, and the American civil rights movement, they concluded that women "have always rebelled for a better way of life."[32]

By 1969, Patton, Beal, and a cohort of other SNCC women channeled their anti-imperialist, gender-inclusive politics through two organizations: the National Black Antiwar Antidraft Union (NBAWADU) and the BWLC. Patton was a founding member of both groups. She instituted NBAWADU in order to secure a "base" of support for black antiwar protests and address the racially specific effects of the war on black soldiers and families. Headquartered in Washington, D.C., the group held rallies and hosted conferences to call attention to the disproportionate number of black men drafted and to ideologically link black American struggles with factions fighting against American imperialism in Vietnam.[33]

As the executive secretary of the organization, Patton cultivated NBAWADU's unique focus on black women's experiences with racism and imperialism. She authored organizational pamphlets such as "For Us Women," which featured articles about how black women "could move to stop [the] system from drafting their sons," support antiwar efforts at home, and cope with the loss of loved ones abroad. In other articles, she foregrounded the parallels between the experiences of black and Vietnamese women under American regimes.[34] Patton also headed workshops on the role of black women in liberation struggles at NBAWADU's national conference in 1968. She encouraged black women to adopt militant, anti-imperialist politics and personas, often referencing Third World women as examples of how to enact these political and social roles.[35] Through Patton's efforts, NBAWADU fostered black women's ideological and organizational connections with other women of color. The organization also served as an intersectional and internationalist space in which SNCC women sharpened their analysis of and identification with the Third World.[36]

Patton encouraged black women to integrate this anti-imperialist frame with their gender-conscious Black Power politics in her BWLC organizing. The idea for the women's caucus developed amid informal discussions among SNCC workers, including Forman, Patton, and Beal. Early meeting notes indicate Patton's plans to gather veteran and young black women activists such as Mae Mallory, Jennifer Lawson, and Faye Bellamy together to "discuss ideology only."[37] After the initial group had established a rigorous theoretical position, they would develop a central committee and organizing platform that could "respond specifically to the needs of black women" within the Black Power movement. The BWLC was part of a proliferation of late 1960s collectives designed to debate and discuss the role of black women in black struggle. SNCC women envisioned it as a space in which they could discuss their relationships with black men and children, political organizing, and political theory.[38]

NBAWADU and the BWLC reflected black women activists' attempts to harness their Black Power, feminist, and internationalist commitments into a cohesive organizational structure and political identity. Coming of age in civil rights organizations that developed under the guidance of postwar, anticolonial activists, black women in SNCC were poised to lead the next phase of black internationalist organizing. Their experiences organizing in rural towns and city centers convinced them of the utility of Black Power politics and the futility of an isolationist approach to black liberation. The gender-specific challenges they faced in the political trenches made a women-centered group and political ideology imperative. As SNCC degenerated, Beal and Patton continued to invest their energy in the BWLC, dedicating initial meetings to examining black women's roles and responsibilities within Black Power, antiwar, and Third World independence struggles. In the process, they laid the organizational and theoretical foundation for the TWWA and the Third World Black Woman ideal.

Black Womanhood and the "Third World Concept"

In January 1969, Patton, along with other members of the organization's Central Committee, issued a call for the first national BWLC meeting to be held in Atlanta, Georgia, in March of that year. Committee members— Dorothy Dewberry, Frances Beal, Sandra F. Scott, and Ann Merritt— announced that this meeting would be the first in a series of gatherings convened to generate new ideas about the role of black women in Black Power organizing. In anticipation of the event, Patton disseminated a list of questions designed to foster debate. The activist argued that the time had come for black women to interrogate the ideological and discursive fictions that upheld Black Power activists' ideas about gender roles. She suggested that her questionnaire could be the basis for challenging prevailing gender constructs and generating new ideas about black womanhood within Black Power and antiwar movements.[39]

Patton's questionnaire was an integral part of the ideological and organizational scaffolding of the TWWA. Through this and other founding documents, BWLC members developed the language and theoretical infrastructure through which future alliance members would foreground the incompatibility of nationalism and sexism and emphasize the ideological bankruptcy of patriarchal approaches to emancipatory projects. Borrowing the term "rock bottom" from SNCC leader James Forman, who, in 1969, used it to describe the student group's ideological standstill, Patton began this conversation by printing "Let's Get Together Sisters. We Are Now at Rock Bottom and We Must Take Time Out Now!" at the top and bottom of the questionnaire.[40] Repurposing the phrase, and applying it to SNCC's stalemate over gender roles and political direction, Patton encouraged her fellow female activists to take on a leading role in developing a new gender-conscious and inclusive ideological and programmatic direction for the organization. Following the "rock bottom" statement, the BWLC leader listed collections of questions that she thought could help generate productive conversations. Categorized under headings such as "Female," "Male-Female," "Philosophy," and "Revolution," Patton argued that her queries had the potential to be the building blocks for a new personal, political, and philosophical approach to defining black womanhood.

Patton opened the questionnaire with the "Female" section, in which she asked, "What is a woman? What is her function and her purpose? . . . What are the functions of a woman in the American system?" The BWLC leader continued this line of questioning by asking SNCC women to think about their definition of womanhood in the context of political organizing. She suggested they contemplate the meaning of femininity and asked, if they accepted the "concept of the revolutionary woman[, would] it diminish [their] femininity?"[41] With these initial questions, Patton encouraged SNCC women to rethink conventional movement gender roles and primed them to take control over their political identifications and develop newer, more nuanced self-conceptions.

The "Revolution" section consisted of a set of inquires designed to push black women to establish their personal and political expectations and needs. Patton asked SNCC organizers to define the meaning of the revolution and verbalize what "the Revolution [would] offer to [their] people." The BWLC leader also encouraged them to clearly articulate their roles within the ideal revolutionary schema. "What do we mean by being a revolutionary?" she asked. "Can there be a revolutionary woman? If so, how does she think? What does she do? How does she move? . . . how does this differ from the roles ascribed to her by the American system?"[42] Patton maintained that a correct understanding of political struggle was a prerequisite for redefining women's role within it. She also underscored the importance of reimagining black womanhood in ways that defied rather than reified the dominant culture's gender roles.

Patton's questions in the "Philosophy" section built on the discussions she forged in NBAWADU and laid the groundwork for her fellow activists to formulate a gender-inclusive, Third World–focused ideological position. The BWLC leader began by asking her readers to define "communalism, socialism, communism," as well as "Fanonism, Nkrumahism, Pan-Africanism, Marxism." She then pivoted to the crux of this line of questioning: "Does the woman have any real role and purpose in these governments and philosophies?" and, if not, "should she?" Should SNCC women find that these existing ideological frameworks did not meet their needs, Patton offered a set of questions designed to help them develop more expansive theoretical constructs. She queried, "Should the black woman believe in the Third World Concept? If so, should she learn from the women in the Congo, Cuba, Algeria, People's China, Vietnam? If not, does she have to outline a new unique revolutionary program for oppressed women in the United

States of America?"[43] The BWLC leader stressed the importance of grounding their conceptions of black women's roles in a specific and inclusive political ideology. She also confirmed black women's ability to develop new ideological frameworks if existing ones did not sufficiently account for their gender-specific oppression and goals.

The BWLC questionnaire, in both form and substance, reflected black women's insurgent approaches to redefining black womanhood and Black Power–era political ideologies. By framing the discussion as a series of questions rather than as a set of statements, Patton suggested that gender roles within SNCC, and the movement at large, were fluid instead of fixed. Her open-ended queries also belied much of the didactic, top-down nature of existing political theorizing, allowing for black women to formulate their own varied responses to their central problematics rather than subscribing to a single mode of thinking. Most importantly, the question format challenged the permanency of existing ontologies of black womanhood within and outside the group and interrogated the emancipatory potential of contemporaneous political ideologies circulating in the public sphere. Not only did this approach prompt women within SNCC to develop new gendered political identities that fit their personal and political needs, it also fostered new forms of feminist organizing *within* Black Power organizations.

This inquiry-centered practice proved indispensable for the ideological and organizational development of the TWWA. Debates over the questions Patton posed helped future members conceive of themselves as political theorists capable of developing new concepts about Black Power, politics, and revolution. It also fostered their interest in redefining gender roles and black womanhood on their own terms—even if this meant developing new organizations and ideologies within which to work. Ultimately, Patton's questionnaire laid the foundation for the group to develop an autonomous political identity and ideological framework that accounted for the intersection of their race, gender, class, and anti-imperialist concerns.

The questionnaire also accelerated SNCC women's interest in identifying as Third World women and activists. As members of SNCC and NBAWADU, they continually asserted the similarities between black and Third World liberation struggles. In formative BWLC meetings, Patton encouraged her fellow activists to discern whether it was productive, or even possible, to build a model of black womanhood based on points of commonality among women of color globally. She also encouraged them to consider whether they could apply the frameworks and organizing models of Third World liberation struggles to their Black Power organizing in the

United States. By urging SNCC women to define their position on "the Third World concept," Patton laid the groundwork for future TWWA members to conceive of themselves as part of a multiracial, multiethnic group. She also encouraged them to develop a political self-conception that was grounded in Black Power struggles while simultaneously advancing their gender-specific concerns through a Third World framework.

Although the Atlanta meeting did not occur, a small collective of SNCC women met in New York in April 1969 to address Patton's questions. Along with a few other young activists, Patton and Beal determined that the primary goal of the BWLC was to develop a clear political philosophy about women's roles in black liberation. In order to create consensus, the collective discussed the main issues facing female Black Power activists. Chief among these were the traditional gender roles espoused by cultural nationalist activists, the personal and political effects of the Moynihan Report, and the importance of reproductive rights. Patton maintained that BWLC members saw "nothing wrong with cultural nationalism" as a theory but rejected the conservative gender roles that advocates espoused. Beal argued that capitalist-driven ideas about family and child-rearing hampered women's political participation. The collective determined that the BWLC would be an "anticaptialist, anti-imperialist" Black Power organization dedicated to achieving the full liberation of black women by rejecting "bourgeois" gender roles.[44] They planned to enact this platform through a series of grassroots political programs that included "Liberation Schools" for black activists and an antiwar draft counseling program for young black men.[45]

This expansive ideology and organizational agenda hastened the BWLC's evolution into the Black Women's Alliance (BWA). By the fall of 1969, members' political platform had garnered the attention of black women who were not affiliated with SNCC. Moreover, BWLC participants' internal conversations highlighted the necessity of expanding the group beyond the confines of SNCC, which was, by 1969, essentially defunct.[46] BWLC leaders severed their formal ties with their parent organization and allowed other black women organizers to join the group. Leaders adjusted the name of the collective to the Black Women's Alliance in order to reflect this change in membership.[47] In the waning months of 1969, the BWA functioned as "a radical black women's organization" and "think tank" designed to create a "revolutionary ideology" aimed at "improv[ing] the conditions of black people and particularly the condition of the black female."[48] During its short existence, BWA members made plans to "develop a political ideology around the oppression of Black Women," organize black laborers in hospitals and the garment industry, and develop committees to address black women's health and reproductive rights.[49]

The following spring, BWA members again found themselves questioning their ideological and organizational approach. According to Frances Beal, in the summer of 1970, several Puerto Rican women asked to join the group. This forced BWA members to reconsider their black-only membership roster. Some members thought that the BWA should remain a separate black women's organization. Others saw commonalities between their experiences and those of their Latina counterparts.[50] Reflecting on this moment, Beal recalled, "When we looked at the Puerto Rican sisters, we saw that they were trying to deal with both their national oppression of living in the United States and a kind of racial and class thing that was separate from just being a part of America as a whole, and then how does your gender fit in when you have this other overriding oppression."[51] Eventually, members concluded that the oppression that both groups of women faced, while not identical, was, in fact, similar. They recognized that they could not "express support for Africa, Asia, and Latin America and, at the same time, ignore non-Black Third World sisters in this country."[52] BWA members voted to open membership to other women of color and again changed the name of the group to reflect its shifting composition. Although it was now a multiracial and multiethnic group, as Stephen Ward has noted, the TWWA "remained grounded in, and responsive to, black political struggles."[53]

TWWA members spent the remaining months of 1970 developing an ideological platform that reflected the group's Black Power roots, Third World solidarities, anti-imperialist politics, and feminist commitments. Members eventually defined the group as an organization dedicated to struggling "against a racist, capitalist, and sexist system that oppresses all minority peoples as well as exploit[s] the majority."[54] In their founding documents, alliance organizers asserted that the "struggle against racism and imperialism [had to] be waged simultaneously with the struggle for women's liberation." They viewed the collective as a unique vehicle for uniting black and Third World women in their common goal of bringing about the liberation of all oppressed people.[55]

By early 1971, the alliance was an organizational force in New York City with a significant membership, consistent community programing, and a national news organ: *Triple Jeopardy*.[56] Leaders Pat Romney, Frances Beal, and Cheryl Johnson proselytized potential recruits at Sunday Afternoon Rap Sessions held at four o'clock in the afternoon at Saint Peter's Church in lower Manhattan.[57] In classes like the Feminine Stink Mystique, a course that addressed "attitudes about [Third World women's] bodies," TWWA leadership encouraged women to question common perceptions about gender roles and their appearance and function in society.[58] Other members, including Mary Stone and Barbara Rice, led political education classes for new recruits and veteran members.[59] In these sessions, members read historical essays and contemporary *Triple Jeopardy* articles in order help develop their analysis of their "triple oppression," or the ways in which their experiences with race, class, and gender discrimination intersected.[60] Alliance organizers Ann Burns and Ana Zentella then applied this intersectional analysis to everyday issues members and their communities faced, such as their lack of access to childcare and to information about birth control. They also participated in strikes, demonstrations, and coalition-building initiatives with local, justice-oriented groups such as the Black Workers Council, the Black Panther Party, El Comite, and Union Latina.[61]

In September 1971, New York member Cheryl Johnson founded the TWWA's first West Coast chapter, which would eventually become more diverse in membership and programming than its Big Apple counterpart. By early 1972, the Bay Area chapter had a core group of fourteen members, including Miriam Ching Yoon Louie, Grace Shimizu, Milagros Huth, and Zelma Toro.[62] The chapter's organizational infrastructure and programming reflected those of its East Coast corollary. Bay Area members created a steady schedule of weekly meetings, political education classes, and consciousness-raising groups. Their "outside activities" included participating in events such as International Women's Day, the 1972 African Liberation Day demonstration, prisoner rights protests, and rallies in support of then-incarcerated Angela Davis. Bay Area organizers also created a coalition with the Black Panther Party to fight high black infant mortality rates in Oakland and unique auxiliary programs, such as the Third World Women's Material Aid Committee, to raise local residents' awareness about African liberation struggles.[63]

The TWWA's expansion to Seattle reflected the vitality and applicability of the group's intersectional ideology and organizational framework. Following a two-day retreat in March 1971, a small group of Seattle-based women formed another chapter of the alliance in the Evergreen State.[64] By the end of that year, the Northwest chapter had a small but growing cohort of dedicated women, led by Mary Stone, who developed the local Free Angela Davis campaign and held events like screenings of the Chinese film *Red Detachment of Women*, in which the heroine becomes a leader of a radical women's militia.[65] Seattle members also led discussion sessions on

"Native American women and the fishing rights struggle" and hosted consciousness-raising sessions on "women in the black movement" as part of their alliance programming.[66] Their other activities included developing a legal defense fund to help local activists pay court fees and collaborating with the Young Workers Liberation League to raise funds to build a hospital for Vietnamese women outside Hanoi.[67] This chapter attracted local interest, however, a lack of shared leadership responsibilities hampered the group, preventing it from enjoying the widespread success of its New York and Bay Area counterparts.[68]

TWWA members across chapters intervened in and reshaped debates over the meaning of black womanhood most profoundly through their newspaper, *Triple Jeopardy*. From 1971 to 1975, the publication was a central site of intellectual production and debate among black women and other women of color. The news organ had a significant reach and influence. In addition to local circulation in New York City, the Bay Area, and Seattle, the paper reached readers in Houston, Baltimore, Detroit, Milwaukee, and Saint Louis. Other readers included communities in Montreal, Canada, and prisoners in New York and California.[69] Publications in *Triple Jeopardy* eluded a single classification. Readers opened the pages of the newspaper to find editorials, articles about community injustices and grassroots mobilization, critiques of U.S. foreign and domestic policy, and interviews with prominent Black Power activists. Editorials often functioned as an ideological call to arms, while shorter articles outlined concrete forms of political action. In whatever form TWWA members presented their analyses, members consistently advocated for an expansive and multifaceted conceptualization of black women and gender roles grounded in the counterhegemonic stance of Black Power's Third World leftist front.

The Third World Black Woman

In the inaugural issue of *Triple Jeopardy*, Frances Beal explained TWWA members' goal of developing a capacious conception of black womanhood within a Third World context. "The task before us," she told readers and potential members in her untitled editorial, "is to develop a sisterhood of third world women which stretches across all countries—A Sisterhood that finds within itself the resolve and strength to actively participate in all phases of the liberation struggles [sic], while at the same time, making sure that the role of women in the new society will be one which will not be oppressive and will not be a continuation of the same kinds of stunning attitudes which are still in mode today."[70] To achieve the community and ideals of womanhood that Beal prophesied, the TWWA engaged in a two-part project in *Triple Jeopardy*: redefining black women's roles within Black Power, feminist, and anticapitalist organizing and aligning their identities, politics, and priorities with those of other women of color.

Alliance members began this effort by situating the organization, its mission, and their ideas about black womanhood within gendered debates circulating in Black Power circles. In their seminal article "Women in the Struggle," founding members reiterated their appreciation of and commitment to the movement's central tenets while simultaneously critiquing patriarchal interpretations and expressions of Black Power principles. Echoing the conversations among BWLC members, the group lauded black men's "rejection of white middle class norms and values" and their investment in redefining black men's and women's political and social roles. However, alliance founders lamented how this "rejection of whiteness" often took "a different turn when it came to the black woman." TWWA members took issue with men who "stated that [black women's] role was a supportive one." They also denounced those men who argued that black women "must become breeders and provide an army" of black activists or that they "had kotex or pussy power," a term activists including Panther leader Eldridge Cleaver deployed to encourage black women to use their sexual prowess to encourage political activity among black men.[71]

More than simply rejecting these ideas, the TWWA established new parameters for black women's political participation. In the same article, members demanded an end to "sex roles regarding training and skills" and called for "all organizations & institutions (including so-called radical, militant and/or so-called revolutionary groups)" to "deal with third world women in their own right as human beings and individuals, rather than as property of men."[72] The TWWA also argued that all organizers and organizations should view black women as full participants "on all levels of the struggle for national liberation," including in the "administrative, political, and military" spheres. TWWA members envisioned black women as politically and ideologically aware activists who were "fully trained and educated in the martial arts as well as the political arena" and who engaged in self-defense in equal measure as men.[73]

If *Triple Jeopardy* articles reenvisioned black women's roles in Black Power organizing, then the alliance's artistic production visually integrated them into a multiethnic political frame. The front page of the first issue of the periodical featured a drawing of three women centered within a round inset, "Racism, Imperialism, Sexism" curling around the circle. The women are gathered together in a triangle formation, facing front. An Asian woman is at the point of the triangle, wearing a patterned dress and holding a rifle with both hands. To the right is a black woman, recognizable by her shaded skin tone and Afro. The Latina on the left side of the frame is similarly outfitted. The figures form a defiant, confrontational, dominating collective, rejecting powerless images of women of color.[74] Clustered together but just as clearly standing as separate entities, similar but not entirely the same, the women in the image are united by their opposition to the white body politic and are literally and figuratively joined together under the banner of their triple oppression: racism, imperialism, and sexism. Such images provided TWWA readership with a visual rendering of the black woman activist that was both singular and multitudinous. She was a freedom fighter and revolutionary in her own right. She was also part of an activist collective and a cooperative reordering of race, gender, and the nation-state that resulted from black women's identification and collaboration with other women of color.

In other cover images, the editorial staff used activist icons to visually link black women's identities and political commitments to those of other ethnic groups. The cover of the February–March 1972 issue of *Triple Jeopardy* featured hand-drawn images of widely recognizable women radicals: Angela Davis and Lolita LeBrón. Davis became the cause célèbre of the Black Power movement after her arrest and trial for her alleged involvement in a courtroom shooting in Marin County, California, in August 1970.[75] LeBrón was a Puerto Rican nationalist convicted and imprisoned for her participation in the March 1954 shooting of five congressmen at the U.S. House of Representatives.[76] Davis's image occupies the left side of the frame. She does not face front; rather, she is positioned in a quarter profile with her head and torso visible to the viewer. While her clothing is nondescript, her Afro, a feature that became a synecdoche for Black Power politics, dominates her side of the frame.[77] LeBrón stares directly at the viewer from the other side of the frame, outfitted in her recognizable style: a scarf tied around her neck and military-style jacket. A series of vertical lines serve as the background for both figures, with a prominent thick line seemingly meant to divide the images of the two women in the middle. Upon closer examination, however, the dividing line becomes a part of the series of vertical demarcations resembling prison bars that appear behind both women. The bars span both sides of the frame, emphasizing the omnipresence of state-sponsored imprisonment.[78]

Front page of Third World Women's Alliance, *Triple Jeopardy*, September–
October 1971. Courtesy of the Third World Women's Alliance Records,
Sophia Smith Collection, Smith College.

Front page of Third World Women's Alliance, *Triple Jeopardy*, February–
March 1972. Courtesy of the Third World Women's Alliance Records,
Sophia Smith Collection, Smith College.

This cover art was emblematic of how TWWA members reconfigured black women's personal and political identities by combining popular icons and well-known liberation struggles in a single frame. Although Davis and LeBrón were pivotal antiracist, antisexist, and anti-imperialist advocates in their own right, their political struggles were temporally and thematically disparate. LeBrón was a leader in the fight for Puerto Rican independence from U.S. control in the 1950s. Davis was primarily known for her antiracist and prison abolitionist organizing in the 1970s. The TWWA collapsed time, space, place, and race in order to visually project a united community of women of color and an expansive understanding of black women's oppression and political identifications. The image mirrored the TWWA's twin goals of redefining black women's roles and envisioning them as part of, but not entirely subsumed within, a radical, ethnically and racially diverse collective. As in the inaugural cover image, the arrangement of Davis and LeBrón side by side in the frame suggests that they are interconnected but not one and the same. The bars that span the frame reinforce this point. They simultaneously remind the reader of the overarching power of state oppression and serve as a demarcation between the two activists' images and the political struggles that they represented.

TWWA members sustained their efforts to reimagine black women's political self-conception within the publication through their mixed-media form. As readers flipped through the newspaper, they encountered layouts that invited them to conceive of black women as part of a global, Third World women's collective. The structure and format of the "Women in the Struggle" article showcased their efforts. Subscribers turned to the middle of the fall 1971 issue to find the title of the article in bold lettering, encased in a layout featuring three images arranged in a diagonal, stretching from the top left to the bottom right of the two-page spread. The first photograph features a group of Cuban women participating in army drills. In the middle of the page, above the "goals & objectives" section of the piece, is an artistic rendering of the profile of a black or African woman wearing a cloth hat and gun. At the bottom right of the layout, to the left of the text describing the group's views on self-defense and self-determination, is a print of an armed Vietnamese woman, recognizable by her traditional straw hat. Engaging the viewer in a single moment of consumption, the image and text framed black and Third World women as politically aware, militant, and ideologically prepared.[79]

This layout exemplified how the alliance created a gendered Third World cartography, wherein region, race, class, and gender converged to disrupt

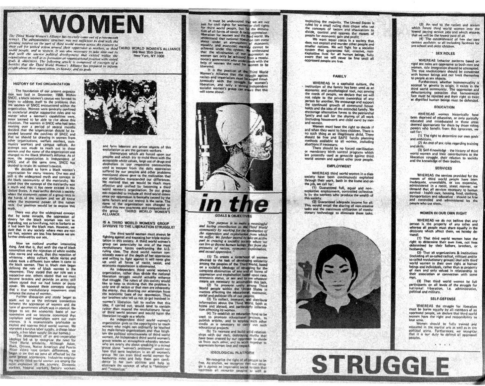

Full page spread of "Women in the Struggle," *Triple Jeopardy*, September–October 1971. Courtesy of the Third World Women's Alliance Records, Sophia Smith Collection, Smith College.

simplistic notions of women's roles and proffer a dynamic and multipositional idea of black women within a global, anti-imperialist context. Photographs and drawings of women engaged in Latin American, Asian, and African liberation struggles permeated the radical black press. *Triple Jeopardy* editors played on their readership's recognition of imagistic tropes, collecting, reordering, and recontextualizing them in order to encourage readers to expand their ideas about black womanhood. By invoking images beyond their moment of origin and placing them alongside textual analyses of women's intersectional oppression and political possibility, they compelled readers to visualize new forms of political identification and embodiment.[80] In this particular layout, the photographs, drawings, and text flow into and through one another, blurring distinctions between ideology and embodiment; obscuring the borders of racial, ethnic, and geographical identities; and creating a new political and aesthetic subjectivity. Yet the center image is that of a black woman, emphasizing the centrality of the black experience within their Third World political frame. When arranged, juxtaposed, and interspersed with images of Puerto Rican, Chinese, Cuban, and Vietnamese women, as they are in this layout and throughout the paper, black women become a part of a fluid group of organizers, guerilla fighters, and radical political actors collectively engaged in political struggle.[81]

The alliance used cover art and collages to establish the idea of a black and Third World collective. Members also published articles in which they emphasized the potential of redefining black womanhood through an intersectional and internationalist frame. In "Slave of a Slave No More" (1973), Frances Beal explained how developing an expansive, Third World–inspired conception of black womanhood enhanced Black Power struggles and women's roles within them. The alliance leader opened her article by drawing on the TWWA founders' tradition of balancing support for black nationalist projects with a critique of activists' masculinist framings of them. Beal indicated that she and the other alliance members appreciated the fact that Black Power organizing had "cultivated a renewed interest in African history" among activists. Yet, she cautioned readers that many "distortions [of this history] continue[d] to go unchecked." In particular, the TWWA disputed the claims of activists who promoted a return to "African" values—a position that cultural nationalists and Pan-Africanists often championed— as a panacea for the rampant inequalities that black Americans faced. By and large, Beal argued, these schemas were manifestations of middle-class black men's political and cultural imaginaries rather than novel revolutionary blueprints. She urged black women to reconsider the "great African drama" that many of their contemporaries glorified. "Nationhood, in most cases, still has a capitalist base," Beal explained, "and so long as it does, there can be no freedom for poor Afro-American and African women."[82] The goals of cultural nationalists and Pan-Africanists were lofty but repressive. Their attempts to replace the dominant order with an "African" one led them to mirror the conservative logic of their oppressors.

Beal argued that this position had disastrous effects on black women's real and imagined roles in emancipatory struggles. The TWWA leader noted that these activists' fidelity to an unrealistic vision of an African homeland subjugated women under the guise of national and cultural emancipation. Far from being liberated in these schemas, the black woman, Beal argued, was the "slave of a slave."[83] She was a victim of the racist, sexist, and capitalist systems that white America perpetuated. She was also enslaved to black men who viewed patriarchy as the remedy to white oppression rather than as a manifestation of it. Not only did this lead the dominant society to frame black women as expendable members of society, it also caused black men to marginalize them in their liberation projects. In the TWWA's estimation, many of their contemporaries had created an ideological framework that re-created rather than rejected the most oppressive aspects of American society. Black women were the primary victims of these idealized projections. They also had the most to gain by rejecting these ideas and developing a more radical political self-conception.

The TWWA leader encouraged black women to approach this project through an intersectional, Third World lens. Beal urged her black women readers to "study to understand how the role of black and other third world women in the home and in society fits into the general picture of third world peoples in this country" and how their Black Power activism "fits into the struggle against exploitation and oppression of all peoples." Examining the black condition from this vantage point, she argued, revealed "the prominent role that the black woman has played in the on-going struggle against racism and exploitation" and showed that they could and should take on a leading role in bringing about black liberation. Armed with this new perspective, black women could take "an active part in changing [their] reality." They could also develop new black-centered emancipatory frameworks that made "the slave of a slave . . . a creature of the past."[84]

Several core themes emerged out of TWWA members' artwork and articles aimed at developing a viable model of black womanhood rooted in an accurate analysis of their race, class, and gender oppression and bolstered by their shared experiences with other women of color. First, whether it was their lionization of movement leaders—including Angela Davis—or their study of African history and black-centered political frames, a commitment to radical black struggles and self-deterministic principles undergirded members' projections of black womanhood. However, when redefining black womanhood, members consistently balanced their investment in nationalist projects with a critique of the conservative gender politics embedded within them. Second, alliance organizers argued that more often than not, existing formulations of Black Power and empowerment did not sufficiently account for black women's historical and contemporary experiences with oppression. Because of this, they insisted on the importance of redefining black women's roles in black political struggle and liberation schemas writ large. In their artwork and mixed-media images, they unfailingly depicted black women enacting the empowered and nontraditional roles that they described in their articles. Finally, members visually and rhetorically represented the commonalities of oppression among women of color and emphasized the potential of women of other ethnicities to provide valuable examples of how black women could redefine and propel nationalist movements. Their print culture projected a model of black womanhood that embraced the central ideas of Black Power, was aligned both ideologically and organizationally with other women of color, and was invested in reproducing these women's strategies in order to combat coexistent oppressive forces. Alliance members argued that this approach not only could generate a more gender-inclusive form of Black Power, it was also a more reliable formula for black women's liberation.

Once TWWA members established the parameters of the Third World Black Woman ideal, they explained how this political identity could transform central Black Power problematics and debates. First and foremost, TWWA members argued that black women's embrace of a Third World perspective could alter their contemporaries' perspective on reproductive rights. The widespread availability of the birth control pill in the 1960s, along with the legalization of abortion in 1973, made childbearing a Black Power issue.[85] Some black nationalists argued that birth control and abortion were tools used in a state-sponsored genocide of black Americans.[86] Others argued that black women could best demonstrate their commitment to black liberation—and swell the number of black liberation fighters—by refusing birth control and having "babies for the revolution."[87] To be sure, the well-documented history of black women's forced sterilization gave some weight to these claims. More often than not, however, black nationalists' resistance to reproductive freedom rehearsed long-standing ideas about women's roles as the literal and metaphorical bearers of the black nation.[88]

In an untitled editorial examining "the two sides of the question of birth control for Third World people," the TWWA explained how their class-conscious, globally minded perspective reformulated the parameters of this debate. Members opened by confirming black nationalists' suspicions of the state. They agreed that the "powerful white minority who [were] imperialists" had been known to use abortion and forced sterilization to control and diminish the black community. But this was only half of the story. Alliance activists also explained that their multiethnic study sessions and organizing had foregrounded new dimensions of this issue. Specifically, they argued that this same "powerful white minority" also kept women of color "ignorant of their bodies and its functioning" and denied them access to the educational and economic resources needed to engage in responsible childbearing practices.[89] As a result, black women often had more children than they wanted or could support. Not only did this deprive them of the ability to practice self-determination and corporal control—principles that Black Power activists universally endorsed—it also kept many black women tethered to poverty and low-paying jobs in the same capitalist system that those who demonized birth control abhorred. Rather than raising the number of black fighters for the nationalist army, black men's disavowal of birth control cost their liberation struggle valuable would-be infantry members.

Alliance organizers then explained how a Third World perspective could offer new approaches to subverting gender-specific imperialist attacks on the black community. The TWWA explained that, for women in African and Asian liberation struggles, motherhood was not the primary axis on which their political legitimacy was measured. In particular, they highlighted Vietnamese women liberation fighters as evidence that female activists "should not be limited to the role of motherhood" and that they "could be providers in other creative ways."[90] Black Power activists across organizations and ideologies heralded the Viet Cong—or the National Liberation Front—as the epitome of revolutionary resistance.[91] TWWA members suggested the Viet Cong could be instructive on multiple fronts, including the theorization of new ideas about black women's roles in political and cultural revolution. They closed the editorial by endorsing a model of black womanhood akin to that of female Vietnamese liberation fighters; one in which "the liberation of their people [was] not based on the quantity of children that they ha[d], but the quality of their day to day input into struggle on every level."[92] Encouraging women to move beyond maternal models of activism could reduce the number of women enduring sterilization at the hands of the state. It could also swell the rank and file of the black liberation movement.

The TWWA also heralded the potential of its internationalist and intersectional framework to advance the movement's anticapitalist and antiimperialist thrusts. The women's group developed during a period in which many activists and organizations were adopting more expansive ideological frames. Increased contact with African, Asian, and Latin American liberation struggles and leaders, coupled with the intractable problem of black poverty at home, propelled activists toward political ideologies that could account for the interrelationship of racism, capitalism, and imperialism. By the 1970s, organizations ranging from the Black Panther Party to CAP had all integrated some form of Marxist-Leninist principles into their racebased organizing. These class-conscious frameworks foregrounded the interconnectedness of U.S.-based minority groups and those laboring under colonial and neocolonial regimes abroad. As women in these organizations often noted, however, they rarely accounted for their gender-specific experiences with imperialist politics and economic oppression.[93]

Alliance members asserted that their women-centered, Third World perspective could more adequately address the economic exploitation that black women and other women of color faced. Their "On the Job" series in *Triple Jeopardy* encapsulated this perspective. In this collection of articles, members featured interviews with different black, Latina, and Asian American women about the oppressive and dehumanizing conditions of their workplaces. For "On the Job with the Black Secretary," they interviewed two black women clerical workers in order to illustrate how their experiences with exploitation were "representative of the exploitation and oppression of third-world women in secretarial positions."[94] In "On the Job with Domestic Workers," they printed the trials of Dorothy Bolden, a black maid who was unionizing her fellow domestic workers in Atlanta. Echoing analyses put forth by postwar women radicals like Ella Baker and Marvel Cooke, Bolden recounted black women's daily difficulties in their attempts to try to find steady, fully compensated work in white women's homes. Editorializing Bolden's testimony, alliance members noted that class, race, and economic discrimination left black women domestics "unable to properly care for their home and children," while being subjected to poor "working conditions for small pay, left-over food and used clothing."[95]

Interviews with black women workers highlighted their mutually reinforcing race, sex, and class exploitation. Other installments featuring Latina and Asian American women indicated that they were not alone. In the September–October 1971 issue, editors published an interview with a Puerto Rican woman who worked at a chicken factory in rural Maryland. In the interview, the young woman told readers about the poor working conditions of the factory and the daily acts of racism and sexism that women of color faced on the job. In addition to the low pay and discrimination she experienced, she explained, her white coworkers "constantly ma[de] jokes about [her] sexual habits and the way [she] looked."[96] "The purpose of these articles," according to *Triple Jeopardy* editors, was to help their readership see that the "oppressive conditions that a telephone operator suffer[ed] [were] similar to [those] of a nurse's aide or factory worker." Equipped with this understanding, they reasoned, black and Third World women could "begin to speak of ways to combat these conditions."[97] Through the series, alliance members provided tangible examples of how black women and other women of color were united by their shared experiences within capitalist oppression. They also deployed the collection of interviews as evidence of the organization's commitment to developing gender-specific analyses of capitalism and imperialism, as well as the need for black women to identify with and mobilize within a poor or working-class Third World community.

The TWWA also used the series to intervene in contemporaneous conversations about racism, capitalism, and black women's roles in combatting these oppressive systems. *Triple Jeopardy* editors argued that black women were not fully aware of the scope and reach of the capitalist system. Accordingly, they did not view themselves as "legitimate members of the labor force" or see "the need to take conscious actions around [their] oppression as workers."[98] This was, in part, a failing of contemporaneous analyses that did not adequately address the particularity of black women's racialized economic oppression or the interrelationship of these abuses and patriarchy. The "On the Job" series, and the myriad other *Triple Jeopardy* articles that TWWA members produced, foregrounded the gender-specific effects of capitalist exploitation, educated black women about its manifestations, and politicized them based on their class identities. Armed with this more expansive, Third World political frame, black women could develop more nuanced analyses of their oppression and mobilize around anticapitalist agendas.

"On the Job" was part of the mosaic of *Triple Jeopardy* articles and artwork that defined the alliance's Third World Black Woman ideal and the political ideology that undergirded it. By 1970, when the alliance was formed, female Black Power activists had long been debating and redefining their roles in child-rearing and the family, political organizing, ideological warfare, self-defense, and the defense of their own communities. In their pamphlet "Third World Women's Alliance: Our History, Our Ideology, Our Goals," TWWA members published their position on these key Black Power–era debates. Whereas many of their counterparts argued that black women's primary roles were familial, the TWWA "encourage[d] alternative forms to the patriarchal family" and asserted women's rights to "decide if and when they wanted to have children." Members noted that their analysis of racism, capitalism, and imperialism across ethnic groups had led them to the conclusion that, "in a capitalist culture, the institution of the family has been used as an economic or psychological tool." The TWWA supported the idea of "communal households and extended families" to lessen the burden of homemaking and child-rearing on black women. They also endorsed black women's desires to dispense with maternal roles all together. Alliance members argued that there should be "free and SAFE family planning methods available to all women, including abortion if necessary," but added that there "should be no forced sterilization or mandatory birth control programs which [have been] used as genocide against third world women and against other poor people."[99]

For the alliance, eliminating rigid ideas about sex roles and child-rearing was a critical first step to in fostering political organizing and transforming the gendered binaries on which much of the era's political organizing rested. The TWWA maintained that "role integration should be dealt with" within organizations in order to advance the movement. Like their counterparts in the Us Organization, CAP, and the Black Panther Party, members argued that women should not be limited to "women's work" and should be included in all aspects of political organizing. They also questioned the idea of gender roles in and of itself. The TWWA argued that activists' emphasis on gender-specific roles in the family, at work, and in political organizing endorsed an implicit heteronormative framework that denied the possibility of other sexual and gender identifications. Members challenged this gendered dichotomy by acknowledging that homosexual and gender-nonconforming peoples were part of the black and Third World community and denouncing the "oppression and dehumanizing ostracism that homosexuals face[d]."[100] By incorporating a heterosexist critique into their ideological platform, the TWWA advanced black women activists' intersectional analyses and identifications. They also began important conversations about how to expand activists' ideas about self-definition and self-determination beyond the binary parameters that other Black Power groups prescribed.

The TWWA also applied this expansive understanding of gender roles to a central Black Power issue: self-defense. They argued that the "struggle for liberation must be borne equally by all members of an oppressed people" and declared that Third World women had "the right and responsibility to bear arms" in order to defend themselves and "all oppressed peoples." This was a point of congruence among alliance members and women in other groups like the Black Panther Party and CAP. In formulating their new ideas about black womanhood, they joined in with other female activists who challenged the "promise of protection" framework, or the idea that black women were in need of black men's social, cultural, or physical security.[101]

Ultimately, examining the central problematics from an intersectional and international approach led the black women leaders of the TWWA to conclude that a single ideological position was too narrow to account for their experiences or emancipatory goals. Throughout the Black Power era, black women had *implicitly* simultaneously identified as nationalists, socialists, and feminists as a way to expand their ideological and activist range. The TWWA explicitly claimed and championed this ideological position. Members boldly proclaimed that they saw no "contradiction in being nationalists, in being feminists, and in being socialists."[102] Rather, the persistent concern of the organization was the formation of a political identity and ideology that confirmed the collective power of black and Third World women and the importance of struggling for women's rights, Black Power, and class liberation simultaneously.

TWWA members consistently argued that their ideological position and political identity were more in line with black women's lived experiences than were other models of womanhood circulating in the public sphere. In both print and public, they challenged their contemporaries' gendered imaginings, arguing that they did not have to "bear children for the revolution . . . walk behind men . . . and stay at home when action [was] happening in the streets."[103] Instead, they defined black womanhood in ways that were similar to those of postwar women like Claudia Jones and Alice Childress, who consistently imagined black women as militant nationalist, working-class, and feminist actors. TWWA leaders claimed that they were unfamiliar with these theorists until well after they established the organization and the Third World Black Woman ideal.[104] Yet there are striking similarities between the ideas about black womanhood that both cohorts of women produced.

The TWWA's theoretics contributed to and extended the Black Power–era gendered imaginary, as well as the shape and scope of women's organizing. The alliance emerged during a period in which many black women publicly voiced their dissatisfaction with the masculinist discourses and political frameworks that permeated the movement.[105] TWWA organizers' outright rejection of activists' ahistorical and conservative prescriptions for women, along with their unabashed support of black women's armed self-defense, political engagement, and ideological acumen, excited black women activists looking for new spaces to assert and enact Black Power ideals. The model of womanhood that the group put forth allowed veteran activists and movement newcomers to envision themselves as part of a collective that valued their rights, roles, and revolutionary potential. It also broadened members' and supporters' political perspectives and commitments by contextualizing black women's individual and domestic concerns in a global and class-conscious political frame.

Adopting the TWWA's expansive understanding of black liberation and women's roles within it afforded members opportunities to practice Black Power's guiding principles in multifaceted ways. Whether it was the TWWA's attempts to advance the black working class through its partnerships with the Black Panther Party, its support of African liberation through its Third World Women's Material Aid Committee, or its efforts to subvert daily acts of racism and sexism through reproductive rights and skill-building classes, the alliance offered a capacious political program through which members could practice self-determination and community control in ways that fit their needs and lived experiences.[106] The Third World Black Woman ideal helped guide them in this pursuit by offering an expansive and empowering model of "women's work" and fostering a global, class-conscious, and feminist approach to everyday acts of resistance.

Organizers continued to promulgate their intersectional political identity and radical political program throughout the 1970s. In both New York and the Bay Area, members expanded their programming and newspaper circulation while also joining forces with other black liberation groups and forming multiracial protest coalitions.[107] TWWA leadership made tentative plans to expand the organization to other cities, including Atlanta, Newark, and Cincinnati.[108] However, government surveillance, lack of funds, and a disparate organizing structure led to the group's demise before members could reach this goal. *Triple Jeopardy* went out of print in 1975. Some New York chapter members continued to meet until 1977; the Bay Area chapter survived slightly longer, ending activities in early 1980.[109]

According to Bay Area member Linda Burnham, TWWA members' black nationalist, feminist, socialist political program and identity positioned them in stark opposition to the Nixon-era policies of the 1970s. It also placed them on the "wrong side of history" when the "Reagan Revolution" dawned in the early 1980s.[110] The Nixon administration looked to combine Republican ideals of private enterprise with Richard Nixon's marginal endorsement of civil rights. The president endorsed federally funded minority business programs and touted the success of a few black corporations and individuals as evidence of U.S. economic vitality and equalizing race relations. Meanwhile, his administration pushed for economic deregulation, free markets, and privatization, ignoring Black Power activists' common claim that capitalism was at the core of economic, racial, and gender inequality.[111]

By the time that Ronald Reagan took office in 1981, Nixon-era policies had reached their apogee. Reagan capitalized on white conservatives' frustration with the previous era's civil rights gains and pursued an implicitly and explicitly antiblack agenda. He endorsed deregulation measures in U.S. and global markets, significant cuts to state and federal social programs that served black communities, and the expansion of policing and prisons. His administration's conservative politics and policies were disastrous for the black community as Reagan reigned over an expanding drug and AIDS crisis, rampant racial income inequality, and a reversion to a geographically and economically segregated social order.[112]

In an effort to combat this conservative political turn, in August 1980, remaining Bay Area TWWA members transformed the group into the Alliance against Women's Oppression (AAWO), a multiracial coalition of women activists.[113] Building on the ideological and organizational legacy of the TWWA, the AAWO mobilized around a women-centered, intersectional agenda aimed at ameliorating the lives of poor white women and women of color.[114] Members continued to enact the TWWA's Third World focus by forming coalitions with international social justice groups like the South African Women's Organization and the Nicaraguan Women's Association.[115] They garnered the most attention for their efforts to restore federal funding for abortions for poor women after the passage of the 1976 Hyde Amendment, which largely barred the use of federal funds for abortion procedures.[116] Despite its strong record on recuperating and advancing rights for women of color, the AAWO ended its activities in early 1990.

After the AAWO dissolved, former TWWA members like Linda Burnham looked for new ways to "sustain a political orientation and vision that, again, trace[d] itself back to the Third World Women's Alliance and then the Black Women's [Liberation Committee]." One of the ways they accomplished this goal was through the creation of the Women of Color Resource Center (WOCRC). Burnham founded the Oakland, California, organization in 1990.[117] The WOCRC functioned as a "political home" for women of color to find "common ground" around the oppression that they faced. Through its community programs, consciousness-raising sessions, educational workshops, and political protests, WOCRC volunteers ensured that the intersectional frameworks that the TWWA developed were not lost in future generations and political communities.[118]

The work of the AAWO and WOCRC illustrates how the TWWA's political identity and ideology was born of Black Power organizing but not confined by it. Founding TWWA members organized during the height of the Black Power era and in the midst of movement debates about birth control, class struggle, reproductive rights, and white cultural hegemony.

Like their activist counterparts, alliance organizers found many male-promulgated models of black womanhood to be too narrow to encompass their experiences or emancipatory visions. Some of their contemporaries attempted to redefine their roles within existing organizational and ideological parameters. TWWA members forged a new identity, ideology, and organization in order to conceptualize more expansive ideas of what a black woman should do and be.

The TWWA's ideal of the Third World Black Woman was both an index of black women's radicalism and a mechanism through which members reshaped Black Power debates and communities. By theorizing black women's liberation from the Third World perspective, alliance organizers demonstrated how central Black Power principles—such as community control and self-determination—translated beyond the political imaginings of black men. Whether it was their artistic renderings of women of color engaged in armed self-defense or their editorials that framed women's access to birth control as a form of self-determination, the TWWA illustrated how, by reimagining black womanhood, activists could generate new ideas about the meaning of Black Power and black empowerment. Ultimately, alliance organizers' reconceptualization of black women as Third World women not only broadened Black Power activists' perceptions of women, gender, and revolution, it also expanded their real and imagined alliances in the fight for global revolution and black liberation.

The TWWA also extended the reach of Black Power ideals and rhetoric beyond the black community. It is often noted that one of the most poignant legacies of Black Power organizing was Native American, Asian American, and Puerto Rican activists' adoption and replication of activists' symbols, rhetoric, and tactics.[119] From the Native American Red Power movement to the Puerto Rican Young Lords, activists across the left developed their own movements and icons that built on and transformed the era's values and tenets.[120] Yet, these were not the only manifestations of Black Power activists' reach and influence. The TWWA encouraged women of color to employ nationalist rhetoric, symbols, and ideas in their own circumstances and communities. They also championed women-led nationalist struggles across the globe through their promotion and exaltation of radical women leaders like Lolita LeBrón. If a central component of Black Power's legacy was the formation of ethnic nationalist movements among communities of color, then it is important to recognize that the TWWA, and black women's organizations more broadly, was a critical part of this discourse.

Despite its popularity and influence, the TWWA's Third World approach was not without pitfalls. Most notably, it was based on an idealized concept of the Third World that "first world minorities" created.[121] In their efforts to forge a U.S.-based Third World front, TWWA members collapsed very real differences between being a black woman in America and being a colonial or neocolonial subject abroad. This framework allowed members to move past ideological and organizational dichotomies, black/white analytical binaries, and prominent race-versus-class debates. However, it also papered over significant political, social, and cultural differences among communities of color and reinforced an undifferentiated minority identity and subject position. As members navigated this fraught ideological terrain, they illustrated how situating black women's struggles in a Third World context could help translate and sustain solidarity across minority communities and in the application of principles such as nationalism, community power, and self-defense on a broader, gender-specific scale. The TWWA's multivalent intellectual and cultural production also sharpened constructions of race, class, and gender oppression among Black Power activists and the black left more broadly.

This intersectional method of defining black womanhood and black liberation grew in popularity during the 1980s and 1990s, in part because of TWWA-inspired organizations such as the AAWO and the WOCRC. Intersectionality, a term coined by Kimberlé Crenshaw, is now a framework through which scholars assess the lives and experiences of black women and other women of color. It is also a rubric through which contemporary activists have developed novel, expansive, and inclusive liberation schemas.[122] Intersectionality, like other contemporary manifestations of black liberation ideologies, stems, in part, from black women's efforts to reshape the gendered imaginary and their goal of revolutionizing power relationships. By redefining black womanhood, black women activists in groups ranging from the UNIA to the TWWA were not simply challenging Black Power-era sexism, they were also arguing that radical conceptions of black womanhood had the potential to expand the terrain of black revolutionary thought and action.

Epilogue

During the Black Power era, ordinary black women from all walks of life developed critical appraisals of the race, class, and gender constructs that governed their lives. They also advanced new ideas about what life might look like if they escaped the crushing weight of white supremacy. Black domestic workers, members of the Black Panther Party, and Black Power feminists all consistently and collectively imagined a new world and their role within it. Yet historical narratives continue to reinforce the idea that black men were the only ones capable of conjuring up new identities and idealized societies. Or, as scholar-activist Angela Davis put it in an October 2013 speech, we are still unable to "imagine and acknowledge what must have been, among these Black women domestic workers, this amazing collective imagination of a future world without racial and gender and economic oppression."[1] Wary of this blind spot, Davis wondered aloud, "How can we counteract the representation of historical agents as powerful individuals, powerful male individuals, in order to reveal the part played, for example, by Black women domestic workers in the Black freedom movement?"[2]

Exploring black women's ideas about black womanhood is one way of performing the counteractive and communal work that Davis suggests is so sorely needed. Black women across the political spectrum developed analyses of their lived conditions, imagined different realities and potentialities, and developed distinct ideas about their roles in bringing this new world into existence. Teasing out the nuances of their emancipatory visions helps us move past patriarchal, individualistic histories of black struggle that rely on singular, sanitized visions of Black Power. It also offers an opportunity to reopen previously foreclosed ideas about the era, namely, that it was a separate and separatist, violent, and male-led movement. Most importantly, black women's ideals and idealistic pursuits offer a road map for how we might rethink the historical and historic uses of Black Power and black radicalism, shining light on the ways that we might move toward differently constituted futures.

Critically examining black women's collective visions about their roles creates new historical openings for thinking about the collectivity and connectivity of the Black Power era. As Davis suggests, popular and political ideas about this period frame it as an individualist, and male-led, march toward "an ultimately triumphant democracy."[3] Black women's theories of black womanhood show us the ideologically grounded, cumulative, and women-driven activism that undergirded and advanced this period in our history. Their sustained commitment to developing intersectional approaches to self-definition foreground the theoretical and activist continuities of this era. Black women's inability to fully eradicate sexism demonstrates the inadequacies of American democratic ideals and some Black Power frameworks.

Despite these shortcomings, for many black women activists, the gendered imaginary proved to be fertile terrain *precisely* because it was a space in which they could both critique existing black political frameworks and envision new ones. Through handbooks, open letters, artwork, and position papers, they envisioned the roles they could play in countering the oppression that governed their daily lives. Whatever form their new vision took, these activists remained committed to black Americans' ongoing quest to assert control over their individual and collective lives and to create new forms of black identity unbridled by white standards or definitions. They also continually emphasized that there could be no revolution without revolutionizing society's ideas about black women's rights and roles.

Far more than simply idealized projections of a utopian community, black women activists' ideas about black womanhood fundamentally reshaped the organizational, ideological, and symbolic course of the Black Power era and its legacy. In this period, as in all historical moments, activists imagined the path to black liberation through gender-specific organizational and social roles. Many male organizers often assigned black women marginal and devalued tasks in black liberation. Black women challenged their traditionalism by reformulating popular, idealized definitions of their political and social roles. By redefining the African Woman or the Black Revolutionary Woman, black women activists developed increasingly progressive and, in some cases, radical conceptions of gendered organizing labor. They also challenged popular claims that black women were inferior or incapable of performing certain types of political or ideological work.

These idealized tropes of black womanhood undergirded activists' real-life efforts to reshape popular Black Power organizations. Armed with a model of womanhood to enact and aspire to, black women populated a range of grassroots and national organizations, took on leadership roles within them, and directly challenged their counterparts' efforts to stymie their political and cultural development. In many cases, they successfully reshaped the political commitments and perspectives of black men. Tracing the effect of black women's gendered theorizing on organizational trajectories shows the essentiality of developing more flexible understandings of the evolution of the Black Power era and its organizations—ones that do not portend the inevitable exclusion or marginalization of black women's political organizing.

Ideologies like Pan-Africanism and revolutionary nationalism undergirded Black Power organizers' protest strategies and agendas. Leaders, ideologues, and activists also used these frameworks to support their claims of the superiority of black men. As they reimagined their roles in political organizing, black women activists often reinterpreted these political philosophies in more expansive and gender-inclusive ways. In other instances, they built a political identity at the intersection of multiple radical political ideologies, fostering new ideological frameworks like intersectionality. Their debates over the definitions and direction of black womanhood show that political theory was a key site of gendered contestation and that activists' gender identity and identifications mediated their ideological interpretations.

Black women's and men's debates over gender roles and hierarchies also reveal that these ideological frameworks were malleable and open to interpretation. Female Black Power activists recognized this and integrated their gender-specific readings of these philosophies into their pronouncements of their political and social roles. Their expanded understandings of these theories gained traction in many Black Power organizations, prompting leaders and organizers to incorporate their perspectives into organizational doctrines. Their influence warns against top-down approaches to Black Power intellectualism, stresses the importance of the reciprocal relationship between Black Power theorizing and activism, and underscores the need to consider black women as consummate Black Power intellectuals.

In envisioning their new roles, black women activists also reimagined the meaning of Black Power itself. The majority of Black Power–era activists adhered to and promoted some form of self-determination, autonomy, and community control in service of creating new emancipatory visions for black people. Black women expanded and formulated gender-specific expressions of these principles through their projections of black womanhood. By demonstrating self-determination through workplace militancy, asserting racial autonomy by identifying as African, or championing community control by fighting for black Americans' equal access to birth control, they continually redefined Black Power and black empowerment. The contours of their gendered imaginings remind us of the pitfalls of continuing to privilege a singular definition of Black Power at the expense of acknowledging the diversity of the era's political, social, and cultural expressions. They also show us that all forms, definitions, and expressions of Black Power were implicitly and often explicitly gendered.

Although they made an indelible impression on the movement, black women's gendered visions fell short of truly defying oppressive structures and organizing frameworks. In an effort to unify black women under a progressive or radical political identity, many of them reinforced traditional gender binaries and glossed over other forms of identification. Ideals like the African Woman or the Militant Black Domestic were what Amy Abugo Ongiri has called "teasingly transgressive and radically unifying revolutionary potentialities," or constructions that heralded their emancipatory potential without acknowledging the material differences and barriers that they elided.[4] Not only did black women activists' tropes of black womanhood sustain traditional gender binaries, they also left little room in their formulations for other forms of identification, namely, nontraditional gender identities and sexualities. Black women's political identity models may have pushed organizations and actors to rethink their commitment to patriarchal practices. They were less successful, however, at reimagining black identity beyond hegemonic gender pairings and sexual identifications.

Their failures and successes at reimagining black identity show that the Black Power era's record on gender relationships was nuanced and complex and defies easy categorization. On the one hand, women did not blindly accept the roles and responsibilities that black men defined for them. On the other, black women's ideas about womanhood were not always or equally radical and transformative. At times, their new perspectives on black womanhood were only slightly less patriarchal that those of their male counterparts. And even when they articulated a radical conception of black womanhood, they were, at times, only able to set organizations and groups on a slightly more progressive course. What a study of their efforts shows, however, is that black men's and women's conversations and contestations about gender roles and Black Power organizing were not inherently antagonistic, nor were they simply static. Male and female activists reached points of congruence and agreement about the centrality of women to political and cultural organizing, and even the most conservative male leaders evolved in their conceptions of gender roles within Black Power organizing.

It is because of this that Black Power occupies a unique place in the black radical imaginary and organizing tradition. Or, as Davis might say, it is now one of "the historical high points" in the history of black revolt.[5]

However, as she aptly noted, the model we have in place does not do justice to the range of freedom dreams that everyday men and women espoused. Yet black radical practices best counter hegemonic systems when we acknowledge and employ the multiplicity of freedom dreams that black women and men created. The destruction of racism, capitalism, sexism, and homophobia will not come from a uniform idea but rather from the recognition and implementation of the array of political imaginings that those fighting against oppression develop. This book, then, is as much about documenting black women's contributions as it is about rethinking how we conceptualize the idea of a singular black intellectual or radical tradition. It is a gesture toward a more expansive idea of these counterhegemonic strains of thought so that we might see how black women's differently constituted ideas might continue to aid us in our ongoing quest for liberation.

Indeed, we all live in Black Power's "incomplete project of freedom," making activists' previous calls for revolution intimately linked to those of today's organizers.[6] As we look for insight into how to organize against mass incarceration, sexual assault, police violence, and the myriad other injustices that black women and men face, we owe it to ourselves and those on the front lines to develop more nuanced and differentiated analyses of Black Power activists' freedom dreams. This means attending seriously to the various ways in which black women developed gender-specific identities and emancipatory visions, rather than subsuming them in suppositions of patriarchy and domination. To not do so is to run the risk of foreclosing imaginative and productive avenues for future visions of black liberation and to reinforce the idea that Black Power was little more than an abstract, disparate, and degenerative movement.

The power in black women's visions of black womanhood, then, is not simply in the new worlds they imagined but also in how they allow us to see new historical and contemporary potentialities in the struggle for collective freedom. In offering new political identities for black women to adopt, black women activists presented a road map for radical activism, a framework for how black men and women might begin to dismantle their complicity in the daily reproduction of patriarchy and capitalism. They showed us that the gendered imaginary was fertile ground on which to rethink black liberation and a generative space for developing truly inclusive versions of black revolution. They also encouraged us to reimagine blackness, womanhood, and liberation anew.

Notes

Introduction

1. *Black Panther*, July 1, 1972, 12.

2. Gayle Dickson often signed her drawings under the penname "Asali." Dickson interview.

3. Kelley, *Freedom Dreams*; Rickford, *We Are an African People*.

4. Van Deburg, *New Day in Babylon*, 26.

5. There is a growing body of literature on the Great Migration. For examples, see Wilkerson, *Warmth of Other Suns*; Boehm, *Making a Way*; and Gregory, *Southern Diaspora*.

6. Higginbotham, *Righteous Discontent*; Ula Taylor, "Street Strollers."

7. Gaines, *Uplifting the Race*; Giddings, *Ida*; Anna Julia Cooper, Lemert, and Bhan, *Voice of Anna Julia Cooper*.

8. For more on Amy Jacques Garvey, see Ula Taylor, *Veiled Garvey*. For more on early black women members of the CP, see McDuffie, *Sojourning for Freedom*; Gore, *Radicalism at the Crossroads*; Lashawn Harris, "Running with the Reds"; and Davies, *Left of Karl Marx*.

9. Winston James, *Holding Aloft the Banner of Ethiopia*, 174; Makalani, *In the Cause of Freedom*, 33; Allen, *Black Women Intellectuals*, 54–57; Zackodink, "Recirculation and Feminist Black Internationalism."

10. For more on this, see McDuffie, *Sojourning for Freedom*; Gore, *Radicalism at the Crossroads*; Von Eschen, *Race against Empire*.

11. Claudia Jones, "On the Right to Self-Determination"; Mary Helen Washington, *Other Blacklist*, 123–64; Farmer, "Mothers of Pan-Africanism."

12. Blain, "'Set the World on Fire,'" 195.

13. For more on McCarthy-era attacks against black women radicals, see McDuffie, *Sojourning for Freedom*; Gore, *Radicalism at the Crossroads*; Mary Helen Washington, "Black Women Write the Popular Front"; Mary Helen Washington, *Other Blacklist*, 123–64; and Lang and Lieberman, *Anticommunism*.

14. Joseph, "Malcolm X's Harlem"; Gaines, *American Africans in Ghana*.

15. Wilkins, "Beyond Bandung"; Mary Helen Washington, *Other Blacklist*, 127–32.

16. John Henrik Clarke, "New Afro-American Nationalism"; Joseph, *Waiting 'Til the Midnight Hour*, xviii; Farmer, "Reframing African American Women's Grassroots Organizing."

17. McDuffie, "'I Wanted a Communist Philosophy'"; Farmer, "Reframing African American Women's Grassroots Organizing."

18. Harley, "'Chronicle of a Death Foretold.'"

19. For more on the Us Organization, see Scot Brown, *Fighting for US*.

20. For more on the Lowndes County Black Panther Party, see Hasan Kwame Jeffries, *Bloody Lowndes*.

21. Woodard, *Nation within a Nation*, 253–54, 160–72; Buffalo, "Revolutionary Life Together."

22. Ward, "Third World Women's Alliance"; Anderson-Bricker, "'Triple Jeopardy.'"

23. For examples of syntheses of the Black Power era and movement, see Joseph, *Waiting 'Til the Midnight Hour*, and Rhonda Y. Williams, *Concrete Demands*. For examples of studies of local struggles, see Hasan Kwame Jeffries, *Bloody Lowndes*; Joseph, *Neighborhood Rebels*; Woodard, *Nation within a Nation*; and Kinchen, *Black Power in the Bluff City*. For international studies, see Swan, *Black Power in Bermuda*; Slate, *Black Power beyond Borders*; and Markle, *Motorcycle on Hell Run*.

24. Joy James, "Framing the Panther"; Joy James, *Shadowboxing*.

25. Davis, *Angela Davis*; Shakur, *Assata*; Elaine Brown, *Taste of Power*.

26. Ula Taylor, *Veiled Garvey*; Fleming, *Soon We Will Not Cry*.

27. Perkins, *Autobiography as Activism*.

28. LeBlanc-Ernest, "'Most Qualified Person'"; Matthews, "'No One Ever Asks.'"

29. Spencer, *Revolution Has Come*; Phillips, "Power of the First Person Narrative," 33–35; Phillips, "Feminist Leadership."

30. Ula Taylor, "Elijah Muhammad's Nation of Islam"; Ula Taylor, "As-salaam Alaikum, My Sister"; Ula Taylor, *Promise of Patriarchy*.

31. Maulana Karenga, interview by author; McCray, "Complements to Kazi Leaders"; Farmer, "Renegotiating the 'African Woman.'"

32. Rhonda Y. Williams, "Black Women, Urban Politics," 81; Nadasen, "'We Do Whatever Becomes Necessary,'" 319.

33. Springer, *Living for the Revolution*; Roth, *Separate Roads to Feminism*.

34. Ward, "Third World Women's Alliance"; Randolph, *Florynce "Flo" Kennedy*.

35. Joseph, "Historiography of the Black Power Movement," 3; Kimberly Nichele Brown, *Writing the Black Revolutionary Diva*, 34.

36. I borrow the term *Black Power–era feminist* from Stephen Ward. See Ward, "Third World Women's Alliance," 120.

37. Joseph, "Rethinking the Black Power Era," 714.

38. Judson L. Jeffries, *Huey P. Newton*; Joseph, *Stokely*; Carmichael, *Stokely Speaks*; Eldridge Cleaver, *Target Zero*; Marable, *Malcolm X*; Asante, *Maulana Karenga*; Ward, *Pages from a Black Radical's Notebook*. A notable exception would be Ward's *In Love and Struggle*, which chronicles Grace Lee Boggs's ideological evolution along with that of her husband, James Boggs.

39. Ula Taylor, "Street Strollers," 154.

40. For a notable text that challenges this framework, see Bay, Griffin, Jones, and Savage, *Toward an Intellectual History*.

41. Davies, *Black Women, Writing, and Identity*, 8. For more on the development of intersectionality during this period, see Beal, "Double Jeopardy"; La Rue, "Black Movement and Women's Liberation"; and Weathers, "Argument for Black Women's

Liberation." Kimberle Crenshaw ("Mapping the Margins") later coined the terms *intersectional* and *intersectionality*.

42. For more on this, see Springer, *Living for the Revolution*.

43. Rhonda Y. Williams, *Concrete Demands*, 260–61; Joseph, *Waiting 'Til the Midnight Hour*, 296–304; Rickford, *We Are an African People*, 253, 267; Collins, *From Black Power to Hip Hop*.

Chapter One

1. Moore, "We Refuse to Be Programmed Anymore," 20.

2. Perlstein, *Justice, Justice*; Rickford, *We Are an African People*, 23–45; "N.Y. Negroes Battle to Educate Ghetto Kids," *Herald-Dispatch*, November 7, 1968, 1.

3. Goudsouzian, *Down to the Crossroads*; Joseph, *Stokely*; Hasan Kwame Jeffries, *Bloody Lowndes*; Rhonda Y. Williams, *Concrete Demands*.

4. Carmichael and Hamilton, *Black Power*, 46.

5. For more on early twentieth-century black nationalism and masculinity, see Leeds, "Toward the 'Higher Type of Womanhood,'" and Kelley, *Race Rebels*, 114.

6. For more on black women domestic workers and their cultural and material links to slavery, see Hunter, *To 'Joy My Freedom*; Sharpless, *Cooking in Other Women's Kitchens*; McElya, *Clinging to Mammy*; Haley, *No Mercy Here*; and LeFlouria, *Chained in Silence*.

7. For more on Marcus Garvey, Garveyism, and globalization, see Garvey, *Garvey and Garveyism*; Grant, *Negro with a Hat*; and Ewing, *Age of Garvey*.

8. Tony Martin, *Race First*, 12.

9. For more on Garveyism at the local level, see Rolinson, *Grassroots Garveyism*; Harold, *Garvey Movement*; Jenkins, "Linking Up the Golden State"; Stephens, "Garveyism in Idlewild"; and McDuffie, "Garveyism in Cleveland, Ohio." It should also be noted that there is a vibrant historiography about Garveyism at the local level outside the United States that is not listed here.

10. Bush, *We Are Not What We Seem*, 100; Rolinson, *Grassroots Garveyism*, 2.

11. For information on Amy Jacques Garvey and black women who joined the UNIA, see Ula Taylor, *Veiled Garvey*; Bair, "True Women, Real Men," 158–60; Tony Martin, *Amy Ashwood Garvey*; McDuffie, "Diasporic Journeys of Louise Little"; and Morris, "Becoming Creole, Becoming Black."

12. Ula Taylor, *Veiled Garvey*, 64–90.

13. Moore, interview by Gilkes, 123.

14. Hill and Bair, *Marcus Garvey Life and Lessons*, 368.

15. Adi, "Negro Question," 158; Makalani, *In the Cause of Freedom*, 133–34.

16. Kelley, *Hammer and Hoe*, 1, 13.

17. Harold, *Garvey Movement*, 117; Rolinson, *Grassroots Garveyism*, 180–82.

18. Wolcott, *Remaking Respectability*, 170; Nadasen, *Household Workers Unite*, 10–11.

19. Baker and Cooke, "Bronx Slave Market," 330; Greenberg, *To Ask for an Equal Chance*, 30; Ransby, *Ella Baker*, 72–73.

20. Nadasen, *Household Workers Unite*, 16; Greenberg, *Or Does It Explode?*, 93–113; Lashawn Harris, "Running with the Reds," 23. For more on black life during the Depression and New Deal eras, see Trotter, *Raw Deal to a New Deal?*

21. Naison, *Communists in Harlem*, 62–63; Kelley, *Hammer and Hoe*, 23–25.

22. Lashawn Harris, "Running with the Reds," 30–31.

23. Moore, interview by Gilkes, 131–32.

24. Solomon, *Cry Was Unity*, 271; "Negroes Assail Italy," *New York Times*, February 16, 1935, 6; "2,000 Parade in Harlem's Protest to Ethiopia Invasion," *Afro-American*, May 11, 1935, 12.

25. Claudia Jones, "Autobiographical History," 13–14.

26. Higashida, *Black Internationalist Feminism*, 35.

27. Kelley, *Race Rebels*, 114; Sangrey, "'One More "S" in the USA.'"

28. Smethurst, *New Red Negro*, 57.

29. McDuffie, *Sojourning for Freedom*, 93.

30. Ibid., 45; Naison, *Communists in Harlem*, 20–21; Shannon King, *Whose Harlem Is This, Anyway?*, 112–13.

31. McDuffie, *Sojourning for Freedom*, 51; Bell Lamb, "Negro Women in Industry," *Negro Champion*, August 8, 1928; Fanny Austin, "Women Day Workers," *Negro Champion*, August 8, 1928.

32. Von Eschen, *Race against Empire*, 19.

33. McDuffie, *Sojourning for Freedom*, 93.

34. Biondi, *To Stand and Fight*, 6.

35. Esther V. Cooper, "Negro Woman Domestic Worker"; McDuffie, "March of Young Southern Black Women," 84; Esther Cooper Jackson, interview by Scott, 5.

36. McDuffie, "Esther V. Cooper's 'Negro Woman Domestic'"; Hughes, "We Demand Our Rights"; Richards, "Fundamentally Determined."

37. Friend and Potter, "The Black and the Red."

38. Thompson, "Toward a Brighter Dawn."

39. McDuffie, *Sojourning for Freedom*, 112–14. Black women's engagement with the CP and Popular Front organizations was extensive and multifaceted. Cooper and Thompson are merely two examples of a diverse group of black women who rose to prominence during this period.

40. Ibid., 93.

41. Gore, *Radicalism at the Crossroads*, 40.

42. Browder, "Negroes and the Right to Self-Determination," 84.

43. Audley Moore, for example, claimed that she joined the CP because it was a "vehicle" through which to organize around Garveyite principles. She also claimed that she became disillusioned with the CP after its leadership abandoned their support of the Black Belt Thesis. Moore, interview by Gilkes, 132.

44. Blain, "'Set the World on Fire.'"

45. On the eve of World War I, in July 1918, W. E. B. Du Bois ("Close Ranks") encouraged black Americans to "close ranks" and join forces with white Americans for the war effort.

46. Claudia Jones, "Autobiographical History," 11.

47. Ibid., 13.

48. Davies, *Claudia Jones, beyond Containment*, xiii–xiv.

49. Davies, *Left of Karl Marx*, 30; Claudia Jones, "Autobiographical History," 14.

50. "On the Right to Self-Determination" was not the first article of this kind that Jones authored. In 1945, she published "Discussion Article," in which she argued that Browder's rejection of the Black Belt Thesis was both "subjective" and "unscientific."

51. Claudia Jones, "Right to Self-Determination," 71.

52. Ibid., 73.

53. Ibid.

54. Harry Haywood (*Black Bolshevik*, 543), a leading CP theorist and architect of the Black Belt Thesis, claimed that after reading an article by Jones, he realized that he "could play a role in restoring [the party's] position on the Afro-American Question."

55. Claudia Jones, "End to the Neglect," 51–54.

56. Ibid.

57. Ibid., 51.

58. Ibid., 55–56.

59. Gore, *Radicalism at the Crossroads*, 74–99; McDuffie, *Sojourning for Freedom*, 161, 169; Charles H. Martin, "Race, Gender, and Southern Justice"; Strain, *Pure Fire*, 30. For a discussion of the Ingram case in the context of racialized sexual assault, see McGuire, *Dark End of the Street*.

60. Claudia Jones, "End to the Neglect," 63.

61. Ibid., 64.

62. Ibid., 55.

63. Lashawn Harris, "Running with the Reds," 23; McDuffie, *Sojourning for Freedom*, 10–12.

64. Claudia Jones, "End to the Neglect," 63.

65. Ibid.

66. Kelley, *Race Rebels*, 114.

67. Davies, *Left of Karl Marx*, 130; Gore, *Radicalism at the Crossroads*, 39–40; McDuffie, *Sojourning for Freedom*, 163.

68. For more on Popular Front organizations' retreat from political militancy and black radicals' response to the McCarthy era, see Lang and Lieberman, *Anticommunism*.

69. "They Dried Their Tears and Spoke Their Minds," *Freedom*, October 1951, 6–7.

70. Sojourners for Truth and Justice, "Constitution," n.d., ca. 1951, Box 15, Folder 26, Louise Thompson Patterson Papers, Stuart A. Rose Manuscripts, Archives, and Rare Book Library, Emory University, Atlanta, Georgia (hereafter referred to as the LTP Papers); McDuffie, "'New Freedom Movement of Negro Women.'"

71. "Our Cup Runneth Over" and "5,000 Negro Women Wanted," n.d., Box 12, Folder 18, LTP Papers. For more on Harriette Moore and her husband, Harry, see Green, *Before His Time*.

72. For more information about the FBI's surveillance of the Sojourners, see FBI SFTJ.

73. Davies, *Left of Karl Marx*, 141–44; Davies, *Claudia Jones, beyond Containment*, xv.

74. McDuffie, "March of Young Southern Black Women," 86, 96–98.

75. Farmer, "Reframing African American Women's Grassroots Organizing."

76. Claudia Jones, "End to the Neglect," 64.

77. Jennings, *Alice Childress*, 8.

78. Mary Helen Washington, *Other Blacklist*, 132; Oral History Interview, Fisk University, 1973, Box 1, Folder 6, Alice Childress Papers, Schomburg Center for Research on Black Culture, New York.

79. Childress, "Candle in a Gale Wind," 112.

80. Mary Helen Washington, *Other Blacklist*, 133–34.

81. Ibid., 134; Jennings, *Alice Childress*, 3–4; Shandell, "Looking beyond Lucasta."

82. Mary Helen Washington, *Other Blacklist*, 134.

83. A key argument of Mary Helen Washington's scholarship is that Childress went to great lengths to erase her association with the CP in her later life. Mary Helen Washington, "Black Women Write the Popular Front," 185; Mary Helen Washington, *Other Blacklist*, 126–27.

84. McDonald, *Feminism*, 52.

85. Childress, "For a Negro Theatre," 61.

86. Ibid., 62.

87. Ibid., 61.

88. Mary Helen Washington, *Other Blacklist*, 136; "Gold through the Trees: CNA Presents Exciting New Dramatic Review," *Freedom*, May 1952, 2.

89. Jennings, *Alice Childress*, 7–8; Childress, *Like One of the Family*.

90. Baker and Cooke, "Bronx Slave Market," 330.

91. Trudier Harris, introduction to *Like One of the Family*, by Childress.

92. Alice Childress, "Like One of the Family," *Freedom*, April 1952, 2, 8.

93. Alice Childress, "All about My Job," in *Like One of the Family*, 33–37.

94. Alice Childress, "The 'Many Others' in History," *Freedom*, February 1952, 3.

95. Childress, "For a Negro Theatre," 61.

96. Alice Childress, "About Those Colored Movies," *Freedom*, June 1952, 8.

97. Alice Childress, "What Does Africa Want? . . . Freedom!" *Freedom*, June 1953, 12.

98. For more on this period, womanhood, liberalism, and race, see Feldstein, *Motherhood in Black and White*; Meyerowitz, *Not June Cleaver*; and Sewell, "Mammies and Matriarchs."

99. Trudier Harris, introduction, xxvi.

100. "Editorial," *Freedom*, March 1955, 1; Mary Helen Washington, *Other Blacklist*, 144.

101. Mary Helen Washington, *Other Blacklist*, 146–47.

102. For examples of *Freedomways* articles, see Esther Cooper Jackson and Pohl, *Freedomways Reader*.

103. Angelou, *Heart of a Woman*, 178; John Henrik Clarke, "New Afro-American Nationalism," 285.

104. Angelou, *Heart of a Woman*, 177.

105. "Nationalists in on Three Disturbances," *New York Amsterdam News*, May 27, 1961; Angelou, *Heart of a Woman*, 756; John Henrik Clarke, "New Afro-American Nationalism," 285; Higashida, *Black Internationalist Feminism*, 54–55.

106. Amiri Baraka, *Autobiography of LeRoi Jones*, 267.

107. Mallory, interview by Lumumba.

108. Ibid.; Claudia Jones, "Autobiographical History," 11.

109. Mallory, interview by Lumumba.

110. "Meeting of Afro-Americans, June 14, 1961," Box 2, Folder 4, Mae Mallory Collection, Walter P. Reuther Library, Wayne State University, Detroit, Michigan (hereafter referred to as the Mallory Collection); Tinson, "'Voice of the Black Protest Movement,'" 3.

111. For more on Robert Williams, Mallory, and the Monroe incident, see Tyson, *Radio Free Dixie*.

112. "Citizens Fire Back at Klan," *Norfolk Journal and Guide*, October 12, 1957, 1; "Williams: Negro Group 'Threatened' at Pool," *Charlotte Observer*, August 22, 1960, 4; Dagbovie, "'God Has Spared Me.'"

113. Tyson, *Radio Free Dixie*, 155–60; "'Eye for an Eye' Type Action on Injustice Rejected by the NAACP," *Atlanta Daily World*, May 7, 1959, 1; "NAACP Suspends Union, N.C., Leader," *Charlotte Observer*, July 9, 1959, 1.

114. Arsenault, *Freedom Riders*, 405–6.

115. Robert F. Williams, *Negroes with Guns*, 48–49.

116. Tyson, *Radio Free Dixie*, 267–69.

117. "'Wanted' Woman in Cleveland Home," *Cleveland Call and Post*, October 21, 1961, 1A.

118. For more analysis of Mallory's prison letters, see Seniors, "Mae Mallory."

119. Mae Mallory, "Of Dogs and Men," in Monroe Defense Committee, *Letters from Prison: The Story of a Frame-Up* (Cleveland, Ohio: Monroe Defense Committee, 1963), 25.

120. Ibid., 26.

121. Ibid., 25.

122. Childress, "Like One of the Family," 8.

123. Mallory, "Of Dogs and Men," 26–27.

124. Ibid., 27.

125. Claudia Jones, "End to the Neglect," 55.

126. Mae Mallory, "Memo from a Monroe Jail," *Freedomways*, Spring 1964, 203.

127. Ibid., 208.

128. For more on Mabel Williams, see Dagbovie, "'God Has Spared Me.'"

129. Mallory, "Memo from a Monroe Jail," 210.

130. "'Wanted' Woman in Cleveland Home," 1A.

131. Mallory, "Memo from a Monroe Jail," 210, 212–14.

132. Mae Mallory, "The Traitors Within," *Did You Know?*, February 22, 1964, 2.

133. "Save Mae from the KKK," n.d., Ephemera on the Monroe Defendants, Special Collections, University of North Carolina at Chapel Hill, Chapel Hill, North Carolina.

134. Ahmad, *We Will Return in the Whirlwind*, 114–15.

135. "Court Voids Conviction of Mrs. Mae Mallory," *Pittsburgh Courier*, February 6, 1965, 19.

136. Organization of Militant Black Women, "License for Murder," n.d., Box 2, Folder 20, Mallory Collection.

Chapter Two

1. Farmer, "Reframing African American Women's Grassroots Organizing"; McDuffie, *Sojourning for Freedom*, 193–220; Gore, "From Communist Politics to Black Power."

2. McDuffie and Woodard, "'If You're in a Country.'"

3. Marable, *Malcolm X*, 305.

4. Mae Mallory, "Statement of Mae Mallory to the Grand Jury Investigating the Assassination of Malcolm X," 1965, Radicalism Collection, Special Collections, Michigan State University, East Lansing, Michigan.

5. Newton and Seale would later drop "for Self-Defense" from the party's title to help rehabilitate the group's image.

6. Seale, *Lonely Rage*, 177; Austin, *Up against the Wall*, 137. Some former Panthers suggest that the rank and file was almost 50 percent women. See Phyllis Jackson, "Black Panther Party," interview by Pambeli, 3.

7. Tyson, *Radio Free Dixie*, 201–2; "Castro Says 'Thanks' for 'Hospitality,'" *New York Amsterdam News*, September 24, 1960, 5; Rhonda Y. Williams, *Concrete Demands*, 71–72.

8. Carson, *In Struggle*, 18–20.

9. Ransby, *Ella Baker*, 239–72.

10. Carson, *In Struggle*, 29.

11. SNCC had both urban and rural chapters across the country. For more information on SNCC and organizers' activities in the South, see Carson, *In Struggle*; Payne, *I've Got the Light of Freedom*; and Hogan, *Many Minds, One Heart*.

12. For more in-depth analyses of SNCC's mobilization in Mississippi, see Moye, *Let the People Decide*, and Hogan, *Many Minds, One Heart*.

13. For more information on the myriad ways in which women contributed to SNCC, see Payne, *I've Got the Light of Freedom*; Robnett, *How Long? How Long?*; Fleming, *Soon We Will Not Cry*; Holsaert et al., *Hands on the Freedom Plow*; and Ford, *Liberated Threads*.

14. Hasan Kwame Jeffries, *Bloody Lowndes*; Grady-Willis, *Challenging U.S. Apartheid*.

15. Crawford, "African American Women."

16. Carson, *In Struggle*, 126.

17. Carmichael, quoted in Hasan Kwame Jeffries, *Bloody Lowndes*, 150–51.

18. Ibid., 152–53.

19. LCFO Black Panther Party, "Party Headquarters: 1966: Gwen Patton, SGA President, Tuskegee Institute," photograph, ComStoBox 24, Folder: Patton Photos, and "The Candidates and What They Do," n.d., ComStoBox 9, Folder: Lowndes Country Freedom Party, Gwen Patton Collection, Special Collections, H. Councill

Trenholm State Technical College, Montgomery, Alabama (hereafter referred to as the Patton Collection).

20. Carson, *In Struggle*, 196. The strongest early proponents of Black Power in SNCC were members of the Atlanta project who worked in the city's black neighborhood of Vine City. SNCC, they argued, should become an all-black organization and white activists should work in their own communities, where racism was "most manifest." "Position Paper," 1966, Box 1, Folder 11, Student Nonviolent Coordinating Committee–Vine City Project (Atlanta, GA) Records, Wisconsin Historical Society, Madison, Wisconsin; Grady-Willis, *Challenging U.S. Apartheid*, 61–65.

21. Hasan Kwame Jeffries, *Bloody Lowndes*, 181–82.

22. Patton, "Born Freedom Fighter," 581.

23. Spencer, "Engendering the Black Freedom Struggle," 95.

24. Nadasen, *Household Workers Unite*, 58; Sharpless, *Cooking in Other Women's Kitchens*, xi.

25. Nadasen, "'We Do Whatever Becomes Necessary'"; McGuire, *Dark End of the Street*.

26. Mara, *Civil Unrest in the 1960s*; Lyons, "Burning Columbia Avenue."

27. Flamm, *Law and Order*, 13–30.

28. Westheider, *Fighting on Two Fronts*; Hall, *Peace and Freedom*; Graham, *Brothers' Vietnam War*.

29. Spencer, "Engendering the Black Freedom Struggle," 96. For more on student protests and their connection with anti-imperialist efforts abroad, see Biondi, *Black Revolution on Campus*, and Ibram H. Rogers, *Black Campus Movement*.

30. For more information on how the Black Power movement spawned black and ethnic studies, see Rojas, *Black Power to Black Studies*; Ibram H. Rogers, *Black Campus Movement*; and Biondi, *Black Revolution on Campus*.

31. Newton, *Revolutionary Suicide*, 62–64, 112; Murch, *Living for the City*, 58–68. For information on Moore's role in founding the African Descendants People's Partition Party, see Audley Moore, "Address to the National Emancipation Proclamation Centennial Observance Committee," October 12, 1962, Carton 4, Reel 15, Folder 35, Social Protest Collection, Bancroft Library, University of California, Berkeley.

32. Spencer, *Revolution Has Come*, 22.

33. Ibid., 33; "Carmichael Hits U.S. Policies at Berkeley Rally," *Los Angeles Times*, October 30, 1966, C1; Bloom and Martin, *Black against Empire*, 39–42.

34. Newton, *Revolutionary Suicide*, 112–13.

35. "What We Want Now! What We Believe," *Black Panther*, May 15, 1967, 3; Seale, *Seize the Time*, 59.

36. Murch, *Living for the City*, 130.

37. "Armed Black Brothers in Richmond Community," *Black Panther*, April 25, 1967, 4; "Remember the Words of Brother Malcolm X," *Black Panther*, May 15, 1967, 7; Newton, "'Intercommunalism,'" 27; Newton, *Revolutionary Suicide*, 110.

38. Bloom and Martin, *Black against Empire*, 51–57; "Why Was Denzil Dowell Killed?," *Black Panther*, April 25, 1967, 1.

39. Newton, *Revolutionary Suicide*, 49–150; "Police Arrest 24 Capital Invaders, Get 11 Weapons," *Sacramento Bee*, May 3, 1967, A4; Bloom and Martin, *Black against Empire*, 58–59.

40. Spencer, "Engendering the Black Freedom Struggle," 96.

41. Ibid., 94–96; Austin, *Up against the Wall*, 70–73; "New Editorial Assistant," *Black Panther*, October 19, 1968, 13.

42. "Audry Hudson," *Black Panther*, July 3, 1967, 4; Spencer, *Revolution Has Come*, 41.

43. LeBlanc-Ernest, "'Most Qualified Person,'" 308.

44. Lee, Bell, and Panigutti, *All Power to the People*. For women's recollections of Panther armed police patrols, see Rudy Johnson, "Joan Bird and Afeni Shakur, Self Styled Soldiers in the Panther's Class Struggle," *New York Times*, July 19, 1970, 53; and Spencer, "Engendering the Black Freedom Struggle," 96. Interviews with Panther women also mention that the Pantherettes was short-lived. See "Panther Sisters on Women's Liberation," 9.

45. For more analysis of the Moynihan Report and its effects on the black community, see Patterson, *Freedom Is Not Enough*.

46. "Armed Black Brothers in Richmond Community," 4.

47. Rhodes, *Framing the Black Panthers*, 92.

48. Spencer, *Revolution Has Come*, 46.

49. Barbara Auther, "Sisters Unite," *Black Panther*, May 15, 1967, 6.

50. Judy Hart, "Black Womanhood No. 1," *Black Panther*, July 20, 1967, 11, 14.

51. Ibid.

52. Ibid.

53. Ibid.

54. *Black Panther*, May 18, 1968, 20.

55. Doss, "'Revolutionary Art'"; Durant, *Black Panther*.

56. Emory Douglas, "Position Paper #1: On Revolutionary Art," *Black Panther*, October 19, 1968, 4.

57. Spencer, "Engendering the Black Freedom Struggle," 94.

58. Doss, "'Revolutionary Art,'" 255.

59. *Black Panther*, December 21, 1968, 4.

60. *Black Panther*, December 21, 1968, 15.

61. Griffin, "'Ironies of the Saint,'" 214.

62. hooks, *Art on My Mind*, 97.

63. See, for example, "Revolutionary Posters," *Black Panther*, October 12, 1968, 4.

64. For more on controlling images and their importance in white supremacist structures, see Collins, *Black Feminist Thought*, 67–90, and Lumsden, "Good Mothers with Guns," 901.

65. Kathleen Neal Cleaver, "Women, Power, and Revolution," 123; Kathleen Neal Cleaver, introduction to *Target Zero*, xiv; Kathleen Neal Cleaver, "Black Scholar Interviews Kathleen Cleaver," 55; Murch, *Living for the City*, 151–52.

66. "Officer Killed, Black Panther Hurt in Duel," *Atlanta Constitution*, October 29, 1967, 7B; "Newton Murder Charge Began with Routine Traffic Check," *Los Angeles Times*, April 1, 1968, A1.

67. Kathleen Neal Cleaver, "Women, Power, and Revolution," 122–23.

68. See, for example, *Black Panther*, September 28, 1968, 20.

69. "Oakland Tense in the Wake of Police, Panthers Battle," *Los Angeles Times*, April 8, 1968, 3; "A Tribute to Lil Bobby," *Black Panther*, May 4, 1968, 1; Bloom and Martin, *Black against Empire*, 118–19.

70. Bloom and Martin, *Black against Empire*, 159.

71. Anderson, "Practical Internationalists," 283–84, 290; Huggins, interview by author.

72. Black Panther Party—Boston Chapter, "Bulletin No. 1," "Bulletin No. 2," n.d., Box 57, Folder 2360, Freedom House Inc. Records, Archives and Special Collections, Northeastern University, Boston, Massachusetts. The "List of Recognized Chapters and Branches and N.C.C.F.s before Spring of 1970" (n.d.) lists Jones as the leader of the Boston chapter. See Box 1, Folder 1, Black Panther Party—Harlem Branch Files, Harlem Branch Collection, Schomburg Center for Research in Black Culture, New York; LeBlanc-Ernest, "'Most Qualified Person,'" 311.

73. Alameen-Shavers, "Woman Question," 46.

74. Jakobi Williams, "'Don't No Woman,'" 35.

75. Bukhari and Whitehorn, *War Before*, 6; Elaine Brown, *Taste of Power*, 186.

76. Abu-Jamal, *We Want Freedom*, 163.

77. Linda Greene, "The Black Revolutionary Woman," *Black Panther*, September 28, 1968, 11.

78. Ibid.

79. Matthews, "'No One Ever Asks,'" 283.

80. Kotlowski, *Nixon's Civil Rights*, 125–26.

81. For more information, see Churchill and Vander Wall, *Agents of Repression*.

82. "Nationwide Harassment of Panthers by Pig Power Structure," *Black Panther*, January 15, 1969, 11–12.

83. "Two Black Panthers Slain in UCLA Hall," *Los Angeles Times*, January 19, 1969, 1; "Brothers Arraigned in UCLA Slayings," *Los Angeles Times*, January 24, 1969, C1.

84. Bloom and Martin, *Black against Empire*, 223; Arend and Jeffries, "Big Easy."

85. Nyasha, interview by author.

86. Newton, "'Intercommunalism,'" 27–28.

87. Ibid.

88. Newton, "Huey Newton Talks to the Movement," 50.

89. Newton, "'Intercommunalism,'" 28.

90. "Panther Sisters on Women's Liberation," 9.

91. Breines, *Trouble between Us*.

92. Ibid. For analysis of the disparate feminist organizations, see Roth, *Separate Roads to Feminism*. For a comprehensive study of black feminist organizations, see Springer, *Living for the Revolution*.

93. Hesford, *Feeling Women's Liberation*, 3.

94. Cleaver, "Black Scholar Interviews Kathleen Cleaver," 56.

95. Phillips, "Feminist Leadership," 189–90.

96. Matthews, "'No One Ever Asks,'" 274; Judson L. Jeffries, "Conversing with Gwen Robinson."

97. Candi Robinson, "Message to Revolutionary Women," *Black Panther*, August 9, 1969, 23.

98. Ibid.

99. Joan Bird was not the only woman to produce autobiographical accounts for the Panther newspaper. There were, in fact, many more women to publish these types of personal autobiographical articles. However, Bird has rarely been the subject of scholarly analysis, meriting the focus on her within this text.

100. "Joan Bird, N.Y. Panther 21 Political Prisoner," *Black Panther*, June 27, 1970, 9.

101. Ibid.

102. Ibid.

103. Party members published contemporaneous and post hoc autobiographical narratives of their politicization. Male accounts include Newton, *Revolutionary Suicide*; Seale, *Seize the Time*; and Eldridge Cleaver, *Soul on Ice*. Women's accounts include Elaine Brown, *Taste of Power*, and Kathleen Neal Cleaver, "Women, Power, and Revolution."

104. Perkins, *Autobiography as Activism*, xiv–xv.

105. Joy James, "Framing the Panther."

106. Sidonie Smith, "Autobiographical Manifestos," 435.

107. Many of Cleaver's female contemporaries took issue with *Soul on Ice*, most notably his claim that raping white women was a political act and one he "perfected" by practicing on African American women.

108. Eldridge Cleaver's involvement with the April 1968 shootout that killed Bobby Hutton was a violation of his parole, making him subject to reincarceration. Cleaver took refuge in Cuba briefly before settling in Algeria and beginning the International Section of the party. For more information, see Kathleen Neal Cleaver, "Back to Africa." For more on the international dimensions of the Black Panther Party, see Clemons and Jones, "Global Solidarity"; Jennifer B. Smith, *International History*; Angelo, "Black Panthers in London"; and Slate, "Dalit Panthers."

109. For a discussion of the New Haven chapter and the death of Alex Rackley, see Bass and Rae, *Murder in the Model City*. For Huggins's role in the incident and her own recollections, see Huggins, interview by Thompson.

110. "Yale Strike Urged to Support Black Panthers," *New York Times*, April 21, 1970, 1; "Strike Rally at Yale," *New York Times*, April 22, 1970, 1.

111. Eldridge Cleaver, "Message to Sister Ericka Huggins of the Black Panther Party," *Black Panther*, July 5, 1969, 12–13.

112. Jakobi Williams, "'Don't No Woman,'" 42–43.

113. Charles E. Jones, "Arm Yourself or Harm Yourself," 23–24.

114. Phillips and LeBlanc-Ernest, "Hidden Narratives," 69–70.

115. "Huey Newton's Conviction Reversed by Coast Court," *New York Times*, May 30, 1970, 1; "Hundreds Greet Newton on Release from Prison," *Washington Post*, August 6, 1970, A3.

116. "Nationwide Harassment of Panthers by Pig Power Structure," *Black Panther*, January 15, 1969, 10. For more on the police murder of Fred Hampton, see Haas, *Assassination of Fred Hampton*.

117. Newton, "'Intercommunalism,'" 30–31.

118. Gwen Hodges, "Survival Pending Revolution," *Black Panther*, January 9, 1971, 3.

119. "Let Us Hold High the Banner of Intercommunalism and the Invincible Thoughts of Huey P. Newton, Minister of Defense and Supreme Commander of the Black Panther Party," *Black Panther*, January 23, 1971, A.

120. Alkebulan, *Survival Pending Revolution*, 29.

121. Newton, "Women's Liberation and Gay Liberation Movements," 157–58.

122. Spencer, *Revolution Has Come*, 98.

123. The two coasts had been at odds over other issues, like the allocation of funds raised for the Panther 21 defense and of funds from newspaper sales. Newton's disavowal of armed revolution exacerbated this already tenuous relationship.

124. "Open Letter to Weatherman Underground from Panther 21," *East Village Other*, January 19, 1971, 3.

125. "Enemies of the People," *Black Panther*, February 13, 1971, 12; "Newton Expels 12 Panthers," *Guardian*, February 20, 1971, 4.

126. Umoja, "Repression Breeds Resistance," 143.

127. "Black Panther Dispute," *Sun Reporter*, March 13, 1971, 2.

128. Spencer, *Revolution Has Come*, 103.

129. Ibid., 111; Bloom and Martin, *Black against Empire*, 362; "Panthers Fear Growing Intraparty Strife," *New York Times*, April 10, 1971, 24.

130. Bloom and Martin, *Black against Empire*, 380.

131. After Newton consolidated the party, members in Oakland filled out a skills survey to assess what role each member should play. A survey of these forms reveals an overwhelmingly female membership. See Box 4, Folders 4–5, Dr. Huey P. Newton Foundation, Inc. Collection, Department of Special Collections and University Archives, Stanford University, Palo Alto, California (hereafter referred to as the HPN Collection).

132. "Oakland—A Base of Operations," *Black Panther*, July 29, 1972, supplement. The Panthers ran a series of articles with this title every week from July 29, 1972, to April 7, 1973, each focused on a different aspect of how members could effect change in the city.

133. The *Black Panther* featured statements of support for Dellums and Chisholm. "Register to Vote for Shirley Chisholm," *Black Panther*, May 13, 1972, front page; "A Survival Program in Congress," *Black Panther*, April 15, 1972, front page; Murch, *Living for the City*, 184.

134. Bloom and Martin, *Black against Empire*, 181–95. For more on the Panthers' health care program, see Alondra Nelson, *Body and Soul*. For more on the wide range of survival programs the Panthers created, see Alkebulan, *Survival Pending Revolution*.

135. Murch, *Living for the City*, 202.

136. "A Program for Survival," *Black Panther*, July 29, 1972, 8. For more on these programs, see Hilliard, *Black Panther Party*.

137. Internal documents among party members about the health clinic reflect Jones's leadership of this section of party activities. For these, see Audrea Jones to Mayor Warren Wilder, no date, Box 17, Folder 7, and Audrea Jones to Comrade Servant [Newton], memo, September 31, 1972, Box 18, Folder 3, HPN Collection.

138. Abron, "'Serving the People'"; Judson L. Jeffries, "Conversing with Gwen Robinson," 142.

139. Elaine Brown, *Taste of Power*, 314–15; Self, *American Babylon*, 309–11; Bloom and Martin, *Black against Empire*, 385.

140. LeBlanc-Ernest, "'Most Qualified Person,'" 318; "Panthers Sweep Berkeley Elections," *Black Panther*, June 10, 1972, 2.

141. Elaine Brown, who joined the party in Los Angeles in 1968, was the editor of the paper from 1970 to 1972. Afterward, Huggins, who served as Brown's assistant in 1971, took over the job. Lumsden, "Good Mothers with Guns," 904.

142. Lula Hudson, "They Told Me I Had to Be Sterilized or Die," *Black Panther*, July 15, 1972, 4; "Winston Salem Welfare Moms Bugged," *Black Panther*, February 7, 1972, 6; "Right on Welfare Moms," *Black Panther*, March 28, 1970, 12.

143. "Our Sisters in Bondage," *Black Panther*, January 13, 1973, 3.

144. "Interview with Margaret Sloan: National Black Feminist Organization Seeks Solutions to Problems of Black Women," *Black Panther*, October 6, 1975, 11; "Angela Davis, a Black Woman in the Liberation Struggle," *Black Panther*, March 11, 1972, front page.

145. "Another Mother for Struggle," *Black Panther*, February 12, 1972, front page.

146. For more on the Soledad Brothers, see George Jackson, *Soledad Brother*; Aptheker, *Morning Breaks*.

147. "Another Mother for Struggle," 10–11.

148. Dickson, interview by author.

149. Phillips and LeBlanc-Ernest, "Hidden Narratives," 73.

150. *Black Panther*, June 3, 1972, 12.

151. Bob Manning, "The Black Panthers Anti-war Survival Conference," *Los Angeles Free Press*, July 21, 1972; *Black Panther*, July 1, 1972, 12.

152. "Leader of Panthers Booked in Assaults," *New York Times*, August 18, 1974, 31.

153. Bloom and Martin, *Black against Empire*, 383.

154. The Oakland Community School was formally the Intercommunal Youth Institute. "The Oakland Community School," n.d., Box 16, Folder 2, HPN Collection; Huggins and LeBlanc-Ernest, "Revolutionary Women, Revolutionary Education," 168–70.

155. For more on the effects of the Panthers' programming in Oakland, see Self, *American Babylon*.

156. Abron, "'Raising the Consciousness of the People,'" 356.

157. "Statement of Elaine Brown Re: The Black Panther Party," November 16, 1977, Box 41, Folder 5, HPN Collection; Elaine Brown, *Taste of Power*, 444–47.

158. Jonina Abron to Ericka Huggins and Huey Newton, "Re: Zimbabwe Medical Drive and ZANU," memo, February 12, 1979, and Jonina Abron to Huey Newton, "Re: Black Veterans Association Rally," memo, March 20, 1979, Box 13, Folder 4, HPN Collection.

159. Abron, "'Raising the Consciousness of the People,'" 357; Bloom and Martin, *Black against Empire*, 389.

Chapter Three

1. Amiri Baraka, "Ideological Statement," 107–8; Woodard, *Nation within a Nation*, 162–63.

2. "African Peoples Congress Will Climax Tomorrow," *Atlanta Daily World*, September 6, 1970, 1; Amiri Baraka, introduction to *African Congress*, ix.

3. Bibi Amina Baraka, "Coordinator's Statement," 177.

4. Maulana Karenga, "Kawaida Philosophy and Practice: Questions for a Life of Struggle," *Los Angeles Sentinel*, August 2, 2007, A7.

5. Scot Brown, *Fighting for US*, 62.

6. Tiamoyo Karenga and Tembo, "Kawaida Womanism," 33.

7. For more information, see Kemper, "Reformers in the Marketplace of Ideas."

8. Ibid., 101–2; "Freedom Rider Tells Experience," *Daily Bruin*, October 3, 1961, 1; "Freedom Ride Described as Brutal Beating," *Daily Bruin*, October 4, 1961, 1.

9. Ogbar, *Black Power*, 128–29; "Malcolm X Scores Metros Style Stories," *Los Angeles Sentinel*, November 29, 1962, A2; Marable, *Malcolm X*, 205–9.

10. "Grand Opening Africa House," *Los Angeles Sentinel*, July 9, 1959, C1; "Africa House Meets Challenge," *Herald-Dispatch*, October 26, 1972, 10; "Africa House Inc., Stresses African Americans' Heritage," *Herald-Dispatch*, December 16, 1967, 1.

11. "Afro-American Assn. Forms L.A. Branch," *Los Angeles Sentinel*, August 15, 1963, A3; Scot Brown, *Fighting for US*, 27–28.

12. Newton, *Revolutionary Suicide*, 60–66; Seale, *Seize the Time*, 20–21.

13. Warden, "The Afro American Association," 14–15; Scot Brown, "'To Unbrainwash an Entire People.'"

14. Scot Brown, *Fighting for US*, 11.

15. Ibid., 28.

16. "Watts Brothers Tell of Incident That Triggered Riot," *Los Angeles Sentinel*, September 9, 1965, A1.

17. Martin Luther King Jr., "Watts," 292.

18. Byron E. Calme, "Black Enigma: A West Coast Militant Talks Tough but Helps Avert Racial Trouble," *Wall Street Journal*, July 26, 1968, 1; Scot Brown, "'To Unbrainwash an Entire People,'" 140.

19. Halisi, *Kitabu*, 3; Scot Brown, *Fighting for US*, 38; Maulana Karenga, interview by author.

20. Hayes and Jeffries, "US Does Not Stand for United Slaves!," 74; Clay Carson, "A Talk with Ron Karenga: Watts Black Nationalist," *Los Angeles Free Press*, September 2, 1966, 12.

21. "An Interview with Hakim Jamal," *Long Beach Free Press*, September–October 1, 1969, 6; Scot Brown, *Fighting for US*, 39.

22. Carson, "Talk with Ron Karenga," 12.

23. Halisi, *Kitabu*, 8.

24. "Holiday for Malcolm X Asked Here," *Los Angeles Times*, May 18, 1967, 29; "Observance Set for Malcolm X," *Los Angeles Sentinel*, February 3, 1966, A1; Scot Brown, *Fighting for US*, 68; Asante, *Maulana Karenga*, 165; Mayes, *Kwanzaa*.

25. "Violence May Benefit Negroes, Rap Brown Says at Rally Here," *Los Angeles Times*, August 14, 1967, 3.

26. "TALO Reiterates Its Position," *Los Angeles Times*, August 6, 1966, B4; Scot Brown, *Fighting for US*, 82; Bloom and Martin, *Black against Empire*, 39.

27. "Black Power Call Is Forging Unity," *Los Angeles Times*, September 24, 1967, F3; "Partial List of Black Congress," *Harambee*, December 1967, 8; "Out on Bail," *Harambee*, December 1967, 1, 8; Elaine Brown, *Taste of Power*, 106–7; Scot Brown, *Fighting for US*, 83.

28. "Operational Unity: Answer to Negro Division," *Los Angeles Sentinel*, June 9, 1968, D1; "Watts Groups Planning Joint Sunrise Services," *Los Angeles Sentinel*, April 13, 1968, B6; "Leaders Picket Manual Arts," *Los Angeles Sentinel*, September 14, 1967, A1; Scot Brown, *Fighting for US*, 84–86.

29. Scot Brown, *Fighting for US*, 42–43.

30. Maulana Karenga, interview by author.

31. Ibid.; Scot Brown, *Fighting for US*, 56.

32. Tiamoyo Karenga, interview by author.

33. Ibid.; Scot Brown, " 'To Unbrainwash an Entire People,' " 141.

34. Halisi, *Kitabu*, 10.

35. White, "Africa on My Mind."

36. Scot Brown, *Fighting for US*, 32–33.

37. Patton, "Black People and the Victorian Ethos."

38. Beal, "Double Jeopardy," 122.

39. See, for example Halisi, *Quotable Karenga*.

40. Scot Brown, *Fighting for US*, 57.

41. Hayes and Jeffries ("US Does Not Stand for United Slaves!," 78) claimed that the *Wall Street Journal* article "Black Enigma: A West Coast Militant Talks Tough but Helps Avert Trouble" was the source of many of these negative portrayals of Karenga. In particular, they noted that this article emphasized that he met with LA police chief Thomas Reddin to quell violence after Dr. King's death—an act interpreted as a betrayal by many in the black community. For evidence of Karenga's attempts to quell violence after Dr. King's death, see "Dr. King's Death Spurs Unity Display by L.A. Negro Groups," *Los Angeles Times*, April 7, 1968, EB.

42. "L.A.P.D. Raids US Headquarters," *Los Angeles Sentinel*, January 1, 1970, A1; "Karenga Wife to Sue Cops," *Los Angeles Sentinel*, February 1, 1968, A1.

43. Agents stated that it was the bureau's "hope" that "counterintelligence measure[s] [would] result in an 'US' and BPP (Black Panther Party) vendetta." SAC [Special Agent in Charge] Los Angeles to Director, memo, November 29, 1968, FBI BN. The sources that discuss the feud, and the FBI's involvement in it, are numerous; therefore, this study will not go into detail about the event. For more information, see Scot Brown, *Fighting for US*; Austin, *Up against the Wall*; and Churchill and Vander Wall, *Agents of Repression*, 37, 112. Karenga also published numerous reports denying that Us premeditated the attack. He maintained that the shootout was "contextual, not conspiratorial." Maulana Karenga, "Response to Muhammad Ahmad," 55.

44. Maulana Karenga, "Kawaida and Its Critics," 131–32.

45. Maulana Karenga, "Black Liberation Movement," 124–25.

46. Ibid.

47. Malaika, "View from the Womans' [sic] Side of the Circle," *Harambee*, April 25 1969, 4.

48. Ibid.

49. Ibid.

50. Ibid.

51. Maulana Karenga, "Black Liberation Movement," 126.

52. Malaika, "Womans' Side of the Circle," 4.

53. Maulana Karenga, "Strategy for Struggle," 17.

54. Scot Brown, *Fighting for US*, 125.

55. Scot Brown, "'To Unbrainwash an Entire People,'" 144.

56. Curvin, *Inside Newark*, 36, 46–47; Tuttle, *How Newark Became Newark*, 156; Buffalo, "Revolutionary Life Together," 84, 86.

57. "Art Festival Will Be Held in Newark," *New York Amsterdam News*, July 23, 1966, 36; Amiri Baraka, *Autobiography of LeRoi Jones*, 336.

58. Amiri Baraka, *Autobiography of LeRoi Jones*, 331; Woodard, *Nation within a Nation*, 65–66. For more on the activists and organizations of the Black Arts movement, see Smethurst, *Black Arts Movement*; Cheryl Clarke, *"After Mecca"*; Smethurst, Sanchez, and Bracey, *SOS/Calling All Black People*.

59. Amiri Baraka, *Autobiography of LeRoi Jones*, 224.

60. "From Congress of African People to Revolutionary Communist League," *Unity and Struggle*, June 1976, 2; Salimu (Nettie) Rogers, interview by Komozi Woodard, 1986, in Komozi, Boehm, and Lewis, *Black Power Movement* [microfilm], Reel 9, Frame 311; Amiri Baraka, interview by Komozi Woodard, January 4, 1986, in ibid., Reel 8, Frame 562.

61. Rogers, interview by Woodard; Woodard, "Message from the Grassroots," 88.

62. Buffalo, "Revolutionary Life Together," 84, 86; Amiri Baraka, *Autobiography of LeRoi Jones*, 344.

63. "C.O.R.E.'s 24th National Convention, June 30, 1967, Part 1," Pacifica Radio Archive, Los Angeles, California; Amiri Baraka, *Autobiography of LeRoi Jones*, 353.

64. "From Congress of African People," 2; Amiri Baraka, *Autobiography of LeRoi Jones*, 350–58.

65. "Newark Mayor Calls in Guard as Riots Spread," *Los Angeles Times*, July 14, 1967, 11; "New Violence in Newark: Stores Burned and Looted," *Newark Star Ledger*, July 14, 1967, 1; Woodard, *Nation within a Nation*, 79–80.

66. Woodard, *Nation within a Nation*, 84.

67. "Newark Meeting on Black Power Attended by 400," *New York Times*, July 21, 1967, 1.

68. Woodard, *Nation within a Nation*, 86.

69. Randolph, *Florynce "Flo" Kennedy*, 115–17.

70. "2 Police Inspectors from Here among the Newark Delegates," *New York Times*, July 22, 1967, 11; Woodard, *Nation within a Nation*, 86–88.

71. Woodard, *Nation within a Nation*, 88.

72. "African Free School Has Its Own Methodology," *New York Amsterdam News*, June 26, 1971, D1; "Newark School Teaches African Culture Class," *Baltimore Afro-American*, January 30, 1971, 12; "African Free School Structure," in Komozi, Boehm, and Lewis, *Black Power Movement*, Reel 2, Frame 577; Rickford, *We Are an African People*, 138–39.

73. Sisters of Black Culture, *Black Woman's Role in the Revolution*, 2.

74. Amiri Baraka, *Autobiography of LeRoi Jones*, 385.

75. Woodard, *Nation within a Nation*, 109–10.

76. Ibid., 101–4; "Newark Negroes Meet on Election," *New York Times*, June 22, 1968, 28; "Newark Negroes Pick 2 Candidates," *New York Times*, June 24, 1968, 23; "From Congress of African People," 2; Scot Brown, *Fighting for US*, 104.

77. Woodard, *Nation within a Nation*, 116–20.

78. "Committee for Unified Newark Organizational Overview," in Komozi, Boehm, and Lewis, *Black Power Movement*, Reel 1, Frame 848; Woodard, *Nation within a Nation*, 135.

79. "African Free School Sets Pre-school for Newark Young," *New York Amsterdam News*, March 25, 1972, B9.

80. "Kawaida Customs and Concepts" and "The Kawaida Wedding," in Komozi, Boehm, and Lewis, *Black Power Movement*, Reel 1, Frame 810; Amiri Baraka, *Autobiography of LeRoi Jones*, 419–20; "African Women Working and Studying toward Nationalism," in Komozi, Boehm, and Lewis, *Black Power Movement*, Reel 2, Frame 581; Woodard, "It's Nation Time in NewArk," 299.

81. "The Political School of Kawaida," in Komozi, Boehm, and Lewis, *Black Power Movement*, Reel 1, Frame 805.

82. Woodard, *Nation within a Nation*, 123.

83. Amiri Baraka, *Autobiography of LeRoi Jones*, 403.

84. Woodard, *Nation within a Nation*, 164–67.

85. "Atlanta Black Congress," *New Pittsburg Courier*, September 19, 1970, 13.

86. Woodard, *Nation within a Nation*, 166–67.

87. Ibid., 160–69.

88. Amiri Baraka, *Autobiography of LeRoi Jones*, 307.

89. "Black Women in the 1970s," *Black NewArk*, December 1973, 7.

90. Shulman, *Seventies*, 159–92; Randolph, *Florynce "Flo" Kennedy*, 98–136; Ward, "Third World Women's Alliance."

91. Roth, *Separate Roads to Feminism*; Echols, *Daring to Be Bad*; Gilmore, *Feminist Coalitions*.

92. "Books Available thru Jihad Productions," in Komozi, Boehm, and Lewis, *Black Power Movement*, Reel 1, Frame 632.

93. Mumininas of the Committee for Unified NewArk, "Mwanamke Mwanachi: The Nationalist Woman," in Komozi, Boehm, and Lewis, *Black Power Movement*, Reel 1, Frame 837.

94. Ibid.

95. Ibid.

96. Ibid.

97. Ibid.

98. Simanga, *Amiri Baraka*, 82–83; Johnson, *Revolutionaries to Race Leaders*, 87; Strickland, "Gary Convention"; Amiri Baraka, "Creation of Political Institutions."

99. Woodard, *Nation within a Nation*, 161; Simanga, *Amiri Baraka*, 85–86.

100. See chapter 4 for more information on these women's collectives.

101. Woodard, *Nation within a Nation*, 218.

102. Amiri Baraka, *Autobiography of LeRoi Jones*, 419.

103. Amiri Baraka, "The Beginning of a National Movement" (presented at the Second Congress of African People National Meeting, San Diego, CA, 1972).

104. Simanga, *Amiri Baraka*, 86–90.

105. Ibid., 90.

106. See, for example, Bibi Amina Baraka, "Social Organization: Ritual Celebrating the Birth of Our Children," *Black NewArk*, October 1972, 3; and Bibi Amina Baraka, "Social Organization: On Afrikan Dress," *Black NewArk*, June 1973, 7.

107. Bibi Amina Baraka, "Social Organization: On Afrikan Women," *Black New-Ark*, August 1973, 2.

108. Ibid.

109. Simanga, *Amiri Baraka*, 86.

110. Malaika, "Social Development," *Black NewArk,* September 1973, 7.

111. Malaika, "Social Development: How Do We Get Out of This Mess?," *Black NewArk*, January–February 1974, 7.

112. "CAP Afrikan Women's Conference . . . Will Be Held in Newark—July 74," *Black NewArk*, January–February 1974, 3.

113. Malaika, "Social Development: The Role of the Black Woman in the Revolution," *Unity and Struggle*, February–March 1974, 11.

114. Ibid.

115. "Forum Planned by Black Women," *New York Times*, June 29, 1974, 63; Malaika, "Social Development: Black Women Organizing to Struggle," *Unity and Struggle*, March 1974, 11.

116. "African Women's Confab Attracts Large Gathering," *Philadelphia Tribune*, July 27, 1974, 12.

117. "African Women Unite," *Unity and Struggle*, August 1974, 11.

118. Ibid.; Simanga, *Amiri Baraka*, 85–86.

119. Amiri Baraka, "The Meaning and Development of Revolutionary Kawaida," in Komozi, Boehm, and Lewis, *Black Power Movement*, Reel 2, Frame 751.

120. Amiri Baraka, "Creating a Unified Consciousness among the Leadership and Putting the Value System and Ideology in Control," in Komozi, Boehm, and Lewis, *Black Power Movement*, Reel 2, Frame 744.

121. Maulana Karenga, "Strategy for Struggle," 17.

122. Amiri Baraka, *Autobiography of LeRoi Jones*, 307; Amiri Baraka, "Creating a Unified Consciousness."

123. Amiri Baraka, "The Organizing Meeting of the Black Women's United Front," in *Black Women's United Front: Congress of Afrikan People on the Woman Question, Position Paper and Speeches from Meeting Held in Detroit, Michigan, January 25, 1975,*

Box 15, Folder: Black Women's United Front, Printed Ephemera Collection on Organizations, Tamiment Library and Robert F. Wagner Labor Archives, New York University, New York.

124. Amiri Baraka, "Revolutionary Party, Revolutionary Ideology," in Komozi, Boehm, and Lewis, *Black Power Movement*, Reel 2, Frame 761.

125. "The Woman Question: Black Women and Struggle," in Komozi, Boehm, and Lewis, *Black Power Movement*, Reel 3, Frame 249; "Black Women's United Front: Black Women Struggle for Democratic Rights," *Unity and Struggle*, October 1975, 4–6.

126. "BWUF Meets in Detroit," *Unity and Struggle*, June 1975, 6; "BWUF 1st Nat'l Assembly Meeting," audio recording, side 1, Box 25, Komozi Woodard–Amiri Baraka Collection, 1931–1998, Auburn Avenue Research Library on African American Culture and History, Atlanta, Georgia; "Black Women Struggle for Democratic Rights," 4–6. For more on Joan Little, see McNeil, "'Joanne Is You,'" 259, 267, and McGuire, "Joan Little," 203.

127. "Black Women's United Front—Forward with the Struggle!," *Unity and Struggle*, November 1975, 7–9; "Women Set Rally Sunday," *Pittsburg Courier*, July 12, 1975, 28; "Black Women's UF to Aid Community," *Pittsburg Courier*, September 20, 1975, 1.

128. "The Woman Question: Black Women and Struggle," in Komozi, Boehm, and Lewis, *Black Power Movement*, Reel 3, Frame 249.

129. Mayes, *Kwanzaa*, xix.

130. Simanga, *Amiri Baraka*, 124.

Chapter Four

1. For more information on The East and its role in CAP, see Konadu, *View from The East*.

2. Alberta Hill, "All-Africa Women's Conference, Dar-es-Salaam, Tanzania," *Black News*, November 1, 1972, 22.

3. Gaines, *American Africans in Ghana*; Meriwether, *Proudly We Can Be Africans*.

4. Pan-African Congress, "Call to Sixth Pan African Congress."

5. Rickford, *We Are an African People*, 132.

6. For more on the different philosophical and activist dimensions of Pan-Africanism, see Kurt B. Young, "Holistic Review of Pan-Africanism," and Walters, *Pan Africanism in the African Diaspora*. In 1897, Trinidadian activist and intellectual Henry Sylvester Williams developed the term *Pan-Africanism* to describe the political, cultural, and social affiliations of the African diaspora and the organizing strategies based on the solidarity and shared destiny of people of African descent. Sherwood, *Origins of Pan-Africanism*.

7. Ula Taylor, *Veiled Garvey*.

8. Sherwood, "Pan-African Conferences, 1900–1953," 107.

9. Monterio, "Sixth Pan-African Congress," 396–97.

10. Sherwood, "Pan-African Conferences, 1900–1953," 110.

11. Forman, *Making of Black Revolutionaries*, 455, 481; Wilkins, "Making of Black Internationalists"; Beal, "Voices of Feminism Oral History Project," interview by

Ross, 145; "International Seminar on Apartheid Racial Discrimination and Colonialism in Southern Africa," ComStoBox 25, Folder: Mae Jackson South Africa, Patton Collection.

12. For more information, see Bloom and Martin, *Black against Empire*; Scot Brown, *Fighting for US*; Woodard, *Nation within a Nation*.

13. "100 Protesters Seize Library at Cornell," *New York Times*, April 28, 1972, 17.

14. "Lincoln Moves on Chrome Issue," *African World*, May 9, 1972, 10; "200 Protest Importation of Chrome," *Atlanta Constitution*, April 20, 1972, 3C.

15. Wilkins, "'Belly of the Beast,'" 196–217. The Youth Organization for Black Unity was originally the Student Organization for Black Unity, founded in North Carolina in 1969. Once it extended its reach to work with nonstudent organizations and took on an explicitly Pan-African focus in 1972, it became the Youth Organization for Black Unity.

16. Rickford, *We Are an African People*, 168–89. For a detailed account of Sadaukai's experience with FRELIMO, see Owusu Sadaukai, "Inside Liberated Mozambique with the FRELIMO Guerillas: Part 1," *African World*, January 8, 1972, 8; "Inside Liberated Mozambique—An Ideology Put into Action, Part 2," *African World*, January 22, 1972, 8.

17. Woodard, *Nation within a Nation*, 173–75; Wilkins, "'Belly of the Beast,'" 134–36.

18. "Locals Back African Liberation Day Rallies," *Pittsburgh Courier*, April 1, 1972, 8.

19. Johnson, *Revolutionaries to Race Leaders*, 190.

20. "Liberation Day Demonstrations Set for D.C., May 27th," *New York Amsterdam News*, April 15, 1972, A10; Johnson, "From Popular Anti-imperialism to Sectarianism," 489.

21. "African Liberation Day," *Contrast*, June 15, 1972, 1.

22. "12,000 Blacks March to Support Africa," *Washington Post*, May 28, 1972, A1.

23. "Blacks Protest South Africa: 35,000 Join Rally," *Chicago Daily Defender*, May 30, 1972, 4.

24. "African Fighters to Get More Help," *Afro-American*, April 1, 1972, 1; "Solidarity Is Goal of Blacks on African Lib Day," *New York Amsterdam News*, June 10, 1972, C5.

25. "ALD: Mass Expression to Learn and Support," *African World*, June 10, 1972, 12; "African Liberation Day Speakers," *African World*, June 10, 1972, 11.

26. Rickford, *We Are an African People*, 184.

27. Ibid., 252; Woodard, *Nation within a Nation*, 179. Other marches took place in Pittsburg, Saint Louis, and Toronto. ALD marchers in the Bay Area stormed the Portuguese embassy before convening in Raymond-Kimball Park to hear Angela Davis's speech on diasporic solidarity. "Locals Back African Liberation Day Rallies," 8; "Liberation Day Planned in Bay Area," *Los Angeles Sentinel*, May 25, 1972, A12.

28. Rickford, *We Are an African People*, 185–88.

29. Mehta, "Images of Exile," 35–36.

30. Lemelle and Kelley, "Introduction: Imagining Home," 4; Leeds, "'Higher Type of Womanhood.'"

31. Wilkins, "'Belly of the Beast,'" 150; Rickford, *We Are an African People*, 182–83.

32. Kuumba, "Engendering the Pan-African Movement," 171.

33. "A Look at Ten Years of an African Women's Organization," *Daily News*, July 24, 1972, 7.

34. "Delegates Ready for Conference," *Daily News*, July 22, 1972, 1.

35. "African Women's Confab: Africa for the Africans at Home and Abroad," *Herald-Dispatch*, September 7, 1972, 1.

36. "African Women's Conference Opens Today," *Daily News*, July 24, 1972, 1.

37. Audley Moore, "Speech to All-Africa Women's Conference," n.d., ca. 1972, Box 39, Folder 2, Preston Wilcox Papers, Schomburg Center for Research in Black Culture, New York.

38. Ibid.

39. Ibid.

40. Ibid.

41. Ibid.

42. Carby, *Race Men*, 5.

43. Moore, "Speech to All-Africa Women's Conference."

44. Rickford, *We Are an African People*, 237.

45. "Women Urged to Forget Prejudices," *Daily News*, August 1, 1972, 1.

46. Alberta Hill, "All-Africa Women's Conference," 22; "African Women's Confab," 1.

47. "ALD Committee Continues to Work," *African World*, August 19, 1972, 14. For more on the ALSC, see Johnson, *Revolutionaries to Race Leaders*; Kadalie, *Internationalism*.

48. Geri Augusto, "The Light and Songs of Freedom: Reflections on SNCC's Legacy to Black Internationalism," unpublished paper in author's possession, 10; Markle, "Drum and Spear Press"; Wilkins, "'Line of Steel,'" 104.

49. "PASP Is Recruiting," *Philadelphia Tribune*, February 26, 1974, 10; Wilkins, "'Belly of the Beast,'" 53–116; Rickford, *We Are an African People*, 161.

50. James Garrett, "A Historical Sketch: The Sixth Pan-African Congress," *Black World*, March 1975, 4.

51. Ibid., 17; Wilkins, "'Line of Steel,'" 100.

52. Markle, "'We Are Not Tourists,'" 244–45.

53. Augusto, interview by author; Augusto, interview by Cobb.

54. Pan-African Congress, "Call to Sixth Pan African Congress."

55. Sylvia Hill and Claude, "Remembering Sixth-PAC," interview by Levy, 41.

56. Ibid., 43; Sylvia Hill, Secretary-General, to "State/District Contact Person Responsible for Distribution of This Application and Questionnaire," memo, December 19, 1973, Box 6, Folder 21, Sixth Pan-African Congress Records, Moorland-Spingarn Research Center, Howard University, Washington, DC (hereafter referred to as 6PAC Records).

57. "North American Region Planning Conference Report," 1973, Box 6, Folder 64, 6PAC Records.

58. Bush, *We Are Not What We Seem*.

59. Bennett, "Pan-Africanism at the Crossroads," 148–50; Kadalie, *Internationalism*, 296; Johnson, *Revolutionaries to Race Leaders*, 155; Rickford, *We Are an African People*, 225–28.

60. "Sixth Pan African Congress Delegate/Observer Questionnaire Application: Lois L. Johnson," n.d., Box 1, Folder 35, 6PAC Records.

61. "Sixth Pan African Congress Delegate/Observer Questionnaire Application: Mrs. Virginia E. Y. Collins," n.d., Box 1, Folder 16, 6PAC Records; Kim Lacey Rogers, *Righteous Lives*; Farmer, "Mothers of Pan-Africanism"; Farmer, "Reframing African American Women's Grassroots Organizing."

62. Minutes from the Midwest Working Meeting, November 23, 24, 1973, Box 2, Folder 16, 6PAC Records.

63. New England District Committee, "Conference Proceedings and Positions," November 3, 1973, Box 2, Folder 21, 6PAC Records.

64. Ibid.

65. "Sunday Morning Meeting Notes, 1/13/74," Box 4, Folder 31, 6PAC Records.

66. Sylvia Hill, "Sixth Pan-African Congress," 35.

67. Cox, quoted in ibid.

68. Claude, "Some Personal Reflections."

69. Ibid.

70. Markle, "'We Are Not Tourists,'" 259; Courtland Cox to Sylvia Hill, March 18, 1974, Box 4, Folder 4, 6PAC Records.

71. Markle, "'We Are Not Tourists,'" 259–60; Augusto, interview by author.

72. Markle, "'We Are Not Tourists,'" 259; Publicity Release, January 17, 1974, Box 3, Folder 85, 6PAC Records.

73. "Interview with Conf. Official: Sixth Pan African Congress in Tanzania," *African World*, May 31, 1974, 5. For more on women and gender in FRELIMO, see Isaacman and Isaacman, *Mozambique*, 91–92. For more information on women and the African Party for the Independence of Guinea and Cape Verde, see Urdang, *Fighting Two Colonialisms*.

74. Julian Elison to Courtland Cox, July 23, 1973, Box 4, Folder 3, 6PAC Records; Sylvia Hill, interview by Minter; Amiri Baraka, "Some Questions."

75. Garrett, "Historical Sketch," 20; Wilkins, "'Line of Steel,'" 106; "Caribbean Radicals out of Dar Talks," *Daily News*, June 13, 1974, 2.

76. Garrett, "Historical Sketch," 20.

77. Markle, "'We Are Not Tourists,'" 249; Wilkins, "'Line of Steel,'" 106; Rodney, *Towards the Sixth Pan-African Congress*.

78. Horne, "Pan-African Congress," 2.

79. Fuller, "Notes," 73–74; Sixth Pan-African Congress Program, June 19–27, 1974, Box 1, Folder 22a, Muriel S. and Otto P. Snowden Papers, Archives and Special Collections, Northeastern University Library, Boston (hereafter referred to as the Snowden Papers).

80. Sixth Pan-African Congress Program, Box 1, Folder 22a, Snowden Papers.

81. "Congress Participants," n.d., Box 3, Folder 3, 6PAC Records. This list of participants breaks down the North American Delegation by gender, indicating that many women attended.

82. "Immigration Form for Special Guests: Audley Moore," n.d., Box 2, Folder 142, 6PAC Records; "Sixth PAC: North American Women," *Daily News*, June 26, 1974, 4. For evidence of Muriel Snowden's participation in the Sixth PAC, see Box 1, Folders 21–22, Snowden Papers.

83. "North America Regional Delegates—Georgia," n.d., Box 3, Folder 2, and "North America Regional Delegates—Michigan," n.d., Box 3, Folder 2, 6PAC Records; "10 Chicago Blacks Will Attend Parley in Tanzania," *Chicago Tribune*, June 13, 1974, N2; Rickford, *We Are an African People*, 235.

84. "Sixth PAC: North American Women," 4.

85. Sixth Pan-African Congress Program, Box 1, Folder 22a, Snowden Papers.

86. "The Role of Women in the Struggle for Liberation," June 24, 1974, Box 4, Folder 32, 6PAC Records.

87. "Women's Contribution to Pan African Struggle," n.d., ca. 1974, Box 4, Folder 32, 6PAC Records.

88. The list of papers presented at "Women in the Struggle" workshops indicates that one of the papers presented was "The Question of Women in the Struggle," presented by Jo Anne Favors from the "USA." Box 4, Folder 32, 6PAC Records.

89. Augusto, interview by author; Pan-African Congress, *Resolutions and Selected Speeches*.

90. "Untitled Position Paper," n.d., ca. 1974, Box 7, Folder 11, 6PAC Records.

91. Ibid.

92. Ibid.

93. Ibid.

94. Ibid.

95. Committee C, "Women's Contribution to the Pan-African Struggle," 1974, general summary of position and resolutions of North America, Box 9, Folder 1, Cleveland L. Sellers Jr. Papers, Avery Research Center for African American History and Culture, College of Charleston, Charleston, South Carolina.

96. For more on Gertrude Wilks and the Nairobi School, see Wilks, *Gathering Together*; Rickford, *We Are an African People*, 100–119.

97. Committee C, "Women's Contribution to the Pan-African Struggle."

98. Ibid.

99. White, "Africa on My Mind"; Rickford, *We Are an African People*, 156–58.

100. Committee C, "Women's Contribution to the Pan-African Struggle." For more on the "natural" roles of women and the Kawaida doctrine, see chapter 3.

101. "Comment," *Daily News*, June 25, 1974, 1.

102. Sylvia Hill, "Observations on the Sixth Pan-African Congress," n.d., Box 6, Folder 63, 6PAC Records.

103. "PAC Must Be Dynamic—Plea," *Daily News*, June 28, 1974, 1.

104. Haki Madhubuti, "Sixth Pan-Afrikan Congress: What Is Being Done to Save the Black Race," *Black Books Bulletin* 2 (Fall 1974): 48.

105. "'Failures' Mar 6th Pan African Congress," *Afro American*, July 27, 1974, 16; "Pilgrimage Reflections—II: 6th Pan African Congress," *Los Angeles Sentinel*, July 18, 1974, A7; "Pan-African Congress Falls Short in Action and Policy," *Chicago Defender*, July 18, 1974, 12.

106. Sylvia Hill, "Observations."

107. Horne, "Pan-African Congress," 2.

108. "Resolution on Women," n.d., ca. 1974, Box 7, Folder 4, 6PAC Records. An edited version of this document was reprinted in the *Resolutions and Selected Speeches* anthology published by the Tanzania Press. See "Resolution on Black Women," in *Resolutions and Selected Speeches*, 197.

109. "Resolution on Women," Box 7, Folder 4, 6PAC Records.

110. Sylvia Hill and Claude, "Remembering Sixth-PAC," interview by Levy, 43.

111. "Sixth PAC: North American Women," 3.

112. Sylvia Hill and Claude, "Remembering Sixth-PAC," interview by Levy, 45.

113. Counts, Hill, and Hill, "Notes on Building International Solidarity," 52; Southern Africa Support Project, *Organizing for Action on Southern Africa*; Sylvia Hill, interview by Cobb.

114. Wilkins, "'Line of Steel,'" 109.

115. Augusto, interview by author.

116. Sylvia Hill and Claude, "Remembering Sixth-PAC," interview by Levy, 46.

117. Markle, "'We Are Not Tourists,'" 287.

118. "Sixth PAC: North American Women," 4.

Chapter Five

1. Cynthia A. Young, *Soul Power*, 3.

2. "Women in the Struggle," *Triple Jeopardy*, September–October 1971, 8–9; Frances Beal, "Slave of a Slave No More," *Triple Jeopardy*, November–December 1973, 11.

3. Rickford, *We Are an African People*, 5.

4. Alice Childress, "What Does Africa Want? . . . Freedom!," *Freedom*, June 1953, 12.

5. Cynthia A. Young, *Soul Power*, 3.

6. Ransby, *Ella Baker*, 98–101.

7. Wilkins, "Making of Black Internationalists," 469.

8. Ibid., 469, 468, 479–83.

9. Carson, *In Struggle*, 142; Hogan, *Many Minds, One Heart*, 243.

10. For more information on the Southern tradition of armed separatist organizing, see Lance E. Hill, *Deacons for Defense*; Umoja, *We Will Shoot Back*; and Cobb, *This Nonviolent Stuff'll Get You Killed*.

11. Carson, *In Struggle*, 196.

12. Hasan Kwame Jeffries, *Bloody Lowndes*, 143–78; Carson, *In Struggle*, 188–89; Bloom and Martin, *Black against Empire*, 111–14.

13. Wood, "Freedom Is Indivisible," 274–78.

14. "Statement by the Student NonViolent Coordinating Committee on the War in Vietnam," January 6, 1966, Reel 4, Segment 48, Lucile Montgomery Papers, Wisconsin Historical Society, Madison; "SNCC Workers on War Crimes Mission: Letters from Hanoi," *Movement*, May 1967, 5; "Report on Bombing of North Vietnam"; Wood, "Freedom Is Indivisible," 261–73.

15. Carson, *In Struggle*, 173–80; Hall, *Peace and Freedom*, 42–45.

16. "Position Paper," 1966, Box 1, Folder 11, Student Nonviolent Coordinating Committee–Vine City Project (Atlanta, GA) Records, Wisconsin Historical Society, Madison; Grady-Willis, *Challenging U.S. Apartheid*, 89.

17. Markle, "Book Publishers for a Pan-African World"; Rickford, *We Are an African People*, 211–12.

18. SNCC International Affairs Commission, "The Indivisible Struggle against Racism, Apartheid and Colonialism," July 24, 1967, position paper, ComStoBox 25, Folder: Mae Jackson—South Africa, Patton Collection.

19. Forman, *Making of Black Revolutionaries*, 481; Carson, *In Struggle*, 269.

20. Cynthia A. Young, *Soul Power*, 9.

21. Wood, "Freedom Is Indivisible," 215–16; Wilkins, "Making of Black Internationalists," 479–83.

22. For more information on the Venceremos Brigade, see Levinson, Brightman, and Berndt, *Venceremos Brigade*. For evidence of future TWWA members' involvement in the brigade, see, Burnham, "Interview with Linda Burnham," by Ross, 22.

23. A large portion of the memos to be discussed at SNCC's Waveland Conference were submitted anonymously. The memo was one of several on the state of the organization and the movement. See "Papers That Should Be in Your Packets, 11/6/64," Box 47, Folder 16, Social Action Vertical File, Wisconsin Historical Society, Madison. For a published transcript of the memo, see Haden, King, and Varala, "SNCC Position Paper."

24. Cynthia Washington, "Different Ends of the Spectrum," 14.

25. Breines, *Trouble between Us*, 19–50; Anderson-Bricker, "'Triple Jeopardy,'" 49–57; Hesford, *Feeling Women's Liberation*, 129–30; Springer, *Living for the Revolution*.

26. Beal, "Double Jeopardy," 112.

27. Ibid.; Ward, "Third World Women's Alliance," 127–28.

28. Patton, "Born Freedom Fighter"; Patton, "Lowndes County Election Fraud."

29. Patton, "Born Freedom Fighter"; Forman, *Sammy Younge, Jr.*; Lucks, *Selma to Saigon*, 112–14.

30. "Statement by Student NonViolent Coordinating Committee."

31. Patton, "Born Freedom Fighter," 582.

32. Faye Bellamy to Gwen Patton, August 1, 1967, and Faye Bellamy to Gwen Patton, September 19, 1967, ComStoBox 22, Folder: Movement, Women's Perspectives, Patton Collection.

33. Gwendolyn Patton, "Why Black People Must Develop Their Own Anti-war and Anti-draft Union . . . Heed the Call," January 1967, ComStoBox 14, Folder: NBAWADU, Patton Collection; Hall, *Peace and Freedom*, 144–45.

34. "For Us Women," n.d., ComStoBox 14, Folder: NBAWADU, Patton Collection.

35. Gwendolyn Patton, "Role of Women in Liberation Struggles," n.d., ComStoBox 23, Folder: Speeches, Patton Collection.

36. Attendance rosters for NBAWADU workshops, such as on the "role of black women in the liberation struggle," list New York SNCC members. "Workshop: Role of Black Women in the Liberation Struggle," NBAWADU National Conference, April 12–14, 1968, ComStoBox 23, Folder: Speeches, Patton Collection.

37. Gwen Patton, "Proposed Outline for a Black Women's Liberation Committee," December 27, 1968, ComStoBox 22, Folder: SNCC Women, Patton Collection.

38. Beal, "Voices of Feminism Oral History Project," interview by Ross, 151; "Just What Is the Black Women's Liberation Committee?," April 17, 1969, Box 3, Folder 24, Frances Beal Collection, National Parks Service, Mary McLeod Bethune Council House, Landover, Maryland (hereafter referred to as the Beal Collection).

39. Gwen Patton to Sisters, January 6, 1969, ComStoBox 23, Folder: Speeches, Patton Collection.

40. Forman, "Rock Bottom," 139.

41. Gwen Patton to Sisters, January 6, 1969.

42. Ibid.

43. Ibid.

44. "Just What Is the Black Women's Liberation Committee?"

45. Ibid.; Anderson-Bricker, "'Triple Jeopardy,'" 60.

46. Beal, "Voices of Feminism Oral History Project," interview by Ross, 155.

47. "Third World Women's Alliance: Our History, Our Ideology, Our Goals," August 1970, Box 4, Folder 29, Beal Collection. Records indicate that SNCC kept its women's group.

48. Frances Beal to Sisters, April 30, 1970, Box 4, Folder 21, Beal Collection.

49. "Memo from National SNCC Office to All SNCC Workers and Programs, Re: Minutes of National SNCC Workers Meeting/June '70," June 19, 1970, Box 24, Folder 3, Beal Collection.

50. Beal, "Voices of Feminism Oral History Project," interview by Ross, 155.

51. Ibid.

52. "Our History, Our Ideology, Our Goals."

53. Ward, "Third World Women's Alliance," 134.

54. "Our History, Our Ideology, Our Goals."

55. Ibid.

56. Frances Beal, New York Coordinator, to All SNCC Workers, October 9, 1970, Box 3, Folder 2, Beal Collection. Because of their intermittent record keeping, it is difficult to ascertain the exact membership numbers of the group. See SAC [Special Agent in Charge], New York, to FBI Director, December 11, 1970, FBI TWWA.

57. TWWA Calendar of Events, n.d., Box 5, Folder 7, Beal Collection.

58. "Sunday Rap Sessions—Summer Schedule," n.d., Box 5, Folder 7, Beal Collection.

59. Minutes of the Political Committee Meeting, June 25, 1971, Box 5, Folder 18, Beal Collection.

60. "Reading List for Orientation Session," n.d., Box 5, Folder 15, Beal Collection.

61. "Third World Anti-war Coalition Planning Meeting," November 10, 1971, Box 4, Folder 4, Beal Collection; Report on Alliance Meeting, May 23, 1974, Box 4, Folder 2, Third World Women's Alliance Records, Sophia Smith Collection, Smith College, Northampton, Massachusetts (hereafter referred to as the TWWA Records).

62. Joon Pyo Lee, "Third World Women's Alliance," 28–35.

63. For more on the Bay Area's activities, see their national reports located in Box 4, Folder 1, TWWA Records; and Kochiyama, Huggins, and Kao, "'Stirrin' Waters 'n' Buildin' Bridges,'" 150–51.

64. "Seattle Third World Women Retreat Agenda," n.d., Box 4, Folder 4, TWWA Records.

65. "History of Seattle Third World Women," n.d., Box 4, Folder 4, TWWA Records.

66. "Seattle Third World Women's Alliance Schedule for June," n.d., Box 4, Folder 4, TWWA Records.

67. "History of Seattle Third World Women"; "A Hospital for Vietnamese Children in Hanoi . . . ," *Triple Jeopardy*, January–February [year unknown], 12.

68. Numerous letters indicate that only one or two women were in charge of running the Seattle chapter, leading to overwork and their inability to expand the chapter.

69. "Distribution List," n.d., Box 5, Folder 39, and Prisoners to TWWA, June 1, 1971, Box 4, Folder 21, Beal Collection.

70. "Editorial," *Triple Jeopardy*, September–October 1971, 16.

71. In an October 1968 speech delivered at Stanford University, Black Panther Party leader Eldridge Cleaver introduced the concept of "pussy power," the idea that black women should manipulate men and force them into political activism by withholding sex. Eldridge Cleaver, "Stanford Speech," 142–43.

72. "Women in the Struggle," 8–9.

73. Ibid.

74. *Triple Jeopardy*, September–October 1971, cover.

75. For more on Davis's trial, see Davis, *Angela Davis*; Aptheker, *Morning Breaks*; and Berger, *Captive Nation*.

76. "5 Congressmen Are Shot in House," *Atlanta Constitution*, March 2, 1954, 1. For more information on LeBrón and her involvement in the shooting, see Committee to Free the 5 Puerto Rican Nationalist Prisoners, *"To Love Me."*

77. Davis, "Afro Images," 23, 26.

78. *Triple Jeopardy*, February–March 1972, cover.

79. "Women in the Struggle," 8–9.

80. Raiford, *Imprisoned in a Luminous Glare*, 22.

81. Strathern, "Cutting the Network," 522.

82. Beal, "Slave of a Slave No More," 5.

83. Ibid.

84. Ibid.

85. The first FDA-approved oral contraceptive became available in 1960. By 1972, married and single women had access to several forms of birth control, including the IUD. Gordon, *Moral Property of Women*.

86. "The Sins of Birth Control," *Muhammad Speaks*, July 16, 1965, 1; "Birth Control for Whom—Negro or White?," *Muhammad Speaks*, July 2, 1965, 1; Jitu Weusi, "An Open Letter," *Black News*, October 1972, 12–14; Jennifer Nelson, *Women of Color*, 56–60.

87. Caron, "Birth Control and the Black Community"; Bambara, "The Pill."

88. Roberts, *Killing the Black Body*, 94–95; Kluchin, *Fit to Be Tied*, 73–113; Rolinson, *Grassroots Garveyism*, 138.

89. Editorial, *Triple Jeopardy*, July–August 1972, 12–13.

90. Ibid.

91. Watkins, *Black Power, Yellow Power*, 47–49; Carson, *In Struggle*, 187–88; "Black Soldiers as Revolutionaries to Overthrow the Ruling Class," *Black Panther*, September 20, 1969, 2.

92. Editorial, *Triple Jeopardy*, July–August 1972, 12–13.

93. For more on black women's groups that articulated a critique of capitalism, see Springer, *Living for the Revolution*.

94. "On the Job with the Black Secretary," *Triple Jeopardy*, March–April 1973, 10–11.

95. "On the Job with Domestic Workers," *Triple Jeopardy*, November–December 1972, 5.

96. "On the Job," *Triple Jeopardy*, September–October 1971, 14.

97. Ibid.

98. Ibid.

99. "Our History, Our Ideology, Our Goals."

100. Ibid.

101. Griffin, "'Ironies of the Saint,'" 214.

102. "Our History, Our Ideology, Our Goals."

103. "Live Like Her," *Triple Jeopardy*, November 1971, 14.

104. McDuffie, *Sojourning for Freedom*, 209.

105. For individual writings about this subject, see Bambara, *Black Woman*.

106. "Skills," *Triple Jeopardy*, September–October 1971, 12; "Anatomy and Physiology," *Triple Jeopardy*, September–October 1971, 7.

107. "National Report," October 1971, Box 4, Folder 1, TWWA Records; Kochiyama, Huggins, and Kao, "'Stirrin' Waters 'n' Buildin' Bridges.'"

108. "National Organizing Report," October 1971, Box 4, Folder 2, TWWA Records.

109. The exact date that the chapters folded is difficult to ascertain. These dates are based on activist interviews and other secondary scholarship. Springer, *Living for the Revolution*, 141; Anderson-Bricker, "'Triple Jeopardy,'" 62–63.

110. Burnham, "Interview with Linda Burnham," by Ross, 24.

111. Laura Warren Hill and Rabig, "History of the Business of Black Power."

112. Collins, *From Black Power to Hip Hop*, 332–33; Alexander, *New Jim Crow*, 48–59; Keeanga-Yamahtta Taylor, *#BlackLivesMatter*, 93–96. For more information on how these policies affected public housing and residential segregation, see Goetz, *New Deal Ruins*.

113. Burnham, "Interview with Linda Burnham," by Ross, 24; Springer, *Living for the Revolution*, 141.

114. "The Political Line of the Alliance against Women's Oppression," Box 5, Folder 9, Alliance against Women's Oppression Records, 1980–1989, Sophia Smith Collection, Smith College, Northampton, Massachusetts (hereafter referred to as the AAWO Records).

115. For more information on the AAWO's alliance with South African women, see Box 9, Folder 4, AAWO Records. For more on their work with the Nicaraguan Women's Association, see Box 10, Folder 2, AAWO Records.

116. Jennifer Nelson, "'All This That Has Happened.'"

117. Burnham, "Interview with Linda Burnham," by Ross, 25.

118. Ibid.

119. Ogbar, *Black Power*, 159.

120. Ogbar, "Rainbow Radicalism." For examples of Panthers' influence on Young Lords, see "13 Point Program and Platform of the Young Lords Organization," in Enck-Wanzer, *Young Lords*, 9–11, where they mimic the form and structure of the Panthers' ten-point plan. For more on the Red Power movement, see Josephy, Nagel, and Johnson, *Red Power*.

121. Cynthia A. Young, *Soul Power*, 14.

122. Aguilar, "Tracing the Roots of Intersectionality"; Crenshaw, "Mapping the Margins."

Epilogue

1. Davis, *Freedom Is a Constant Struggle*, 64.

2. Ibid., 66.

3. Ibid., 66, 65.

4. Ongiri, "We Are Family," 281.

5. Davis, *Freedom Is a Constant Struggle*, 64.

6. Hartman, "Venus in Two Acts," 4.

Bibliography

Manuscript Collections

Ann Arbor, Michigan
  University of Michigan, Ann Arbor, Special Collections Library
    Joseph A. Labadie Collection
Atlanta, Georgia
  Auburn Avenue Research Library on African American Culture and History
    Komozi Woodard–Amiri Baraka Collection
  Emory University, Stuart A. Rose Manuscripts, Archives, and Rare Book Library
    Louise Thompson Patterson Papers
Berkeley, California
  University of California, Berkeley, Bancroft Library, Special Collections
    Social Protest Collection
Boston, Massachusetts
  Northeastern University, Archives and Special Collections
    Freedom House Inc. Records
    Muriel S. and Otto P. Snowden Papers
Chapel Hill, North Carolina
  University of North Carolina at Chapel Hill, Special Collections
    Ephemera on the Monroe Defendants
Charleston, South Carolina
  College of Charleston, Avery Research Center for African American History and
      Culture
    Cleveland L. Sellers Jr. Papers
Detroit, Michigan
  Wayne State University, Walter P. Reuther Library
    Mae Mallory Collection
East Lansing, Michigan
  Michigan State University, Special Collections
    Radicalism Collection
Landover, Maryland
  Mary McLeod Bethune Council House, National Parks Service
    Frances Beal Collection
Madison, Wisconsin
  Wisconsin Historical Society
    Lucile Montgomery Papers
    Social Action Vertical File

Student Nonviolent Coordinating Committee–Vine City Project (Atlanta, GA) Records
Montgomery, Alabama
  H. Councill Trenholm State Technical College, Special Collections
    Gwen Patton Collection
New York, New York
  New York University, Tamiment Library and Robert F. Wagner Labor Archives
    Printed Ephemera Collection on Organizations
  Schomburg Center for Research in Black Culture
    Black Panther Party—Harlem Branch Files
    Alice Childress Papers
    Preston Wilcox Papers
Northampton, Massachusetts
  Smith College, Sophia Smith Collection
    Alliance against Women's Oppression Records
    Third World Women's Alliance Records
    Voices of Feminism Oral History Project
Palo Alto, California
  Stanford University, Department of Special Collections and University Archives
    Dr. Huey P. Newton Foundation, Inc. Collection
Washington, DC
  Howard University, Moorland-Spingarn Research Center
    Sixth Pan-African Congress Records

Newspapers

African World

Afro-American (Baltimore, MD)

Atlanta Constitution

Atlanta Daily World

Black NewArk (Newark, NJ)

Black News (New York, NY)

Black Panther (Oakland, CA)

Charlotte Observer

Chicago Defender

Cleveland Call and Post

Contrast (Toronto, Canada)

Daily Bruin (University of California, Los Angeles)

Daily News (Dar es Salaam, Tanzania)

Did You Know? (Monroe, NC)

East Village Other (New York, NY)

Freedom (New York, New NY)

Guardian

Harambee (Los Angeles, CA)

Herald-Dispatch (Los Angeles, CA)

Long Beach Free Press

Los Angeles Free Press

Los Angeles Sentinel

Los Angeles Times

Muhammad Speaks (Chicago, IL)

Negro Champion (New York, NY)

Newark Star Ledger (Newark, NJ)

New Pittsburg Courier

New York Amsterdam News

New York Times

Norfolk Journal and Guide (Norfolk, VA)

Sacramento Bee

Sun Reporter (San Francisco, CA)

Triple Jeopardy (New York, NY)

Unity and Struggle (Newark, NJ)

Wall Street Journal

Washington Post

Interviews

Author

Geri Stark Augusto, November 28, 2015.
Gayle Dickson, October 2, 2010.
Sylvia Hill, August 3, 2010.
Ericka Huggins, November 12, 2010.
Maulana Karenga, March 7, 2017.
Tiamoyo Karenga, February 20, 2017.
Kiilu Nyasha, August 10, 2010.

Published and Archived

Augusto, Geri. Interview by Charles Cobb. *No Easy Victories*. Accessed February 14, 2017. http://www.noeasyvictories.org/interviews/int10_augusto.php.

Hill, Sylvia. Interview by Charles Cobb. *No Easy Victories*. Accessed February 14, 2017. http://www.noeasyvictories.org/interviews/int16_hill.php.

———. Interview by William Minter. *No Easy Victories*. Accessed February 14, 2017. http://www.noeasyvictories.org/interviews/int11_hill.php.

Huggins, Ericka. Interview by Fiona Thompson. Individual Memoirs in Politics and Government. Bancroft Library, University of California, Berkeley.

Mallory, Mae. Interview by Malaika Lumumba. Ralph J. Bunche Oral History Collection, Moorland-Spingarn Research Center, Howard University, Washington, DC.

Moore, Audley. Interview by Cheryl Gilkes. In *The Black Women Oral History Project*, vol. 8, edited by Ruth Edmonds Hill, 111–201. Westport, CT: Meckler, 1990.

Audio and Video Recordings

"C.O.R.E.'s 24th National Convention, June 30, 1967, Part 1." Pacifica Radio Archive, Los Angeles, California.

Friend, Beth, and Charles Potter. "The Black and the Red." Los Angeles: Pacifica Radio Archive, 1983.

Lee, Lee Lew, Kristin Bell, and Nico Panigutti. *All Power to the People: The Black Panther Party and Beyond*. Directed by Lee Lew Lee. 1996; New York: Filmmakers Library, 2000. DVD.

FBI Records

FBI BN	File No. 100-448006 (Black Nationalist Hate Groups)
FBI SFTJ	File No. 100-384225 (Sojourners for Truth and Justice)
FBI TWWA	File No. 157-19982 (Third World Women's Alliance)

Articles, Books, and Pamphlets

Abron, Jonina M. "'Raising the Consciousness of the People': The Black Panther Intercommunal News Service, 1967–1980." In *Voices from the Underground: Insider Histories of the Vietnam Era Underground Press*, edited by Ken Wachsberger, 335–68. Tempe, AZ: Mica's Press, 1993.

———. "'Serving the People': The Survival Programs of the Black Panther Party." In *The Black Panther Party (Reconsidered)*, edited by Charles E. Jones, 177–92. Baltimore: Black Classic, 1998.

Abu-Jamal, Mumia. *We Want Freedom: A Life in the Black Panther Party*. Cambridge, MA: South End, 2004.

Adi, Hakim. "The Negro Question: The Communist International and Black Liberation in the Interwar Years." In *From Toussaint to Tupac: The Black International since the Age of Revolution*, edited by Michael O. West, William G. Martin, and Fanon Che Wilkins, 155–78. Chapel Hill: University of North Carolina Press, 2009.

Aguilar, Delia D. "Tracing the Roots of Intersectionality." *Monthly Review*, December 4, 2012.

Ahmad, Muhammad. *We Will Return in the Whirlwind: Black Radical Organizations, 1960–1975*. Chicago: Charles H. Kerr, 2007.

Alameen-Shavers, Antwanisha. "The Woman Question: Gender Dynamics within the Black Panther Party." *Spectrum: A Journal on Black Men* 5, no. 1 (Fall 2016): 33–62.

Alexander, Michelle. *The New Jim Crow: Mass Incarceration in the Age of Colorblindness*. New York: New Press, 2012.

Alkebulan, Paul. *Survival Pending Revolution: The History of the Black Panther Party*. Tuscaloosa: University of Alabama Press, 2007.

Allen, Carol. *Black Women Intellectuals: Strategies of the Nation, Family, and Neighborhood in the Works of Pauline Hopkins, Jessie Fauset, and Marita Bonner*. New York: Garland, 1998.

Anderson, Reynaldo. "Practical Internationalists: The Story of the Des Moines, Iowa, Black Panther Party." In *Groundwork: Local Black Freedom Movements in America*, edited by Jeanne Theoharis and Komozi Woodard, 282–99. New York: New York University Press, 2005.

Anderson-Bricker, Kristen. "'Triple Jeopardy': Black Women and the Growth of Feminist Consciousness in SNCC, 1964–1975." In *Still Lifting, Still Climbing: African American Women's Contemporary Activism*, edited by Kimberly Springer, 49–69. New York: New York University Press, 1999.

Angelo, Ann-Marie. "The Black Panthers in London, 1967–1972: A Diasporic Struggle Navigates the Black Atlantic." *Radical Historical Review* 103 (2009): 17–35.

Angelou, Maya. *The Heart of a Woman*. New York: Bantam Books, 1993.

Aptheker, Bettina. *The Morning Breaks: The Trial of Angela Davis*. New York: International, 1975.

Arend, Orissa, and Judson L. Jeffries. "The Big Easy Was Anything but for Panthers." In *On the Ground: The Black Panther in Communities across America*, edited by Judson L. Jeffries, 224–72. Jackson: University of Mississippi Press, 2010.

Arsenault, Raymond. *Freedom Riders: 1961 and the Struggle for Racial Justice*. New York: Oxford University Press, 2006.

Asante, Molefi Kete. *Maulana Karenga: An Intellectual Portrait*. Cambridge, MA: Polity, 2009.

Augusto, Geri. "The Light and Songs of Freedom: Reflections on SNCC's Legacy to Black Internationalism." Paper in author's possession.

Austin, Curtis J. *Up against the Wall: Violence in the Making and Unmaking of the Black Panther Party*. Fayetteville: University of Arkansas Press, 2006.

Bair, Barbara. "True Women, Real Men: Gender, Ideology and Social Roles in the Garvey Movement." In *Gendered Domains: Rethinking Public and Private in Women's Histories, Essays from the Seventh Berkshire Conference on the History of Women*, edited by Dorothy O. Helly and Susan M. Reverby, 158–66. Ithaca, NY: Cornell University Press, 1992.

Baker, Ella, and Marvel Cooke. "The Bronx Slave Market." *Crisis* 42 (1935): 330–31, 340.

Bambara, Toni Cade. "The Pill: Genocide or Liberation." In *The Black Woman: An Anthology*, repr. ed., edited by Toni Cade Bambara, 203–12. New York: Washington Square, 2005.

———, ed. *The Black Woman: An Anthology*. Repr. ed. New York: Washington Square, 2005.

Baraka, Amiri. *Autobiography of LeRoi Jones*. New York: Lawrence Hill Books, 1997.

———. "Ideological Statement of the Congress of African Peoples." In *African Congress: A Documentary of the First Modern Pan-African Congress*, edited by Amiri Baraka, 107–11. New York: William Morrow, 1972.

———. Introduction to *African Congress: A Documentary of the First Modern Pan-African Congress*, vii–x. Edited by Amiri Baraka. New York: William Morrow, 1972.

———. "Some Questions about the Sixth Pan-African Congress." *Black Scholar* 6, no. 2 (October 1974): 42–46.

———. "Toward the Creation of Political Institutions for All African Peoples." *Black World* 21 (October 1972): 54–78.

Baraka, Bibi Amina. "Coordinator's Statement." In *African Congress: A Documentary of the First Modern Pan-African Congress*, 177–79. New York: William Morrow, 1972.

Bass, Paul, and Douglas W. Rae. *Murder in the Model City: The Black Panthers, Yale, and the Redemption of a Killer*. New York: Basic Books, 2006.

Bay, Mia E., Farah J. Griffin, Martha Jones, and Barbara D. Savage, eds. *Toward an Intellectual History of Black Women*. Chapel Hill: University of North Carolina Press, 2015.

Beal, Frances M. "Double Jeopardy: To Be Black and Female." In *The Black Woman: An Anthology*, repr. ed., edited by Toni Cade Bambara, 109–22. New York: Washington Square, 2005.

———. "Excerpts from the Voices of Feminism Oral History Project: Interview with Frances Beal." By Loretta J. Ross. *Meridians: Feminism, Race, Transnationalism* 8, no. 2 (2008): 126–65.

Bennett, Lerone, Jr. "Pan-Africanism at the Crossroads." *Ebony*, September 1974, 148–60.

Berger, Dan. *Captive Nation: Black Prison Organizing in the Civil Rights Era.* Chapel Hill: University of North Carolina Press, 2014.

Biondi, Martha. *The Black Revolution on Campus.* Berkeley: University of California Press, 2012.

———. *To Stand and Fight: The Struggle for Civil Rights in Postwar New York City.* Cambridge, MA: Harvard University Press, 2003.

Blain, Keisha N. "'We Want to Set the World on Fire': Black Nationalist Women and Diasporic Politics in the New Negro World, 1940–1944." *Journal of Social History* 49, no. 1 (2015): 194–212.

Bloom, Joshua, and Waldo E. Martin Jr. *Black against Empire: The History and Politics of the Black Panther Party.* Berkeley: University of California Press, 2013.

Boehm, Lisa Krissoff. *Making a Way out of No Way: African American Women and the Second Great Migration.* Jackson: University Press of Mississippi, 2009.

Breines, Wini. *The Trouble between Us: An Uneasy History of White and Black Women in the Feminist Movement.* New York: Oxford University Press, 2006.

Browder, Earl. "On the Negroes and the Right to Self-Determination." *Communist* 23 (January 1944): 83–85.

Brown, Elaine. *A Taste of Power: A Black Woman's Story.* New York: Pantheon Books, 1992.

Brown, Kimberly Nichele. *Writing the Black Revolutionary Diva: Women's Subjectivity and the Decolonizing Text.* Bloomington: Indiana University Press, 2010.

Brown, Scot. *Fighting for US: Maulana Karenga, the US Organization, and Black Cultural Nationalism.* New York: New York University Press, 2003.

———. "'To Unbrainwash an Entire People': Malcolm X, Cultural Nationalism, and the US Organization in the Era of Black Power." In *Malcolm X: A Historical Reader*, edited by James L. Conyers Jr. and Andrew P. Smallwood, 137–46. Durham, NC: Carolina Academic Press, 2008.

Buffalo, Audreen. "A Revolutionary Life Together: Amina and Amiri Talk Frankly about Their Marriage." *Essence*, May 1985, 82–86, 210–16.

Bukhari, Safiya, and Laura Whitehorn. *The War Before: The True Life Story of Becoming a Black Panther, Keeping the Faith in Prison, and Fighting for Those Left Behind.* New York: Feminist Press at the City University of New York, 2009.

Burnham, Linda. "Interview with Linda Burnham: Voices of Feminism Oral History Project." By Loretta J. Ross. *Black Scholar* 36, no. 1 (2006): 19–26.

Bush, Rod. *We Are Not What We Seem: Black Nationalism and Class Struggle in the American Century.* New York: New York University Press, 1999.

Carby, Hazel. *Race Men.* Cambridge, MA: Harvard University Press, 1999.

Carmichael, Stokely. *Stokely Speaks: From Black Power to Pan-Africanism.* New York: Random House, 1971.

Carmichael, Stokely, and Charles V. Hamilton. *Black Power: The Politics of Liberation in America*. New York: Random House, 1967.

Caron, Simone M. "Birth Control and the Black Community in the 1960s: Genocide or Power Politics?" *Journal of Social History* 31 (1998): 545–69.

Carson, Clayborne. *In Struggle: SNCC and the Black Awakening of the 1960s*. Cambridge, MA: Harvard University Press, 1981.

Childress, Alice. "A Candle in a Gale Wind." In *Black Women Writers: Arguments and Interviews*, edited by Mari Evans, 111–16. London: Pluto, 1983.

——. "For a Negro Theatre." *Masses and Mainstream*, February 1951, 61–64.

——. *Like One of the Family: Conversations from a Domestic's Life*. Brooklyn, NY: Independence, 1956.

Churchill, Ward, and Jim Vander Wall. *Agents of Repression: The FBI's Secret Wars against the Black Panther Party and the American Indian Movement*. Cambridge, MA: South End, 1988.

Clarke, Cheryl. *"After Mecca": Women Poets and the Black Arts Movement*. New Brunswick, NJ: Rutgers University Press, 2005.

Clarke, John Henrik. "The New Afro-American Nationalism." *Freedomways* 1, no. 3 (Fall 1961): 285–95.

Claude, Judy. "Some Personal Reflections on the Sixth Pan-African Congress." *Black Scholar* 37, no. 4 (2008): 48–49.

Cleaver, Eldridge. *Soul on Ice*. New York: McGraw-Hill, 1968.

——. "Stanford Speech." In *Post Prison Writings and Speeches*, edited by Eldridge Cleaver, 113–46. New York: Random House, 1969.

——. *Target Zero: A Life in Writing*. Edited by Kathleen Neal Cleaver. New York: Palgrave Macmillan, 2006.

Cleaver, Kathleen Neal. "Back to Africa: The Evolution of the International Section of the Black Panther Party (1969–1972)." In *The Black Panther Party (Reconsidered)*, edited by Charles E. Jones, 211–56. Baltimore: Black Classic, 1999.

——. "The Black Scholar Interviews Kathleen Cleaver." *Black Scholar* 3, no. 4 (December 1971): 54–59.

——. Introduction to *Liberation, Imagination, and the Black Panther Party: A New Look at the Panthers and Their Legacy*, vii–xiv. Edited by Kathleen Neal Cleaver and George Katsiaficas. New York: Routledge, 2001.

——. Introduction to *Target Zero: A Life in Writing*, by Eldridge Cleaver, xi–xxvi. Edited by Kathleen Neal Cleaver. New York: Palgrave Macmillan, 2006.

——. "Women, Power, and Revolution." In *Liberation, Imagination, and the Black Panther Party: A New Look at the Panthers and Their Legacy*, edited by Kathleen Neal Cleaver and George Katsiaficas, 123–27. New York: Routledge, 2001.

Clemons, Michael L., and Charles E. Jones. "Global Solidarity: The Black Panther Party in the International Arena." *New Political Science* 21, no. 2 (1999): 177–203.

Cobb, Charles E., Jr. *This Nonviolent Stuff'll Get You Killed: How Guns Made the Civil Rights Movement Possible*. Repr. ed. Durham, NC: Duke University Press, 2015.

Collins, Patricia Hill. *Black Feminist Thought: Knowledge, Consciousness, and the Politics of Empowerment*. New York: Routledge, 2002.

———. *From Black Power to Hip Hop: Racism, Nationalism, and Feminism.* Philadelphia: Temple University Press, 2006.

Committee to Free the 5 Puerto Rican Nationalist Prisoners. *"To Love Me, Is to Love My Country": Lolita Lebron, Her Story, Her Struggle.* Chicago: Committee to Free the 5 Nationalists, 1954.

Cooper, Anna Julia, Charles C. Lemert, and Esme Bhan. *The Voice of Anna Julia Cooper: Including a Voice from the South and Other Important Essays, Papers, and Letters.* Lanham, MD: Rowman and Littlefield, 1998.

Cooper, Esther V. "The Negro Woman Domestic Worker in Relation to Trade Unionism." Master's thesis, Fisk University, 1940.

Counts, Cecelie, Sylvia Hill, and Sandra Hill. "Notes on Building International Solidarity in the United States." *Black Scholar* 15, no. 6 (November/December 1984): 44–52.

Crawford, Vicki. "African American Women in the Mississippi Freedom Democratic Party." In *Sisters in the Struggle: African American Women in the Civil Rights–Black Power Movement,* edited by Bettye Collier-Thomas and V. P. Franklin, 121–38. New York: New York University Press, 2001.

Crenshaw, Kimberlé. "Mapping the Margins: Intersectionality, Identity Politics, and Violence against Women of Color." *Stanford Law Review* 43, no. 6 (July 1991): 1241–99.

Curvin, Robert. *Inside Newark: Decline, Rebellion, and the Search for Transformation.* New Brunswick, NJ: Rutgers University Press, 2014.

Dagbovie, Pero Gaglo. "'God Has Spared Me to Tell My Story': Mabel Robinson Williams and the Civil Rights–Black Power Movement." *Black Scholar* 43, no. 1/2 (Spring 2013): 69–88.

Davies, Carole Boyce. *Black Women, Writing, and Identity: Migrations of the Subject.* New York: Routledge, 1994.

———, ed. *Claudia Jones, beyond Containment: Autobiographical Reflections, Essays, and Poems.* Boulder, CO: Lynn Rienner, 2011.

———. *Left of Karl Marx: The Political Life of Black Communist Claudia Jones.* Durham, NC: Duke University Press, 2008.

Davis, Angela Y. "Afro Images: Politics, Fashion, and Nostalgia." In *Soul: Black Power, Politics, and Pleasure,* edited by Monique Guillory and Richard C. Green, 23–31. New York: New York University Press, 1998.

———. *Angela Davis: An Autobiography.* New York: Random House, 1974.

———. *Freedom Is a Constant Struggle: Ferguson, Palestine, and the Foundations of a Movement.* Chicago: Haymarket Books, 2016.

Doss, Erika. "'Revolutionary Art Is a Tool for Liberation': Emory Douglas and Protest Aesthetics at the *Black Panther.*" *New Political Science* 21, no. 2 (1999): 245–59.

Du Bois, W. E. B. "Close Ranks." *Crisis* 16 (July 1918): 111.

Durant, Sam, ed. *Black Panther: The Revolutionary Art of Emory Douglas.* New York: Rizzoli, 2007.

Duziak, Mary. *Cold War Civil Rights: Race and the Image of American Democracy.* Princeton, NJ: Princeton University Press, 2000.

Echols, Alice. *Daring to Be Bad: Radical Feminism in America, 1967–1975.* Minneapolis: University of Minnesota Press, 1989.

Enck-Wanzer, Darrel, ed. *The Young Lords: A Reader.* New York: New York University Press, 2010.

Ewing, Adam. *The Age of Garvey: How a Jamaican Activist Created a Mass Movement and Changed Global Black Politics.* Princeton, NJ: Princeton University Press, 2014.

Farmer, Ashley D. "Mothers of Pan-Africanism: Audley Moore and Dara Abubakari." *Women, Gender, and Families of Color* 4, no. 2 (Fall 2016): 274–95.

———. "Reframing African American Women's Grassroots Organizing: Audley Moore and the Universal Association of Ethiopian Women, 1957–1963." *Journal of African American History* 101, no. 1/2 (Winter/Spring 2016): 69–96.

———. "Renegotiating the 'African Woman': Women's Cultural Nationalist Theorizing in the Us Organization and the Congress of African People, 1965–1975." *Black Diaspora Review* 4, no. 1 (Winter 2014): 76–112.

Feldstein, Ruth. *Motherhood in Black and White: Race and Sex in American Liberalism, 1930–1965.* Ithaca, NY: Cornell University Press, 2000.

Flamm, Michael W. *Law and Order: Street Crime, Civil Unrest, and the Crisis of Liberalism in the 1960s.* New York: Columbia University Press, 2005.

Fleming, Cynthia Griggs. *Soon We Will Not Cry: The Liberation of Ruby Doris Smith Robinson.* Lanham, MD: Rowman and Littlefield, 1998.

Ford, Tanisha C. *Liberated Threads: Black Women, Style, and the Global Politics of Soul.* Chapel Hill: University of North Carolina Press, 2015.

Forman, James. *The Making of Black Revolutionaries.* Seattle: University of Washington Press, 1997.

———. *The Political Thought of James Forman.* Detroit: Black Star, 1970.

———. "Rock Bottom." In *The Political Thought of James Forman*, 137–150. Detroit: Black Star, 1970.

———. *Sammy Younge, Jr.: The First Black College Student to Die in the Black Liberation Movement.* New York: Grove, 1968.

Fuller, Hoyt W. "Notes from a Sixth Pan-African Journal." *Black World*, October 1974, 70–81.

Gaines, Kevin K. *American Africans in Ghana: Black Expatriates and the Civil Rights Era.* Chapel Hill: University of North Carolina Press, 2006.

———. *Uplifting the Race: Black Leadership, Politics, and Culture in the Twentieth Century.* Chapel Hill: University of North Carolina Press, 1996.

Garrett, James. "A Historical Sketch: The Sixth Pan-African Congress." *Black World*, March 1975, 5–20.

Garvey, Amy Jacques. *Garvey and Garveyism.* New York: Collier Books, 1970.

Giddings, Paula. *Ida: A Sword among Lions.* New York: Amistad, 2008.

Gilmore, Stephanie, ed. *Feminist Coalitions: Historical Perspectives on Second-Wave Feminism in the United States.* Urbana: University of Illinois Press, 2008.

Goetz, Edward G. *New Deal Ruins: Race, Economic Justice, and Public Housing Policy.* Ithaca, NY: Cornell University Press, 2013.

Gordon, Linda. *The Moral Property of Women: A History of Birth Control Politics in America*. Urbana: University of Illinois Press, 2002.

Gore, Dayo F. "From Communist Politics to Black Power: The Visionary Politics and Transnational Solidarities of Victoria 'Vicki' Ama Garvin." In *Want to Start a Revolution? Radical Black Women in the Black Freedom Struggle*, edited by Dayo F. Gore, Jeanne Theoharis, and Komozi Woodard, 72–94. New York: New York University Press, 2009.

———. *Radicalism at the Crossroads: African American Women Activists in the Cold War*. New York: New York University Press, 2011.

Goudsouzian, Aram. *Down to the Crossroads: Civil Rights, Black Power, and the Meredith March against Fear*. New York: Farrar, Straus, and Giroux, 2014.

Grady-Willis, Winston A. *Challenging U.S. Apartheid: Atlanta and Black Struggles for Human Rights, 1960–1977*. Durham, NC: Duke University Press, 2006.

Graham, Herman. *The Brothers' Vietnam War: Black Power, Manhood and the Military Experience*. Gainesville: University of Florida Press, 2003.

Grant, Colin. *Negro with a Hat: The Rise and Fall of Marcus Garvey and His Dream of Mother Africa*. New York: Oxford University Press, 2008.

Green, Ben. *Before His Time: The Untold Story of Harry T. Moore, America's First Civil Rights Martyr*. New York: Free Press, 1999.

Greenberg, Cheryl Lynn. *Or Does It Explode? Black Harlem in the Great Depression*. New York: Oxford University Press, 1991.

———. *To Ask for an Equal Chance: African Americans in the Great Depression*. Lanham, MD: Rowman and Littlefield, 2009.

Gregory, James N. *The Southern Diaspora: How the Great Migrations of Black and White Southerners Transformed America*. Chapel Hill: University of North Carolina Press, 2005.

Griffin, Farah Jasmine. "'Ironies of the Saint': Malcolm X, Black Women, and the Price of Protection." In *Sisters in the Struggle: African American Women in the Civil Rights–Black Power Movement*, edited by Bettye Collier-Thomas and V. P. Franklin, 214–29. New York: New York University Press, 2001.

Haas, Jeffrey. *The Assassination of Fred Hampton: How the FBI and the Chicago Police Murdered a Black Panther*. Chicago: Lawrence Hill Books, 2010.

Haden, Casey, and Mary King, with Maria Varala. "SNCC Position Paper (Women in the Movement)." In Sara Evans, *Personal Politics: The Roots of Women's Liberation in the Civil Rights Movement and the New Left*, 233–35. New York: Random House, 1979.

Haley, Sarah. *No Mercy Here: Gender, Punishment, and the Making of Jim Crow Modernity*. Chapel Hill: University of North Carolina Press, 2016.

Halisi, Imamu, ed. *Kitabu: Beginning Concepts in Kawaida*. Los Angeles: Temple of Kawaida, 1971.

———, ed. *The Quotable Karenga*. Los Angeles: Saidi, 1967.

Hall, Simon. *Peace and Freedom: The Civil Rights and Antiwar Movements of the 1960s*. Philadelphia: University of Pennsylvania Press, 2005.

Harley, Sharon. "'Chronicle of a Death Foretold': Gloria Richardson, the Cambridge Movement, and the Radical Black Activist Tradition." In *Sisters in the*

Struggle: African American Women in the Civil Rights–Black Power Movement, edited by Bettye Collier-Thomas and V. P. Franklin, 174–96. New York: New York University Press, 2001.

Harold, Claudrena N. *The Rise and Fall of the Garvey Movement in the Urban South, 1918–1942*. New York: Routledge, 2007.

Harris, Lashawn. "Running with the Reds: African American Women and the Communist Party during the Great Depression." *Journal of African American History* 94, no. 1 (Winter 2009): 21–43.

Harris, Trudier. Introduction to *Like One of the Family: Conversations from a Domestic's Life*, by Alice Childress, xi–xxxiv. Brooklyn, NY: Independence, 1956.

Hartman, Saidiya. "Venus in Two Acts." *Small Axe* 12, no. 2 (2008): 1–14.

Hayes, Floyd W., III, and Judson L. Jeffries. "US Does Not Stand for United Slaves!" In *Black Power: In the Belly of the Beast*, edited by Judson L. Jeffries, 67–92. Urbana: University of Illinois Press, 2006.

Haywood, Harry. *Black Bolshevik: Autobiography of an Afro-American Communist*. Chicago: Liberator, 1978.

Hesford, Victoria. *Feeling Women's Liberation*. Durham, NC: Duke University Press, 2013.

Higashida, Cheryl. *Black Internationalist Feminism: Women Writers of the Black Left, 1955–1995*. Urbana: University of Illinois Press, 2011.

Higginbotham, Evelyn Brooks. *Righteous Discontent: The Women's Movement in the Black Baptist Church, 1880–1920*. Cambridge, MA: Harvard University Press, 1994.

Hill, Lance E. *Deacons for Defense: Armed Resistance and the Civil Rights Movement*. Chapel Hill: University of North Carolina Press, 2004.

Hill, Laura Warren, and Julia Rabig. "Toward a History of the Business of Black Power." In *The Business of Black Power: Community Development, Capitalism, and Corporate Responsibility in Postwar America*, edited by Laura Warren Hill and Julia Rabig, 15–44. Rochester, NY: University of Rochester Press, 2012.

Hill, Robert A., and Barbara Bair, eds. *Marcus Garvey Life and Lessons: A Centennial Companion to the Marcus Garvey and Universal Negro Improvement Association Papers*. Berkeley: University of California Press, 1987.

Hill, Sylvia. "Sixth Pan-African Congress: Progress Report on Congress Organizing." *Black Scholar* 5, no. 7 (April 1974): 35–39.

Hill, Sylvia, and Judy Claude. "Remembering Sixth-PAC: Interviews with Sylvia Hill and Judy Claude, Organizers of the Sixth Pan-African Congress." By La TaSha Levy. *Black Scholar* 37, no. 4 (Winter 2008): 39–47.

Hilliard, David, ed. *The Black Panther Party: Service to the People Programs*. Albuquerque: University of New Mexico Press, 2008.

Hogan, Wesley C. *Many Minds, One Heart: SNCC's Dream for a New America*. Chapel Hill: University of North Carolina Press, 2007.

Holsaert, Faith S., Martha Prescod Norman Noonan, Judy Richardson, Betty Garman Robinson, Jean Smith Young, and Dorothy M. Zellner, eds. *Hands on the Freedom Plow: Personal Accounts by Women in SNCC*. Urbana: University of Illinois Press, 2010.

hooks, bell. *Art on My Mind: Visual Politics*. New York: New Press, 1995.

Horne, David Lawrence. "The Pan-African Congress: A Positive Assessment." *Black Scholar* 5, no. 10 (July–August 1974): 2–11.

Huggins, Ericka, and Angela D. LeBlanc-Ernest. "Revolutionary Women, Revolutionary Education: The Black Panther Party's Oakland Community School." In *Want to Start a Revolution? Radical Black Women in the Black Freedom Struggle*, edited by Dayo F. Gore, Jeanne Theoharis, and Komozi Woodard, 161–84. New York: New York University Press, 2009.

Hughes, Alvin C. "We Demand Our Rights: The Southern Negro Youth Congress, 1937–1949." *Phylon* 48, no. 1 (1987): 38–50.

Hunter, Tera W. *To 'Joy My Freedom: Southern Black Women's Lives and Labors after the Civil War*. Cambridge, MA: Harvard University Press, 1997.

Isaacman, Allen, and Barbara Isaacman. *Mozambique: From Colonialism to Revolution, 1900–1982*. Boulder, CO: Westview, 1983.

Jackson, Esther Cooper. "An Interview with Esther Jackson." By Della Scott. *Abafazi: The Simmons College Journal of Women of African Descent* 9, no. 1 (Fall/Winter 1998): 2–9.

Jackson, Esther Cooper, and Constance Pohl, eds. *Freedomways Reader: Prophets in Their Own Country*. Boulder, CO: Westview, 2000.

Jackson, George. *Soledad Brother: The Prison Letters of George Jackson*. New York: Coward-McCann, 1970.

Jackson, Phyllis. "The Black Panther Party . . . from a Sister's Point of View: An Interview of Dr. Phyllis Jackson." By Mzuri Pambeli. *Positive Action*, March–April 2007, 3–4.

James, Joy. "Framing the Panther: Assata Shakur and Black Female Agency." In *Want to Start a Revolution? Radical Black Women in the Black Freedom Struggle*, edited by Dayo F. Gore, Jeanne Theoharis, and Komozi Woodard, 138–60. New York: New York University Press, 2009.

———. *Shadowboxing: Representations of Black Feminist Politics*. New York: Palgrave Macmillan, 1999.

James, Winston. *Holding Aloft the Banner of Ethiopia: Caribbean Radicalism in the Early Twentieth Century*. New York: Verso Books, 1998.

Jeffries, Hasan Kwame. *Bloody Lowndes: Civil Rights and Black Power in Alabama Black Belt*. New York: New York University Press, 2009.

Jeffries, Judson L. "Conversing with Gwen Robinson." *Spectrum: A Journal on Black Men* 5, no. 1 (Fall 2016): 137–45.

———. *Huey P. Newton: The Radical Theorist*. Jackson: University Press of Mississippi, 2002.

Jenkins, Robin Dearmon. "Linking Up the Golden State: Garveyism in the San Francisco Bay Area, 1919–1925." *Journal of Black Studies* 39, no. 2 (2008): 266–80.

Jennings, La Vinia Delois. *Alice Childress*. New York: Twain, 1995.

Johnson, Cedric. "From Popular Anti-imperialism to Sectarianism: The African Liberation Support Committee and Black Power Radicals." *New Political Science* 25, no. 4 (December 2003): 477–507.

———. *Revolutionaries to Race Leaders: Black Power and the Making of African American Politics*. Minneapolis: University of Minnesota Press, 2007.

Jones, Charles E. "Arm Yourself or Harm Yourself: People's Party II and the Black Panther Party in Houston, Texas." In *On the Ground: The Black Panther Party in Communities across America*, edited by Judson Jeffries, 3–40. Jackson: University Press of Mississippi, 2010.

———. "Global Solidarity: The Black Panther Party in the International Arena." *New Political Science* 21, no. 2 (1999): 177–203.

Jones, Claudia. "Autobiographical History." In *Claudia Jones, beyond Containment: Autobiographical Reflections, Essays, and Poems*, edited by Carole Boyce Davies, 10–16. Boulder, CO: Lynn Rienner, 2011.

———. "Discussion Article." *Political Affairs* 25 (August 1945): 718–20.

———. "An End to the Neglect of the Problems of the Negro Woman!" *Political Affairs* 28 (June 1949): 51–67.

———. "On the Right to Self-Determination for the Negro People in the Black Belt." *Political Affairs* 35 (January 1946): 66–77.

Joseph, Peniel E. "Malcolm X's Harlem and Early Black Power Activism." In *Neighborhood Rebels: Black Power at the Local Level*, edited by Peniel E. Joseph, 21–43. New York: Palgrave Macmillan, 2010.

———, ed. *Neighborhood Rebels: Black Power at the Local Level*. New York: Palgrave Macmillan, 2010.

———. "Rethinking the Black Power Era." *Journal of Southern History* 75, no. 3 (2009): 707–16.

———. *Stokely: A Life*. New York: Basic Civitas, 2014.

———. "Toward a Historiography of the Black Power Movement." In *The Black Power Movement: Rethinking the Civil Rights–Black Power Era*, edited by Peniel E. Joseph, 1–26. New York: Routledge, 2006.

———. *Waiting 'Til the Midnight Hour: A Narrative History of Black Power in America*. New York: Henry Holt, 2006.

Josephy, Alvin M., Joane Nagel, and Troy R. Johnson, eds. *Red Power: The American Indians' Fight for Freedom*. Lincoln: University of Nebraska Press, 1999.

Kadalie, Modibo M. *Internationalism, Pan-Africanism, and the Struggle of Social Classes: Raw Writings from the Notebook of an Early Nineteen Seventies African American Radical Activist*. Savannah, GA: One Quest, 1999.

Karenga, Maulana Ron. "Kawaida and Its Critics: A Sociohistorical Analysis." *Journal of Black Studies* 8, no. 2 (December 1977): 125–48.

———. "A Response to Muhammad Ahmad on the US/Panther Conflict." *Black Scholar* 9, no. 10 (July–August 1978): 55–57.

———. "A Strategy for Struggle: Turning Weakness into Strength." *Black Scholar* 5, no. 3 (November 1973): 8–21.

———. "Us, Kawaida, and the Black Liberation Movement in the 1960s: Culture, Knowledge, and Struggle." In *Engines of the Black Power Movement: Essays on the Influence of Civil Rights Actions, Arts, and Islam*, edited by James L. Conyers, 95–133. Jefferson, NC: McFarland, 2007.

Karenga, Tiamoyo, and Chimbuko Tembo. "Kawaida Womanism: African Ways of Being Woman in the World." *Western Journal of Black Studies* 36, no. 1 (Winter 2012): 33–47.

Kelley, Robin D. G. *Freedom Dreams: The Black Radical Imagination*. Boston: Beacon, 2002.

———. *Hammer and Hoe: Alabama Communists during the Great Depression*. Chapel Hill: University of North Carolina Press, 1990.

———. *Race Rebels: Culture, Politics, and the Black Working Class*. New York: Free Press, 1996.

Kemper, Kurt Edward. "Reformers in the Marketplace of Ideas: Student Activism and American Democracy in Cold War Los Angeles." PhD diss., Louisiana State University, 2000.

Kinchen, Shirletta J. *Black Power in the Bluff City: African American Youth and Student Activism in Memphis, 1965–1975*. Knoxville: University of Tennessee Press, 2016.

King, Martin Luther, Jr. "Watts." In *The Autobiography of Martin Luther King Jr.*, edited by Clayborne Carson, 292–96. New York: Warner Books, 1998.

King, Shannon. *Whose Harlem Is This, Anyway? Community Politics and Grassroots Activism during the New Negro Era*. New York: New York University Press, 2015.

Kluchin, Rebecca M. *Fit to Be Tied: Sterilization and Reproductive Rights in America, 1950–1980*. New Brunswick, NJ: Rutgers University Press, 2009.

Kochiyama, Yuri, Ericka Huggins, and Mary Uyematsu Kao. "'Stirrin' Waters 'n' Buildin' Bridges': A Conversation with Ericka Huggins and Yuri Kochiyama." *Amerasia Journal* 35, no. 1 (2009): 140–67.

Konadu, Kwasi. *A View from The East: Black Cultural Nationalism and Education in New York City*. Syracuse, NY: Syracuse University Press, 2009.

Kotlowski, Dean J. *Nixon's Civil Rights: Politics, Principle, Policy*. Cambridge, MA: Harvard University Press, 2001.

Kuumba, M. Bahati. "Engendering the Pan-African Movement: Field Notes from the All-African Women's Revolutionary Union." In *Still Lifting, Still Climbing: African American Women's Contemporary Activism*, edited by Kimberly Springer, 167–88. New York: New York University Press, 1999.

Lang, Clarence, and Robbie Lieberman, eds. *Anticommunism and the African American Freedom Movement: "Another Side of the Story."* New York: Palgrave Macmillan, 2009.

La Rue, Linda. "The Black Movement and Women's Liberation." *Black Scholar* 1, no. 7 (May 1970): 36–42.

LeBlanc-Ernest, Angela. "'The Most Qualified Person to Handle the Job': Black Panther Party Women, 1966–1982." In *The Black Panther Party (Reconsidered)*, edited by Charles E. Jones, 305–36. Baltimore: Black Classic, 1998.

Lee, Joon Pyo. "The Third World Women's Alliance 1970–1980: Women of Color Organizing in a Revolutionary Era." Master's thesis, Sarah Lawrence College, 2007.

Leeds, Asia. "Toward the 'Higher Type of Womanhood': The Gendered Contours of Garveyism and the Making of Redemptive Geographies in Costa Rica, 1922–1941." *Palimpsest: A Journal on Women, Gender, and the Black International* 2, no. 1 (2013): 1–27.

LeFlouria, Talitha L. *Chained in Silence: Black Women and Convict Labor in the New South*. Chapel Hill: University of North Carolina Press, 2015.

Lemelle, Sidney J., and Robin D. G. Kelley. "Introduction: Imagining Home: Pan-Africanism Revisited." In *Imagining Home: Class, Culture, and Nationalism in the African Diaspora*, edited by Sidney J. Lemelle and Robin D. G. Kelley, 1–16. New York: Verso, 1995.

Levinson, Sandra, Carol Brightman, and Jerry Berndt. *Venceremos Brigade: Young Americans Sharing the Life and Work of Revolutionary Cuba: Diaries, Letters, Interviews, Tapes, Essays, Poetry by the Venceremos Brigade*. New York: Simon and Schuster, 1971.

Lucks, Daniel S. *Selma to Saigon: The Civil Rights Movement and the Vietnam War*. Lexington: University of Kentucky Press, 2014.

Lumsden, Linda. "Good Mothers with Guns: Framing Black Womanhood in *The Black Panther*, 1968–1980." *Journalism and Mass Communication Quarterly* 86, no. 4 (Winter 2009): 900–922.

Lyons, Courtney Ann. "Burning Columbia Avenue: Black Christianity, Black Nationalism, and 'Riot Liturgy' in the 1964 Philadelphia Race Riot." *Pennsylvania History: A Journal of Mid-Atlantic Studies* 77, no. 3 (2010): 324–48.

Madhubuti, Haki. "Sixth Pan-Afrikan Congress: What Is Being Done to Save the Black Race." *Black Books Bulletin* 2 (Fall 1974): 44–51.

Makalani, Minkah. *In the Cause of Freedom: Radical Black Internationalism from Harlem to London, 1917–1939*. Chapel Hill: University of North Carolina Press, 2011.

Mara, Wil. *Civil Unrest in the 1960s: Riots and Their Aftermath*. New York: Cavendish Square, 2009.

Marable, Manning. *Malcolm X: A Life of Reinvention*. New York: Viking, 2011.

Markle, Seth. "Book Publishers for a Pan-African World: Drum and Spear Press and Tanzania's Ujamaa Ideology." *Black Scholar* 37, no. 4 (2008): 16–26.

———. *A Motorcycle on Hell Run: Tanzania, Black Power, and the Uncertain Future of Pan-Africanism, 1964–1974*. Ann Arbor: Michigan State University Press, 2017.

———. "'We Are Not Tourists': The Black Power Movement and the Making of Socialist Tanzania, 1960–1974." PhD diss., New York University, 2011.

Martin, Charles H. "Race, Gender, and Southern Justice: The Rosa Lee Ingram Case." *American Journal of Legal History* 29, no. 3 (July 1985): 251–68.

Martin, Tony. *Amy Ashwood Garvey: Pan-Africanist, Feminist, and Mrs. Marcus Garvey Wife No. 1; or, A Tale of Two Amies*. Dover, MA: Majority, 2007.

———. *Race First: The Ideological and Organizational Struggles of Marcus Garvey and the Universal Negro Improvement Association*. Westport, CN: Greenwood, 1976.

Matthews, Trayce Ann. "'No One Ever Asks What a Man's Role in the Revolution Is': Gender and the Politics of the Black Panther Party, 1966–1971." In *The Black Panther Party (Reconsidered)*, edited by Charles E. Jones, 267–304. Baltimore: Black Classic, 1998.

Mayes, Keith A. *Kwanzaa: Black Power and the Making of the African American Holiday Tradition*. New York: Routledge, 2009.

McCray, Kenja. "Complements to Kazi Leaders: Female Activists in Kawaida-Influenced Cultural-Nationalist Organizations, 1965–1987." PhD diss., Georgia State University, 2017.

McDonald, Kathlene. *Feminism, the Left, and Postwar Literary Culture.* Jackson: University Press of Mississippi, 2012.

McDuffie, Erik S. "The Diasporic Journeys of Louise Little: Grassroots Garveyism, the Midwest, and Community Feminism." *Women, Gender, and Families of Color* 4, no. 2 (2016): 146–70.

———. "Esther V. Cooper's 'The Negro Woman Domestic in Relation to Trade Unionism': Black Left Feminism and the Popular Front." *American Communist History* 7, no. 2 (2008): 203–9.

———. "Garveyism in Cleveland, Ohio and the History of the Diasporic Midwest, 1920–1975." *African Identities* 9, no. 2 (2011): 163–81.

———. "'I Wanted a Communist Philosophy, but I Wanted Us to Have a Chance to Organize Our People': The Diasporic Radicalism of Queen Mother Audley Moore and the Origins of Black Power." *African and Black Diaspora: An International Journal* 3, no. 2 (2010): 181–95.

———. "The March of Young Southern Black Women: Esther Cooper Jackson, Black Left Feminism, and the Personal and Political Costs of Cold War Repression." In *Anticommunism and the African American Freedom Movement: "Another Side of the Story,"* edited by Robbie Lieberman and Clarence Lang, 81–114. New York: Palgrave Macmillan, 2009.

———. "A 'New Freedom Movement of Negro Women': Sojourning for Truth, Justice, and Human Rights during the Early Cold War." *Radical History Review* 101 (2008): 81–106.

———. *Sojourning for Freedom: Black Women, American Communism, and the Making of Black Left Feminism.* Durham, NC: Duke University Press, 2011.

McDuffie, Erik S., and Komozi Woodard. "'If You're in a Country That's Progressive, the Woman Is Progressive': Black Women Radicals and the Making of the Politics and Legacy of Malcolm X." *Biography* 36, no. 3 (Summer 2013): 507–39.

McElya, Micki. *Clinging to Mammy: The Faithful Slave in Twentieth-Century America.* Cambridge, MA: Harvard University Press, 2007.

McGuire, Danielle L. *At the Dark End of the Street: Black Women, Rape, and Resistance—A New History of the Civil Rights Movement from Rosa Parks to the Rise of Black Power.* New York: Vintage Books, 2010.

———. "Joan Little and the Triumph of Testimony." In *Freedom Rights: New Perspectives on the Civil Rights Movement*, edited by Danielle L. McGuire and John Dittmer, 191–222. Lexington: University Press of Kentucky, 2011.

McNeil, Genna Rae. "'Joanne Is You and Joanne Is Me': A Consideration of African American Women and the 'Free Joan Little' Movement, 1974–1975." In *Sisters in the Struggle: African American Women in the Civil Rights–Black Power Movement*, edited by Bettye Collier-Thomas and V. P. Franklin, 259–79. New York: New York University Press, 2001.

Mehta, Brinda. "Images of Exile and the Female Condition in Nawal El Saadawi's *The Fall of the Imam* and *Memoirs from the Women's Prison*." In *Migrating Words and Worlds: Pan-Africanism Updated*, edited by E. Anthony Hurley, Renée Larrier, and Joseph McLaren, 25–50. Trenton, NJ: African World, 1999.

Meriwether, James Hunter. *Proudly We Can Be Africans: Black Americans and Africa, 1935–1961*. Chapel Hill: University of North Carolina Press, 2002.

Meyerowitz, Joanne, ed. *Not June Cleaver: Women and Gender in Postwar America, 1945–1960*. Philadelphia: Temple University Press, 1994.

Monterio, Anthony. "The Sixth Pan-African Congress: Agenda for African-Afro-American Solidarity." In *A Freedomways Reader: Afro-America in the Seventies*, edited by Ernest Kaiser, 396–411. New York: International, 1977.

Moore, Queen Mother [Audley]. "We Refuse to Be Programmed Anymore." In *Before the Fall: A Discussion of Schools in Conflict with Community*, edited by Stanley F. Wanat and Michael R. Cohen, 19–25. Ithaca, NY: Cornell University Press, 1969.

Morris, Courtney Desiree. "Becoming Creole, Becoming Black: Migration, Diasporic Self-Making, and the Many Lives of Madame Maymie Leone Turpeau de Mena." *Women, Gender, and Families of Color* 4, no. 2 (Fall 2016): 171–95.

Moye, J. Todd. *Let the People Decide: Black Freedom and White Resistance Movements in Sunflower County, Mississippi, 1945–1986*. Chapel Hill: University of North Carolina Press, 2004.

Murch, Donna Jean. *Living for the City: Migration, Education, and the Rise of the Black Panther Party in Oakland, California*. Chapel Hill: University of North Carolina Press, 2010.

Nadasen, Premilla. *Household Workers Unite: The Untold Story of African American Women Who Built a Movement*. Boston: Beacon, 2015.

———. "'We Do Whatever Becomes Necessary': Johnnie Tillmon, Welfare Rights, and Black Power." In *Want to Start a Revolution? Radical Black Women in the Black Freedom Struggle*, edited by Dayo F. Gore, Jeanne Theoharis, and Komozi Woodard, 317–38. New York: New York University Press, 2009.

Naison, Mark. *Communists in Harlem during the Depression*. Urbana: University of Illinois Press, 1983.

Nelson, Alondra. *Body and Soul: The Black Panther Party and the Fight against Medical Discrimination*. Minneapolis: University of Minnesota Press, 2011.

Nelson, Jennifer. "'All This That Has Happened to Me Shouldn't Happen to Nobody Else': Loretta Ross and the Women of Color Reproductive Freedom Movement of the 1980s." *Journal of Women's History* 22, no. 3 (2010): 136–60.

———. *Women of Color and the Reproductive Rights Movement*. New York: New York University Press, 2003.

Newton, Huey P. "Huey Newton Talks to the Movement about the Black Panther Party, Cultural Nationalism, SNCC, Liberals, and White Revolutionaries." In *The Black Panthers Speak*, 2nd ed., edited by Phillip S. Foner, 50–56. New York: Da Capo, 1995.

———. "'Intercommunalism,' a Statement by Huey P. Newton." In *In Search of Common Ground: Conversations with Erik H. Erikson and Huey P. Newton*, edited by Kai T. Erikson, 23–44. New York: W. W. Norton, 1973.

———. *Revolutionary Suicide*. New York: Penguin Books, 2009.

———. "The Women's Liberation and Gay Liberation Movements." In *The Huey P. Newton Reader*, edited by David Hilliard and Donald Weise, 157–59. New York: Seven Stories, 2002.

Ogbar, Jeffery O. G. *Black Power: Radical Politics and African American Identity*. Baltimore: Johns Hopkins University Press, 2004.

———. "Rainbow Radicalism: The Rise of Radical Ethnic Nationalism." In *The Black Power Movement: Rethinking the Civil Rights–Black Power Era*, edited by Peniel E. Joseph, 193–228. New York: Routledge, 2006.

Ongiri, Amy Abugo. "We Are Family: Black Nationalism, Black Masculinity, and the Black Gay Cultural Imagination." *College Literature* 24, no. 1 (February 1997): 280–94.

Pan-African Congress. "The Call to the Sixth Pan African Congress." In *Resolutions and Selected Speeches from the Sixth Pan-African Congress*, edited by Tanzania Publishing House, 219–22. Dar es Salaam: Tanzania Publishing House, 1976.

———. *Resolutions and Selected Speeches from the Sixth Pan-African Congress*. Edited by Tanzania Publishing House. Dar es Salaam: Tanzania Publishing House, 1976.

"Panther Sisters on Women's Liberation." *Movement*, September 1969, 8–10.

Patterson, James T. *Freedom Is Not Enough: The Moynihan Report and America's Struggle over Black Family Life from LBJ to Obama*. New York: Basic Books, 2010.

Patton, Gwen. "Black People and the Victorian Ethos." In *The Black Woman: An Anthology*, edited by Toni Cade Bambara, 179–85. New York: New American Library, 1970.

———. "Born Freedom Fighter." In *Hands on the Freedom Plow: Personal Accounts by Women in SNCC*, edited by Faith S. Holsaert, Martha Prescod Norman Noonan, Judy Richardson, Betty Garman Robinson, Jean Smith Young, and Dorothy M. Zellner, 572–86. Urbana: University of Illinois Press, 2010.

———. "Lowndes County Election Fraud." *Liberator*, December 1966, 8–9.

Payne, Charles M. *I've Got the Light of Freedom: The Organizing Tradition and the Mississippi Freedom Struggle*. Berkeley: University of California Press, 1996.

Perkins, Margo V. *Autobiography as Activism: Three Black Women of the Sixties*. Jackson: University of Mississippi Press, 2000.

Perlstein, Daniel H. *Justice, Justice: School Politics and the Eclipse of Liberalism*. New York: P. Lang, 2004.

Phillips, Mary. "The Feminist Leadership of Ericka Huggins in the Black Panther Party." *Black Diaspora Review* 4, no. 1 (Winter 2014): 187–221.

———. "The Power of the First Person Narrative: Ericka Huggins and the Black Panther Party." *Women's Studies Quarterly* 43, no. 3/4 (Fall/Winter 2015): 33–51.

Phillips, Mary, and Angela LeBlanc-Ernest. "The Hidden Narratives: Recovering and (Re)visioning the Community Activism of Men in the Black Panther Party." *Spectrum: A Journal on Black Men* 5, no. 1 (Fall 2016): 63–89.

Raiford, Leigh. *Imprisoned in a Luminous Glare: Photography and the African American Freedom Struggle*. Chapel Hill: University of North Carolina Press, 2011.

Randolph, Sherie M. *Florynce "Flo" Kennedy: The Life of a Black Feminist Radical*. Chapel Hill: University of North Carolina Press, 2015.

Ransby, Barbara. *Ella Baker and the Black Freedom Movement: A Radical Democratic Vision*. Chapel Hill: University of North Carolina Press, 2003.

"Report on Bombing of North Vietnam, Testimony by Charles Cobb and Julius Lester." In *Against the Crime of Silence: Proceedings of the Russell International War Crimes Tribunal*, edited by John Duffett, 206–10. New York: O'Hare Books, 1968.

Rhodes, Jane. *Framing the Black Panthers: The Spectacular Rise of a Black Power Icon*. New York: New Press, 2007.

Richards, Johnetta. "Fundamentally Determined: James E. Jackson and Esther Cooper Jackson and the Southern Negro Youth Congress, 1937–1946." *American Communist History* 7, no. 2 (2008): 191–202.

Rickford, Russell. *We Are an African People: Independent Black Education, Black Power, and the Radical Imagination*. New York: Oxford University Press, 2016.

Roberts, Dorothy. *Killing the Black Body: Race, Reproduction and the Making of Liberty*. New York: Vintage Books, 1997.

Robnett, Belinda. *How Long? How Long? African American Women in the Struggle for Civil Rights*. New York: Oxford University Press, 1997.

Rodney, Walter. *Towards the Sixth Pan-African Congress: Aspects of the International Class Struggle in Africa, the Caribbean, and Latin America*. Atlanta, GA: Institute for the Black World, 1975.

Rogers, Ibram H. *The Black Campus Movement: Black Students and the Racial Reconstitution of Higher Education, 1965–1972*. New York: Palgrave Macmillan, 2012.

Rogers, Kim Lacey. *Righteous Lives: Narratives of the New Orleans Civil Rights Movement*. New York: New York University Press, 1993.

Rojas, Fabio. *From Black Power to Black Studies: How a Radical Social Movement Became an Academic Discipline*. Baltimore: Johns Hopkins University Press, 2007.

Rolinson, Mary G. *Grassroots Garveyism: The Universal Negro Improvement Association in the Rural South, 1920–1927*. Chapel Hill: University of North Carolina Press, 2007.

Roth, Benita. *Separate Roads to Feminism: Black, Chicana, and White Feminist Movements in America's Second Wave*. New York: Cambridge University Press, 2004.

Sangrey, Trevor Joy. "'Put One More "S" in the USA': Communist Pamphlet Literature and the Productive Fiction of the Black Belt Thesis." PhD diss., University of California, Santa Cruz, 2012.

Seale, Bobby. *A Lonely Rage: The Autobiography of Bobby Seale*. New York: Times Books, 1978.

———. *Seize the Time: The Story of the Black Panther Party and Huey P. Newton*. New York: Random House, 1970.

Self, Robert O. *American Babylon: Race and the Struggle for Postwar Oakland.* Princeton, NJ: Princeton University Press, 2003.

Seniors, Paula Marie. "Mae Mallory and 'the Southern Belle Fantasy Trope' at the Cuyahoga County Jail, 21st and Payne/PAIN." In *From "Uncle Tom's Cabin" to "The Help": Critical Perspectives on White-Authored Narratives of Black Life*, edited by Claire Garcia, Vershawn Ashanti Young, and Charise Pimentel, 101–31. New York: Palgrave Macmillan, 2015.

Sewell, Christopher J. P. "Mammies and Matriarchs: Tracing Images of the Black Female in Popular Culture 1950s to Present." *Journal of African American Studies* 17, no. 3 (September 2013): 308–26.

Shakur, Assata. *Assata: An Autobiography.* Chicago: Lawrence Hill Books, 1987.

Shandell, Jonathan. "Looking beyond Lucasta: The Black Dramas of the American Negro Theatre." *African American Review* 42, no. 3/4 (Fall 2008): 533–47.

Sharpless, Rebecca. *Cooking in Other Women's Kitchens: Domestic Workers in the South, 1865–1960.* Chapel Hill: University of North Carolina Press, 2010.

Sherwood, Marika. *Origins of Pan-Africanism: Henry Sylvester Williams, Africa, and the African Diaspora.* New York: Routledge, 2011.

———. "Pan-African Conferences, 1900–1953: What Did 'Pan-Africanism' Mean?" *Journal of Pan African Studies* 4, no. 10 (January 2012): 106–26.

Shulman, Bruce. *The Seventies: The Great Shift in American Society, Culture, and Politics.* New York: Free Press, 2001.

Simanga, Michael. *Amiri Baraka and the Congress of African People: History and Memory.* New York: Palgrave Macmillan, 2015.

Sisters of Black Culture. *Black Woman's Role in the Revolution.* Newark, NJ: Jihad Productions, 1969.

Slate, Nico, ed. *Black Power beyond Borders: The Global Dimensions of the Black Power Movement.* New York: Palgrave Macmillan, 2012.

———. "The Dalit Panthers: Race, Caste, and Black Power in India." In *Black Power beyond Borders: The Global Dimensions of the Black Power Movement*, edited by Nico Slate, 127–43. New York: Palgrave Macmillan, 2012.

Smethurst, James Edward. *The Black Arts Movement: Literary Nationalism in the 1960s and 1970s.* Chapel Hill: University of North Carolina Press, 2005.

———. *The New Red Negro: The Literary Left and African American Poetry, 1930–1946.* New York: Oxford University Press, 1999.

Smethurst, James Edward, Sonia Sanchez, and John H. Bracey, eds. *SOS/Calling All Black People: A Black Arts Movement Reader.* Amherst: University of Massachusetts Press, 2014.

Smith, Jennifer B. *An International History of the Black Panther Party.* New York: Taylor and Francis, 1999.

Smith, Sidonie. "Autobiographical Manifestos." In *Women, Autobiography, and Theory: A Reader*, edited by Sidonie Smith and Julia Watson, 433–40. Madison: University of Wisconsin Press, 1998.

"SNCC Workers on War Crimes Mission: Letters from Hanoi." *Movement*, May 1967, 5.

Solomon, Mark. *The Cry Was Unity: Communists and African Americans, 1917–36.* Jackson: University of Mississippi Press, 1998.

Southern Africa Support Project. *Organizing for Action on Southern Africa: Bringing the Struggle Home.* Washington, DC: Southern Africa Support Project, 1998.

Spencer, Robyn C. "Engendering the Black Freedom Struggle: Revolutionary Black Womanhood and the Black Panther Party in the Bay Area, California." *Journal of Women's History* 20, no. 1 (Spring 2008): 90–113.

———. *The Revolution Has Come: Black Power, Gender, and the Black Panther Party in Oakland.* Durham, NC: Duke University Press, 2016.

Springer, Kimberly. *Living for the Revolution: Black Feminist Organizations, 1968–1980.* Durham, NC: Duke University Press, 2005.

Stephens, Ronald J. "Garveyism in Idlewild, 1927 to 1936." *Journal of Black Studies* 34, no. 4 (2004): 462–88.

Strain, Christopher B. *Pure Fire: Self-Defense as Activism in the Civil Rights Era.* Athens: University of Georgia Press, 2005.

Strathern, Marilyn. "Cutting the Network." *Journal of the Royal Anthropological Institute* 2 (September 1996): 517–35.

Strickland, William. "The Gary Convention and the Crisis of American Politics." *Black World* 21 (October 1972): 18–26.

Swan, Quito. *Black Power in Bermuda: The Struggle for Decolonization.* New York: Palgrave Macmillan, 2009.

Taylor, Keeanga-Yamahtta. *From #BlackLivesMatter to Black Liberation.* Chicago: Haymarket Books, 2016.

Taylor, Ula. "As-salaam Alaikum, My Sister, Peace Be unto You: The Honorable Elijah Muhammad and the Women Who Followed Him." *Race and Society* 1, no. 2 (1998): 177–96.

———. "Elijah Muhammad's Nation of Islam: Separatism, Regendering, and a Secular Approach to Black Power after Malcolm X (1965–1975)." In *Freedom North: Black Freedom Struggles outside the South, 1940–1980*, edited by Jeanne F. Theoharis and Komozi Woodard, 177–98. New York: Palgrave Macmillan, 2003.

———. *The Promise of Patriarchy: Women and the Nation of Islam.* Chapel Hill: University of North Carolina Press, 2017.

———. "Street Strollers: Grounding the Theory of Black Women Intellectuals." *Afro-Americans in New York Life and History* 30, no. 2 (July 2006): 153–71.

———. *The Veiled Garvey: The Life and Times of Amy Jacques Garvey.* Chapel Hill: University of North Carolina Press, 2002.

Thompson, Louise. "Toward a Brighter Dawn." *Woman Today*, April 1936, 14, 30.

Tinson, Christopher N. "'The Voice of the Black Protest Movement': Notes on the 'Liberator' Magazine and Black Radicalism in the Early 1960s." *Black Scholar* 37, no. 4 (Winter 2008): 3–15.

Trotter, Joe William, Jr. *From Raw Deal to a New Deal? African Americans, 1929–1945.* New York: Oxford University Press, 1996.

Tuttle, Brad R. *How Newark Became Newark: The Rise, Fall, and Rebirth of an American City.* New Brunswick, NJ: Rivergate Books, 2009.

Tyson, Timothy. *Radio Free Dixie: Robert F. Williams and the Roots of Black Power.* Chapel Hill: University of North Carolina Press, 1999.

Umoja, Akinyele Omowale. "Repression Breeds Resistance: The Black Liberation Army and the Radical Legacy of the Black Panther Party." *New Political Science* 22, no. 2 (1999): 131–55.

———. *We Will Shoot Back: Armed Resistance in the Mississippi Freedom Movement.* New York: New York University Press, 2013.

Urdang, Stephanie. *Fighting Two Colonialisms: Women in Guinea-Bissau.* New York: Monthly Review Press, 1979.

Van Deburg, William L. *New Day in Babylon: The Black Power Movement and American Culture, 1966–1975.* Chicago: University of Chicago Press, 1992.

Von Eschen, Penny M. *Race against Empire: Black Americans and Anticolonialism, 1937–1957.* Ithaca, NY: Cornell University Press, 1997.

Walters, Ronald W. *Pan Africanism in the African Diaspora: An Analysis of Modern Afrocentric Political Movements.* Detroit: Wayne State University Press, 1993.

Ward, Stephen M. *In Love and Struggle: The Revolutionary Lives of James and Grace Lee Boggs.* Chapel Hill: University of North Carolina Press, 2016.

———, ed. *Pages from a Black Radical's Notebook: A James Boggs Reader.* Detroit: Wayne State University Press, 2011.

———. "The Third World Women's Alliance: Black Feminist Radicalism and Black Power Politics." In *The Black Power Movement: Rethinking the Civil Rights–Black Power Era,* edited by Peniel E. Joseph, 119–44. New York: Routledge, 2006.

Warden, Don. "The Afro American Association: The California Revolt." *Liberator,* March 1963, 14–15.

Washington, Cynthia. "We Started from Different Ends of the Spectrum." *Southern Exposure* 4, no. 4 (Winter 1977): 14–18.

Washington, Mary Helen. "Alice Childress, Lorraine Hansberry, and Claudia Jones: Black Women Write the Popular Front." In *Left of the Color Line: Race, Radicalism, and Twentieth Century Literature of the United States,* edited by Bill Mullen and James Smethurst, 183–204. Chapel Hill: University of North Carolina Press, 2003.

———. *The Other Blacklist: The African American Literary and Cultural Left of the 1950s.* New York: Columbia University Press, 2014.

Watkins, Rychetta. *Black Power, Yellow Power, and the Making of Revolutionary Identities.* Jackson: University Press of Mississippi, 2012.

Weathers, Mary Ann. "An Argument for Black Women's Liberation as a Revolutionary Force." In *Words of Fire: An Anthology of African-American Feminist Thought,* edited by Beverly Guy Sheftall, 158–62. New York: New Press, 1995.

Westheider, James E. *Fighting on Two Fronts: African Americans and the Vietnam War.* New York: New York University Press, 1997.

White, E. Frances. "Africa on My Mind: Gender, Counter Discourse, and African American Nationalism." *Journal of Women's History* 2, no. 1 (Spring 1990): 73–97.

Wilkerson, Isabel. *The Warmth of Other Suns: The Epic Story of America's Great Migration*. New York: Random House, 2010.

Wilkins, Fanon Che. "Beyond Bandung: The Critical Nationalism of Lorraine Hansberry, 1950–1965." *Radical Historical Review* 95 (2006): 191–210.

———. "'In the Belly of the Beast': Black Power, Anti-imperialism, and the African Liberation Solidarity Movement, 1968–1975." PhD diss., New York University, 2001.

———. "'A Line of Steel: The Organization of the Sixth Pan-African Congress and the Struggle for International Black Power, 1969–1974." In *The Hidden 1970s: Histories of Radicalism*, edited by Dan Berger, 97–114. New Brunswick, NJ: Rutgers University Press, 2010.

———. "The Making of Black Internationalists: SNCC and Africa before the Launching of Black Power, 1961–1965." *Journal of African American History* 92, no. 4 (2007): 468–91.

Wilks, Gertrude Dyer. *Gathering Together: Born to Be a Leader*. LaVergne, TN: Xlibris, 2010.

Williams, Jakobi. "'Don't No Woman Have to Do Nothing She Don't Want to Do': Gender, Activism, and the Illinois Black Panther Party." *Black Women, Gender and Families* 6, no. 2 (Fall 2012): 29–54.

Williams, Rhonda Y. "Black Women, Urban Politics, and Engendering Black Power." In *The Black Power Movement: Rethinking the Civil Rights–Black Power Era*, edited by Peniel E. Joseph, 79–103. New York: Routledge, 2006.

———. *Concrete Demands: The Search for Black Power in the 20th Century*. New York: Routledge, 2015.

Williams, Robert F. *Negroes with Guns*. New York: Marzania and Munsell, 1962.

Wolcott, Victoria W. *Remaking Respectability: African American Women in Interwar Detroit*. Chapel Hill: University of North Carolina Press, 2001.

Wood, Julia Erin. "Freedom Is Indivisible: The Student Non-violent Coordinating Committee (SNCC), Cold War Politics, and International Liberation Movements." PhD diss., Yale University, 2011.

Woodard, Komozi. "It's Nation Time in NewArk: Amiri Baraka and the Black Power Experiment in Newark, New Jersey." In *Freedom North: Black Freedom Struggles outside the South, 1940–1980*, edited by Jeanne F. Theoharis and Komozi Woodard, 287–309. New York: Palgrave Macmillan, 2003.

———. "Message from the Grassroots: The Black Power Experiment in Newark, New Jersey." In *Groundwork: Local Black Freedom Movements in America*, edited by Jeanne F. Theoharis and Komozi Woodard, 72–96. New York: New York University Press, 2005.

———. *A Nation within a Nation: Amiri Baraka (LeRoi Jones) and Black Power Politics*. Chapel Hill: University of North Carolina Press, 1999.

Woodard, Komozi, Randolph Boehm, and Daniel Lewis, eds. *The Black Power Movement*. Pt. 1, *Amiri Baraka, from Black Arts to Black Radicalism*. Bethesda, MD: University Publications of America, 2000. Microfilm.

Young, Cynthia A. *Soul Power: Culture, Radicalism, and the Making of a U.S. Third World Left*. Durham, NC: Duke University Press, 2006.

Young, Kurt B. "Towards a Holistic Review of Pan-Africanism: Linking the Idea and the Movement." *Nationalism and Ethnic Politics* 16, no. 2 (2010): 141–63.

Zackodink, Teresa. "Recirculation and Feminist Black Internationalism in Jessie Fauset's 'The Looking Glass' and Amy Jacques Garvey's 'Our Women and What They Think.'" *Modernism/Modernity* 19, no. 3 (September 2012): 437–59.

Index

"About Those Colored Movies" (Childress), 38–39

Abron, Jonina, 81, 90

Abunuwas, Maisha, 98

Abubakari, Dara (Virginia Y. Collins), 141

Africa House (Los Angeles), 95

African Descendants People's Partition Party, 55, 207n31

African Free School, 9, 107, 108–9

African Liberation Day (ALD), 127, 130–33, 138–39, 141, 156, 173, 219n27

African Liberation Support Committee (ALSC), 138, 141, 145, 156, 220n47

African Party for the Independence of Guinea and Cape Verde (PAIGC), 144, 221n73

African Woman ideal: Afrikan Women's Conference, 120–23; black women's theories of, 3, 93, 110, 111–18, 121, 122; cultural nationalism and, 16, 92, 93–94, 125; end of ideal, 124; Kawaida doctrine and, 99–100, 108–9, 110, 111–14, 119, 121; polygamous relationships and, 99, 122. *See also* Baraka, Amina (Sylvia Robinson); Committee for Unified Newark (CFUN); Congress of African People (CAP); cultural nationalism; gendered imaginary; Us Organization

African World (newspaper), 130, 164

Afrikan Women's Conference (1974), 120–23

Afro-American Association, 55, 96, 98

Ahmad, Muhammad, 48–49

Alexander, Sanford and Patricia, 95–96

"All about My Job" (Childress), 37

All-Africa Women's Conference (AAWC): anti-imperialism organ-

izing and, 135–36; Audley Moore speech at, 134–38, 156; overview of, 133–34; Pan-African consciousness and, 114–15, 127, 133–38, 156–57; participant demographics, 133–34

Allen, Austin, 77

Alliance against Women's Oppression (AAWO), 190, 192, 228n115

American Negro Theatre (ANT), 34

"An End to the Neglect of the Problems of the Negro Woman!" (Jones), 29–31, 32–33

Angelou, Maya, 41

Augusto, Geri (Stark), 139–40, 143–44, 145–46, 152–53, 156, 163

Auther, Barbara, 59, 66

Baker, Ella, 23, 51–52, 162, 185

Baltimore Africo American (newspaper), 40

Bandung Afro-Asian Conference (1955), 161

Baraka, Amina (Sylvia Robinson): African Free School and, 9, 107–9; Black Arts movement and, 104–5; CFUN and, 93–94, 107–9; Muminina (Newark) and, 108–9; Newark Black Arts programming, 104–5; "On Afrikan Women" article, 115, 116–17; "Social Organization" column, 115, 116–17; United Sisters and, 107, 108–9

Baraka, Amiri: BART/S and Black Arts movement and, 104–5; CAP and, 109–10, 114, 145; CFUN and, 93–94, 107–8; image of, 146; Karenga and, 104–5, 108; Kawaida interpretations, 105, 114–15, 122–23; Newark Black Power Conference and, 105–7;

Community control, 8, 9, 20, 21, 61, 65, 96, 107–8, 189, 191, 195–96

Community education/political education: African Free School, 9, 107, 108–9; BART/S, 104; BPP and, 67, 81, 90; BWLC and, 171; Nairobi School, 151; Oakland Community School, 90, 212n154; Pan-African Skills Project, 138; Spirit House, 104–5, 107; *Triple Jeopardy* (newspaper) as, 172–73, 174; UNIA and, 22; United Sisters, 107, 108; Us Organization and, 98–99

Congress of African People (CAP): African liberation movements and, 109–10, 114–15; African Woman ideal and, 93–94, 120–21; Afrikan Women's Conference, 120–23; anti-imperialism and, 120–23; Baraka leadership, 114–15; Black Power ideals, 93; BWUF and, 122–23; CFUN and, 109–10; coalition building and, 109; development and expansion, 108–9; The East and, 127, 142, 218n1; formation of, 109–10; founding of, 93, 109–10; gender roles within, 93, 110–11; global conception of gender roles, 115–17; Malaika, 110, 115–19, 120–21; Marxism and, 123–24; Muminina, 110, 117–19; National Black Political Conference, 114; patriarchal practices and, 122–23; Revolutionary Kawaida and, 122–23; "Social Organization" articles (Baraka), 115, 116–17; Women's Division, 11, 108–10, 116–17, 119, 125, 132; women's liberation movements and, 110–11. *See also* Baraka, Amina (Sylvia Robinson); Baraka, Amiri; Committee for Unified Newark (CFUN)

Congress of Racial Equality (CORE), 95, 97–98, 105, 121, 131

"Conversations from Life" series (Childress), 36–40

Cooke, Marvel, 23, 185

Cooper, Anna Julia, 6

Counts, Cecelie, 156

Cox, Courtland, 140, 143

Crenshaw, Kimberlé, 192, 200n41

Cruse, Harold, 104

Cuba, 43, 51, 90, 133, 158, 161, 164, 169, 210n108

Cultural Association for Women of African Heritage (CAWAH), 8, 41, 42

Cultural nationalism: African identity and, 94, 99–100; class-conscious politics and, 115; foundations of, 93–94, 95–104; gendered imaginary and, 14, 16, 125–26; gender roles and, 94, 99–103, 113, 119–20, 122; internationalism and, 109, 115; Kwanzaa, 97, 99, 124; Newark, NJ and, 104–10; Nguzo Saba and women's interpretations of, 97, 100–103, 111–17; Pan-Africanism and, 127–28; patriarchal practices and, 94, 103–4, 115, 119–20, 122–23; polygamous relationships and, 99, 122. *See also* African Woman ideal; Committee for Unified Newark (CFUN); Congress of African People (CAP); Karenga, Maulana (Ronald Everett); Kawaida doctrine; Us Organization

Damu, Regina, 98

Davis, Angela, 10, 82, 131, 173, 176, 182, 193–94, 196–97, 219n27, 226n75

Davis, Irving, 138

Dellums, Ron, 81, 211n133

Democratic National Convention (DNC), 52–53

Devine, Annie, 52–53

Dewberry, Dorothy, 145, 168

Dickson, Gayle (Asali), 1–3, 85–89

Domestic Workers Union (DWU), 23

"Double Jeopardy: To Be Black and Female" (Beal), 164, 165, 200n41

Douglas, Emory, 61–62, 66

Mallory, Mae: BWLC and, 167; early life and activism, 41–42; Freedom Riders and, 42–43; image of, 146; incarceration of, 43; Malcolm X association, 50; Monroe incident protest and participation, 42–43; movement to free Mallory, 48–49; Pan-Africanist organizing, 129–30; self-defense and, 42–43, 46–48; Sixth PAC participation, 145, 146; working-class women and, 13–14, 44–49

Mallory, Mae, writings by: "Memo from a Monroe Jail," 45–48; "Of Dogs and Men," 43–45; prison letters, 43–49, 205n118

Mao Zedong, 70, 161

Marxism, 123–24, 169

Matilaba (Tarika Lewis), 57, 62–66, 67–68, 88, 91

Matthews, Connie, 79–80

Mayfield, Julian, 46

McCarthyism, 8, 33–34, 35, 40, 42, 49, 201n13, 203n68

"Memo from a Monroe Jail" (Mallory), 45–48

Merritt, Ann, 168

"Message to Revolutionary Women" (Robinson), 72–73

"Message to Sister Ericka Huggins" (Eldridge Cleaver), 76–77

"Message to the Grassroots" (Malcolm X), 8

Methodology, 12, 14–16, 18–19

Militant Negro Domestic ideal: Black Belt Thesis and, 26, 27–28; black domestic workers as, 28–34; Black Power and, 40–49; black women's theories of, 28–34, 36–40, 43–49; Bronx Slave Market, 23–24, 27, 51; development of, 20–21; domestic worker militancy, 21, 28–34, 43–49; Garveyism and, 21, 22–23; internationalism and, 21, 40–41; intersectional approaches and, 31, 49; masculinist narratives and, 21, 25;

print media on, 36–40, 43–49; radicalization/radical networks of, 22–28, 40–41; self-defense and, 21, 47–48. *See also* gendered imaginary

Mississippi Freedom Democratic Party (MFDP), 52–53

Mississippi Freedom Summer (1964), 52, 53, 164

Monroe Defense Committee (MDC), 43, 47

Moore, Audley: AAWC speech, 134–38, 149, 150, 156; African Descendants People's Partition Party and, 55, 207n31; ALD protest, 132; CAP and, 93, 104–5, 109; CP membership, 7, 34, 202n43; development of Black Power framework and, 20–21; Garveyism and, 7, 22, 34, 55, 202n43; Muhammad Ahmad and, 48; New England District Committee and, 142; Pan-Africanism and, 134–37, 156; Second Black Power Conference, 106; Sixth PAC and, 138, 142, 143, 145, 156; Sojourners for Truth and Justice and, 33–34; UAEW and, 141

Moore, Harriette, 33, 203n71

Moore, Renee "Peaches," 70

Morgan, Ruby, 77

Moynihan Report (*The Negro Family: A Case for National Action*), 58, 59, 79, 99, 149, 165, 171, 208n45

Mozambique Liberation Front (FRELIMO), 131, 144, 219n16, 221n73

Msemaji, Ahera, 98

Muhammad Speaks (newspaper), 56

Mulford Act (1967), 57

Muminina, the, 98, 108–9, 110, 111–14, 119, 121

National Association for the Advancement of Colored People (NAACP), 23, 33, 42, 51, 95, 97–98

National Black Antiwar Antidraft Union (NBAWADU), 166–67, 169–71, 224n36